Hitler's Gateway to the Atlantic

Hitler's Gateway to the Atlantic

German Naval Bases in France 1940–1945

by

Lars Hellwinkel

Translated by Geoffrey Brooks

Seaforth
PUBLISHING

Opposite title page: *U588* commanded by Kptlt Viktor Vogel entering
St-Nazaire in 1942. (Bundesarchiv, 101II-MW-6029-31A)

Copyright © Christoph Links Verlag GmbH 2012
English translation © Seaforth Publishing 2014

First published in Great Britain in 2014 by
Seaforth Publishing,
Pen & Sword Books Ltd,
47 Church Street,
Barnsley S70 2AS

First published in 2012 under the title *Hitlers Tor zum Atlantik* by Ch. Links Verlag

www.seaforthpublishing.com

British Library Cataloguing in Publication Data
A catalogue record for this book is available
from the British Library

ISBN 978 1 84832 199 1

Typeset and designed by M.A.T.S., Leigh-on-Sea, Essex
Printed and bound by CPI Group (UK) Ltd, Croydon, CR0 4YY

Contents

Introduction

The image that springs to mind when thinking about the French Atlantic and Biscay ports in the Second World War is one of German U-boats running into or departing from the huge U-boat bunkers built for their protection.

At the outbreak of war the German U-boat arm had fifty-seven submarines, of which only about half were suitable for operations in the Atlantic. As the war went on, Admiral Karl Dönitz, the Commander-in-Chief of the U-boat arm, transformed the U-boat into one of the most important weapons available to the Kriegsmarine in the naval war against Great Britain.

The German maritime armaments industry was redirected to step up U-boat production, and by the end of the war 1,110 boats had been turned out. Of these 757 were lost and with them 29,000 submariners, a casualty rate of almost 70 per cent.[1] Although most of these men ultimately died for no purpose, particularly towards the end of the war, to this day the myth of a blood brotherhood surrounding the U-boat fleet persists.

In Germany, the autobiographical novel *Das Boot*, written by former war correspondent Lothar-Günther Buchheim, and Wolfgang Petersen's film based on the book, revived the myth, although the film gave rise to much controversy amongst U-boat veterans.[2] The fascination with U-boats remains undiminished, as can be seen from the growing number of U-boat museums on the German coast, from the World War II boat at Laboe to submarines of the former post-war Bundesmarine, and the Soviet Cold War spy boat at Hamburg.

So what was it really like to serve aboard a U-boat? Looking at an exhibition of Buchheim's photographs, what are particularly striking are the facial portraits of the crewmen. These faces reflect anxiety as depth charges explode, are etched with the fear that an Allied bomber might yet attack the boat before it reaches port, or are joyful at having completed a voyage safely once more.

The bases themselves remain in the background, rather as if they were merely stage sets. The memoirs of individual U-boatmen are concerned mainly with wartime voyages and life aboard; one learns little or nothing about the ports and how the crew lived in the period between putting in and sailing again. Against Buchheim's well-known photographs of the bridge watch on the tower, swamped by monstrous seas crossing the bow, bearded men in the torpedo rooms, or indoor boxing in the U-boat bunker, the images of picturesque Breton stone houses and precipitous rocky cliffs seem out of place. Nor is much known about the French who had daily contact with U-boatmen for over four years.

Sources pose a problem for a sociohistorical investigation into everyday activities and life in the naval bases. More than sixty years after the end of the war, most of the participants, French and German, have passed on. Only a handful of them set down their experiences for posterity in writing, and in most cases these were former officers. The published experiences of simple sailors and yard workers are modest in scale and usually sparing in their references to the French. Thus the French rarely find mention in German memoirs, and in French literature, the Germans are generally discussed in their role as occupiers.

The official archives are of little help, because the major part of the Kriegsmarine documentation relating to the yards was destroyed when the central office of naval construction in Berlin was bombed. All military documentation, charts and photographs held in the bases along the Biscay coast were destroyed before the final surrender in May 1945. Thus all that the German Federal Archive BA/MA has to offer is the war diary for 1942 kept privately by the senior yard director of the main U-boat base at Lorient. Hardly any files survived from the no less important naval base of Brest. The *Seekriegsleitung* War Diary made available in facsimile by the official German archive makes only limited references to events at that port. Information specific to the region can be extracted from the almost complete archived war diaries of the commanding admirals and naval commanders in France, but on the other hand almost nothing by way of documentation exists in the archives from the subordinate service offices, such as the harbour commanders or naval commanders, the real points of intersection between the French and Germans. Thus the history of the French Atlantic bases during the German occupation relies on the few published memoirs of those involved.[3] This is presumably also the reason why up until now only individual German historians have tried to get close to this subject. At the present time, therefore, we find only the works of Sönke Neitzel on the construction and use of the U-boat bunkers and an investigation by this author into the history of the Kriegsmarine base at Brest.[4]

In France, on the other hand, particularly when it comes to the two naval bases, Brest and Lorient, there is comprehensive material available in the French navy archives, amongst them files from the technical directorates of the two naval arsenals, as well as the relevant French Admiralty staffs in Vichy and Paris. For the mercantile ports, St-Nazaire, La Pallice and Bordeaux and the private shipyards, however, there are neither files nor academic investigations available: for example, into the role of the French shipbuilding industry under German occupation. French historians have favoured a culture of reminiscence, with, quite understandably, a leaning towards everyday life under the occupation and what the French Resistance did, rather than the activities of the occupying forces. The fact is that the naval bases with their purely industrial orientation were places of intensive co-operation between occupiers and occupied: their use by the occupying force was only possible with recourse to the French yards, suppliers and labour force.

Of the thousands of workers who worked directly or indirectly for the Germans during the occupation, nobody wanted to discuss this aspect of the war after the Liberation, above all those involved. And so the history of the French Atlantic ports enters the debate regarding the economic and political collaboration of Vichy France with the German Reich. The subject of this book is accordingly less about the details of U-boat bunker construction and the U-boat war, and much more about the general development of the German naval bases facing the Atlantic, from the first strategic considerations in 1925 to the occupation of the French coast in the summer of 1940, and the capitulation of the last Atlantic redoubt in May 1945. In addition, there is a sociohistorical consideration of life around the bases, with a glance at modern attitudes towards this history in the ports concerned.

The text which follows is a completely revised and expanded version of my 2006 dissertation on the German Kriegsmarine base at Brest, accepted by the Christian-Albrecht University, Kiel and the Université de Bretagne Occidentale, Brest, which was published in 2010 by Dr Dieter Winkler.[5] I am grateful to the Christoph Links publishing house for accepting this manuscript into their schedule, and to all colleagues, especially reader Stephan Lehrem, for their untiring patience and the expert advice and industry made during the production of this book.

1

The Dream of the Gateway to the Atlantic

The French Atlantic Coast

The Imperial High Seas Fleet was scuttled at Scapa Flow in 1919 without having once challenged the Royal Navy to a decisive naval encounter, with the exception of the battle of Jutland, during the First World War. After the war the search began for an explanation for the apparent failure in German naval planning. Within the navy it was finally admitted that it had simply got 'tangled up' in the fleet-building plans of Admiral Tirpitz, which were concentrated wholly on the construction of large armoured ships which then spent the war drifting round their anchors in harbour.[1]

Although the Reichsmarine of the Weimar Republic had been reduced by the Treaty of Versailles to a few old ships of the line (ie, pre-dreadnought battleships built around 1906) and cruisers, in 1925

Brest: the roadstead and harbour, c.1925. (Author collection)

Vizeadmiral Wolfgang Wegener, c.1925.
(Privatarchiv Hans-Ulrich Wegener,
Münich)

discussions began regarding the more offensive use of the fleet within the framework of cruiser warfare against mercantile shipping. The trigger for this was a memorandum by the then Inspector of Naval Gunnery, Vizeadmiral Wolfgang Wegener. In his reflections he proposed improvements in strategic-geographic exits, instead of dallying with purely tactical planning 'in the nerve-racking Narrows of the German Bight' as the head of the Naval Archive, Vizeadmiral von Manthey, had put it so fittingly in the autumn of 1932.[2] As Wegener saw it, the Imperial Admiralty had not been in a position to look beyond the 'Heligoland exercise roadstead'.[3]

Instead, when war broke out they should have attempted, in common with the army, to head westwards as far as the Atlantic. For Wegener, the only worthwhile target for such an operation was to capture the French naval base at Brest, using which, as he saw it, the German navy could have conducted naval warfare in the true sense of the word and thus woken up 'to life'.[4] On the other hand, choosing to remain in the narrow corset of the North Sea and Baltic was the same as a total rejection of naval warfare.

These theories were listened to eagerly, particularly by the younger officers of the Reichsmarine, especially since the strategic errors of the Imperial Navy, though common knowledge, were rarely discussed.[5] In 1931 the later Commander-in-Chief of the Kriegsmarine, Grossadmiral Erich Raeder, who had entered the navy in the same year as Wegener, dismissed Wegener's theory as 'a miserable concoction',[6] yet it was the same Raeder who at the beginning of the Second World War made anti-shipping warfare (*Kreuzerkrieg*) the foundation of German naval policy, owing to the modest means available. He had not, however, done anything to provide for the necessary geographic exits, which the noted American naval theoretician Admiral Alfred Thayer Mahan had declared at the end of the nineteenth century to be essential for successful attacks on enemy shipping routes.[7] The fate of the Panzerschiff *Admiral Graf Spee*, which was scuttled after a battle with British cruisers off the River Plate, far from any German repair or supply base, seems in retrospect a confirmation of this theory.

Equally, in the discussion of Wegener's memorandum it must be remembered that at the time when his ideas were published, the Reichsmarine had neither the necessary ships for wide-ranging operations, nor was it the time, only a few years after the First World War, to discuss the use of naval forces in the Atlantic. The tactical planning then was concentrated on the North Sea and Baltic, where the old battleships and cruisers with which the Reichsmarine had been left were supposed to be used only for coastal defence.[8] Even so, in the winter of 1925/26 the attention of the naval planners was refocused for the first time on the Atlantic. In a war game encompassing the expected conflict with Poland, it was reckoned that the enemy could count on the support of France. The plan therefore was to operate auxiliary cruisers off the African coast, in order to tie down French naval forces in this region and prevent their arrival in the Baltic.

This scenario was taken up anew in the 1932 war game. This time, besides the elimination of Polish naval forces by the German fleet, consideration was given to using the three new Panzerschiffe ('pocket battleships') of the *Deutschland* class to attack French troop transports from North Africa and to disrupt French sea routes.[9] Although the *Deutschland* (in service in 1931), the *Admiral Scheer* (1934) and the *Admiral Graf Spee* (1936) had been limited to a theoretical 10,000 tonnes displacement by the Treaty of Versailles, their fast diesels gave them a large radius of action which, from the navy's point of view, also solved the problem of the absence of overseas bases. Thus these three ships were always given a role in subsequent war games. In May 1938 the German naval planners were for the first time warned by Hitler to consider a future naval war against Britain.[10] Here again the conclusion was drawn that a war on shipping, with its diversionary effect on enemy naval forces, was 'the most promising' form of warfare against the materially far superior Royal Navy.[11] Whether that kind of naval warfare could actually be decisive against Britain was a question left open.

Fregattenkapitän Hellmuth Heye, entrusted with planning at Naval War Operations (Skl), restated the case for bases beyond the North Sea. He thought that harbours in the central or south Atlantic were the most favourable, and thus he suggested the recovery of the former German colonies in Africa or the use of Spanish or Italian bases in west and east Africa in the event of a conflict. When the question of France resurfaced in the deliberations of his colleagues in the operations division, Heye placed great value on an advance by the army towards the Channel coast, and if possible even further to the French naval base at Brest, in future naval planning.

Brest, with its great natural roadstead, and the French navy shipyards remained the longed-for ideal in German naval considerations. In the war game of spring 1939 the advantages of using the French port of Brest and the Spanish port of El Ferrol in the event of a possible conflict with Great Britain and France were investigated. The Commander of the Fleet Division at the German Admiralty, Konteradmiral Werner Fuchs, disowned this idea at the post mortem on the war game. For Fuchs, the seizure of the Brest naval base did not even enter the discussion because the impregnable Maginot Line blocked the path of the army.[12] On the other hand, setting up a German naval base at Polarnoye in the Barents Sea seemed much more promising to him.[13] The Chief of Staff at Skl, Admiral Otto Schniewind, spoke out against this remote harbour on the northern Soviet coast and argued for Brest as 'the more favourable solution'.[14]

After his conversations with Hitler, Grossadmiral Raeder had not reckoned on war before 1944.[15] When on 3 September 1939 war broke out against the two large European sea powers, Britain and France, apparently coming as a complete surprise to the Kriegsmarine, the naval planners had other concerns than thinking about creating a better strategic outlet into the Atlantic. The Kriegsmarine was still under construction. The two new battleships *Scharnhorst* and *Gneisenau*, still working up, three Panzerschiffe and two heavy cruisers faced a total of twenty-two heavy units of the combined British and French fleets.[16] Raeder accorded them

Kiel harbour, 1938: the battleships *Scharnhorst* (in foreground) and *Gneisenau*. (Stadtarchiv, Kiel)

no special significance, and made the well-known observation that German surface forces, even when fully deployed, could do no more than prove that 'they knew how to die with credit'.[17] At the time nobody amongst the German planners thought that fate would side so favourably with the Kriegsmarine.

According to Hitler's policy instruction of 31 August 1939, the main task of the Kriegsmarine was warfare against shipping, with its centre of gravity levelled towards Britain.[18] This was primarily the task of the U-boat arm, whose submarines would first have to pass around the British Isles in order to reach British supply routes. Thus the question of creating superior bases was resurrected. In order to consider such a possibility, on 5 October 1939 the Chief of Staff at Skl, Vizeadmiral Schniewind, met with the Chief of the Army General Staff, General Franz Halder.[19] To Schniewind's question about a possible advance towards the Channel or Normandy, and even further to Brittany, Halder replied that an operation of that kind would exceed the capabilities of the army; success would be doubtful since the time required could not be calculated, bearing in mind the depth of the territory. This put a premature end to Kriegsmarine dreams of a base on the Atlantic. When in November 1939 Hitler enquired regarding the wishes of the Kriegsmarine as respects future bases on the Dutch-Belgian Channel coast, and was told by Raeder that this region was too dangerous for U-

The attack on France: German troops in the department of Marne, May 1940. (Bundesarchiv, 101I-055-1572-30/Schweizer)

boat operations and therefore without interest, the Kriegsmarine looked north once more.

The Skl instruction of January 1940 for the occasion of a German attack on France mentioned only mining operations in the Scheldt, around the island of Texel and the port of Den Helder.[20] Operation *Weserübung*, the attack on Denmark and Norway, secured both countries for the German Wehrmacht in April 1940.[21] The Kriegsmarine, which had an important role in the escort of troop transports and the occupation of the Norwegian ports, suffered heavy losses off Narvik and Oslo, including the heavy cruiser *Blücher* and several destroyers.

When the army attacked France on 10 May 1940, the Kriegsmarine was completely unprepared for this offensive. The then Commander of Minesweepers West, Kapitän zur See Friedrich Ruge, mentions in his memoirs that he was taken utterly by surprise. He only found out about developments while listening to the news on the radio that morning. 'The navy did not seem to be involved, I had received no orders, and no orders came.'[22] The Kriegsmarine only made three U-boats available for *Fall Gelb*, of which *U9* sank the French submarine *Doris* and two independent steamers off Terschelling.[23]

While the attention of Skl was still concentrated on Norway and plans were being made for the new fleet base at Trondheim, events in the west unfolded rapidly. On 15 May 1940 the Dutch army surrendered, and on

Wreck of the French destroyer *L'Adroit* sunk off Dunkirk by German aircraft, May 1940. (Author collection)

21 May the first German troops reached the French Channel coast at Abbeville.[24] Contrary to the opinion held previously by Raeder in November 1939, Skl now saw the opportunity for operations from the Dutch coast as 'especially good' and sent S-boats (motor torpedo boats) which had been intended to operate from Norway to Den Helder and the Hook of Holland.[25] These S-boats were the only Kriegsmarine surface vessels to take part in the campaign in the west. On 23 May they sank the large French destroyer *Jaguar*, and in the wake of the evacuation from Dunkirk, the British destroyer *Wakeful* and the French destroyer *Sirocco*. The majority of the seventy-two Allied vessels lost at Dunkirk were sunk by the Luftwaffe.[26] Nevertheless, the Allies succeeded in evacuating 338,266 men across the Channel to England, amongst them 123,000 French.[27]

At the situation conference on 21 May 1940, Raeder set out the Kriegsmarine's plans to make Trondheim the future main base of the German fleet.[28] Seven days later King Leopold of the Belgians capitulated with his army, and on 5 June after the resolution of *Fall Rot*, the German army began the further occupation of France.[29] Paris was occupied on 14 June. There was no serious resistance: the French army was in disarray. Thus 7th Panzer Division under General Erwin Rommel set out unopposed on 17 June for the French naval base at Cherbourg 240km (150 miles) to the west. Hitler had ordered the capture of this base as well as the occupation of the ports at Brest, Lorient and St-Nazaire in his Instruction Nr 15 on 14 June.[30]

Opposite: German soldiers in front of the Eiffel Tower, Paris, June 1940. (Author collection)

Below: German flak post near the railway pier terminus at Cherbourg, June 1940. (Author collection)

The occupation in the summer of 1940

As German troops headed for the Atlantic coast, the French navy prepared to abandon its bases. On 15 June 1940 the naval prefecture at Brest and Lorient was ordered to terminate all current shipyard work and to make all warships under construction or repair ready for sea as quickly as possible.[31] At the same time the British Expeditionary Force began evacuating troops from Cherbourg, St Malo, Brest, St-Nazaire and La Pallice.[32] At Rennes the commission which had been set up by the Reynaud government to create a 'Breton redoubt', led by the Under Secretary of State at the Defence Ministry, General Charles de Gaulle, concluded that the erection of such a defensive outpost was totally pointless given the rapidity of the German advance. De Gaulle left for Britain the same day from Brest, while the French government withdrew south to Bordeaux.

On the night of 17 June the French government under Marshal Philippe Pétain asked the German Reich for an armistice. At that Hitler ordered the Wehrmacht to occupy France as far as the Verdun–Toul–Belfort line, the former western border of the German Reich in the Middle Ages, and to seize the ports of Cherbourg and Brest, together with the armaments centre at Le Creusot.[33] This sealed the fate of the French naval bases. As the German advance to the Atlantic continued, the French navy began the greatest evacuation in its history. At the time there lay in the port and

The German advance into northern France, June 1940. (Author collection)

roadstead at Brest no less than eighty-three French warships, amongst them the new battleship *Richelieu*, and seventy-six merchant ships under the flags of France, Belgium, Holland and Norway.[34] The naval prefect, Vice Admiral Marcel Traub, was informed of the French government's armistice request and received orders to get all seaworthy ships to sea immediately. Concurrently, the senior British naval officer from London was instructed to evacuate all British troops by the evening of 17 June.[35] The Royal Navy was particularly anxious to prevent the new battleship *Richelieu* from falling into German hands, and the Brest dockyard readied her for sea in great haste for the transfer to north Africa.

Richelieu took the cadets and personnel of the French naval academy into the west African port of Dakar, while most of the auxiliary cruisers, destroyers, torpedo boats, submarines and naval yachts arrived at Casablanca. The smaller surface vessels such as minesweepers, patrol boats and the many harbour boats and tenders fled to southern England.[36] The heavy-gun submarine *Surcouf*, in dock for a major overhaul, and the old battleship *Paris* were removed from dry dock and made for Plymouth at slow speed, the *Surcouf* only on her electric motors.

In order to impede the French naval units in their headlong flight, the Luftwaffe mined the waters off Brest, Lorient and La Rochelle, the Loire estuary and the Gironde.[37] This measure was immediately sharply criticised by Naval Group Command West (Group West) and, looking at

Announcement of the armistice, 22 June 1940. (Author collection)

the later use of the bases by the Kriegsmarine, it does seem that Skl attempted to distance itself from the aerial minelaying.[38] On the other hand, the Germans had no other means available to disrupt Allied ship movements. Faced with the increasing probability of finding only empty harbours along the coast, Skl decided on a ruse. On the afternoon of 19 June 1940 a signal in the name of the Commander-in-Chief of the French Fleet, Admiral Darlan, was transmitted on the French frequencies ordering the French ships back to harbour: 'Order, break off all military operations. Stop. All warships to make at once for the nearest French port. Stop. Do not, I repeat, do not, follow British instructions. Stop.'[39]

This signal had no effect. Neither this ruse nor Luftwaffe minelaying could prevent the flight of the French fleet. At Brest and Lorient the only victims of the German mines were two tugs, and at Chenal du Four northwest of Brest the state yacht *Vauquois*, though this went down with great loss of life because of the numbers of soldiers and civilian evacuees aboard. According to the official Royal Naval history, the reason that the evacuation of the ports went off so smoothly, in spite of the mines, was the small number of German bombers present.[40] In one of the few attacks by German aircraft on shipping movements off the French ports, the British troop transporter *Lancastria* was sunk near St-Nazaire on 17 June, at least three thousand soldiers losing their lives. Because of the death toll, Churchill decided to withhold the announcement of the loss of the ship so as not to further undermine morale at home.

On the evening of 18 June the destruction of the harbour installations was begun at Brest. The last remaining ships were sunk. Off Dunkirk the damaged destroyer *Cyclone* blocked the Tourville dry dock and in the backwaters of the naval arsenal the submarines *Ouessant* and *Achille* were scuttled in the river in front of their crews. For sailors such as the young French lieutenant commander, Jean Philippon, No. 2 watchkeeping officer of the *Ouessant*, it was a tragic day: 'It was the end of a world, of our world, and nothing had prepared us for it.'[41] Some crew members wanted to avenge the shame of having had to sink their boat without a fight; rifles and revolvers were issued, but ultimately it was recognised how futile it would be to oppose the war-hardened German units, and during the night the sailors gradually drifted away from the naval arsenal.[42] In the great construction dock the incomplete hull of the new battleship *Clémenceau* remained behind.

In the workshops the employees destroyed the machinery. Important files were burned, the breech-blocks of the guns sunk in the harbour, dock gates and cranes blown up. On the plateau behind the naval academy the fuel reserves of the French navy went up in flames, and burning oil flowed down to the harbour. In their work of destruction French sailors were supported by British demolition squads. These demolition specialists were

Burning French navy oil tanks, Brest, June 1940. (Author collection)

there to ensure that their French ally left no important installation to fall into enemy hands undamaged. The British team at Brest took it upon themselves to destroy the quay installations needed for the evacuation and only when threatened with force did they submit to the authority of the French.[43] Off St-Nazaire the British destroyer *Vanquisher* kept the newly-constructed battleship *Jean Bart* under surveillance to ensure that it either sailed or was destroyed in dry dock at the Penhoët shipyard, while at Bordeaux a second destroyer ensured the destruction of the oil supplies there.

After the last French warships had left Brest, on the orders of the French Admiral (West), Admiral Jean de Laborde, only the French naval prefect, the Commandant of the Arsenal Brohan and the technical directors of the arsenal remained behind. On the evening of 18 June orders from the French Admiralty to defend the base finally reached the naval prefect.[44] With the help of the remaining soldiers, improvised barricades were set up on the approach roads to Brest using buses and lorries. Because most of the heavy weapons had already been destroyed, the defenders were left with only some light guns and rifles, but no armour-piercing ammunition. Ultimately, the resistance at these barricades was not a defensive measure but a gesture for French honour. They could only hold up the German advance very briefly, for the German panzers simply drove round the French positions.[45]

On the afternoon of 19 June the French naval prefect at Brest was ordered by telephone to surrender the port or it would be bombed. When Vice Admiral Traub finally capitulated, the port was a wasteland and the military installations unusable.[46] Off the entrance to the Goulet, the small channel between the port and the open Atlantic, the French destroyer *Mistral* and the state yacht *Commandant Duboc* cruised up and down until the latter came under fire from German artillery and the two ships pulled back to the open sea.[47]

As at Brest, the naval prefect at Lorient had received orders to resist, and set up two defensive positions on the access roads. On 21 June, at one of these barricades near the suburb of Guidel to the northwest of the city, a skirmish took place with German reconnaissance units in the presence of the naval prefect, during which seven French sailors lost their lives. Even here, however, the defenders could do nothing beyond a symbolic act of resistance to halt the German advance. On the afternoon of the same day the naval prefect at Lorient capitulated. As at Brest, all seaworthy ships had already been evacuated and the gates of the dry dock blown up. A huge column of smoke hung over the port, and fuel oil which had flowed down from the ruptured oil tanks burned on the surface waters of the naval arsenal.

At St-Nazaire, just before the first German troops arrived, the French navy managed to ready the new battleship *Jean Bart*, only launched in March, for sea. She was only 75 per cent complete, without heavy guns and her engines untried, but she sailed on 19 June, making a successful maiden voyage to Morocco.

First measures

The German troops at Brest first occupied the central squares and important public buildings such as the town hall, and the main post office with its telephone exchange. At the town hall the French tricolour was hauled down and replace with the swastika flag. The naval prefecture was thoroughly searched, although Vice Admiral Traub was allowed to remain in office. Only in the telephone exchange and in the courtyard of the prefecture were German sentries posted. The French senior lieutenant and future British agent at Brest, Jean Philippon, witnessed the occupation of the arsenal from a window of the port administration office: 'Their motor-cycles with sidecar and light vehicles were positioned on both banks of the Penfeld [the arsenal river], at the rear entrance to the arsenal. In a few minutes they were everywhere, and their motor-cycle despatch riders circled through the quay installations.'[48] French soldiers were disarmed and confined to barracks, but officers were allowed to go where they liked in the streets and in uniform.[49]

German naval officers, NCOs and police of the Degenhardt Commission, naval arsenal, Brest, June 1940. (Bundesarchiv, 101II-MW-5683-21)

In order to assess the usefulness of the conquered Belgian and French ports, OKM had appointed a 'special plenipotentiary' shortly before the German attack on France. Kapitän zur See Degenhardt's Commission consisted of three officers from the seaman, engineering and administration branches respectively, an interpreter, three NCOs, seven ratings and the fighting forces behind.[50] First destination was Antwerp, then after a stop at Bruges the Commission followed the coast round and looked over the ports at Ostend, Dunkirk, Calais and Boulogne. On the way to Le Havre Degenhardt learned of the imminent capitulation of the French capital and decided on a detour to Paris, where on the evening of 14 June, with six naval men, he occupied the French Navy Ministry on the Place de la Concorde. From Paris the survey continued to the French submarine yard at Le Trait near Rouen and then via Le Havre to Cherbourg. The naval shipyard was to be occupied by the Naval Assault Troop Detachment 'Gotenhafen' which Naval Command Northern France had already ordered to Cherbourg for this purpose. This was done without seeking the agreement of the army; the detachment found itself alone in an unsecured region waiting for a German infantry unit to turn up before proceeding in safety into Cherbourg. There, as in the other ports of the Atlantic coast, Degenhardt arrived as the first representative of the Kriegsmarine.

Together with securing the shipyard installations and the seizure of materiel and prizes, his particular interest was to ensure that the approaches to the ports were mine-free. The mine situation was the subject of discussion with the French naval prefect in Brest, still holding office on 21 June, in which the French admiral declined to involve the French navy in minesweeping on the grounds that the mines were German.[51] The French admiral also refused outright Degenhardt's demand that he should attempt to convince the garrison on the offshore island of Ushant to surrender.

At Lorient Degenhardt found the French much more accommodating. He negotiated there with the technical director of the arsenal, Ingenieur Général Antoine, an engineering officer described in the German report as 'very loyal', whom Degenhardt was able to convince to enter into 'practical collaboration'.[52] Antoine agreed to make ready two auxiliary minesweepers in the harbour for minesweeping off Lorient. The director of the naval commissariat, on the other hand, had previously categorically declined all contact with the German occupiers.

On 21 June the new Naval Commander Brittany arrived in Brest. In his war diary, Vizeadmiral Lothar von Arnauld de la Perière set out his gloomy first impression of the port: 'Oil tanks at Brest, gunned by the British, are burning with a large column of smoke. No ships in the harbour.'[53] In the

The evacuated naval arsenal at Brest – in the background smoke billows from the French navy's burning fuel supplies, June 1940. (Author collection)

German sailors preparing French depth charges for operational use,
Atlantic coast, 1940. (Author collection)

arsenal a chaotic scene met his eyes: 'Inestimable quantities of material.
Guns found for the most part ruined ... Severe damage to all kinds of
installation. Many sunken vessels, cranes, etc, workers celebrating.
Everywhere great disorder.'[54] The French navy demolition squads had been
hard at work: not a single dock was usable, and the quay installations and
the arsenal river were blocked by sunken shipping.

In the midst of this chaos, on 23 June the naval commander received the
order to set up a U-boat base at Brest. The day before Group West had
required preparations to be taken in hand to use the base as quickly as
possible as a new base for German U-boats to operate in the Atlantic.[55]
Besides repair facilities and the organisation of supplies, mine-free access
into the port was necessary. Above all, the uncertain mine situation
presented the German naval centres in France with a problem, for there
was no information on the exact locations where the Luftwaffe had
dropped mines off the French ports. These were now a danger for German
naval craft. Worse still, only one minesweeping flotilla was available to
search for them because most of the German coastal security units were
in Norway.[56] The boats of 2nd R-boat Flotilla (*Räumboot*, or small
minesweeper) checked the ports on the Channel coast first and arrived at
Brest on 28 June. Meanwhile the German naval centres in Brittany had
begun looking at their own boats with a view to using them as auxiliary

minesweepers. Although in Brest and the Brest Bight there was not a single seaworthy boat to be found, several French steam trawlers were commandeered in the fishery harbour at Lorient.

By 6 August here alone the Kriegsmarine had impounded twenty-two vessels for the formation of new minesweeping flotillas at Cherbourg, Brest, Lorient, St-Nazaire and La Rochelle.[57] The trawlers were fitted with towing apparatus for minesweeping, mountings on deck for MGs (machine guns) or small calibre guns for use as anti-submarine defence or flak, and racks for depth charges. For fitting out these vessels there was no shortage of French equipment. At Brest alone there were forty otters,[58] 300 floats and 150 lines, as well as 4,000 serviceable depth charges of various sizes.[59] The conversion work on the trawlers was done in the naval arsenal. French yard workers set up the gun positions on deck and built the racks and guide rails for the depth charges.[60] There was a shortage of shipboard guns and so under German supervision the French gunnery workshops fitted a number of French 7.5cm field-gun barrels on traversable mountings.[61] A colourful collection of captured guns were forced into service. Thus the newly constituted Harbour Defence (*Hafenschutz*) Flotilla Brest had German and British signal pistols, French and Spanish revolvers and rifles, eight French Hotchkiss MGs and a Swiss

German VP- (*Vorposten*) boats in the naval arsenal at Brest, 1940. Notice the circular gun platforms on the foredeck of the outer boats. (Archiv Hans-Joachim Spallek, Lübeck)

2cm Oerlikon.[62] A similar situation reigned in the Channel coast flotillas where, for example, a patrol boat (*Vorpostenboot*, or VP-boat) of 15th VP-boat Flotilla was equipped with a German MG, a French First World War MG, two water-cooled Austrian MGs and a British MG as shipboard flak, while at the stern on a rotatable chassis was a German 3.7cm anti-tank gun.[63]

Converting these differing vessels into auxiliary minesweepers took time, and by the time that the first of them were commissioned, the eight motor minesweepers of 2nd R-boot Flotilla had undertaken the main task of minesweeping along the Biscay coast. They also accompanied the first U-boats into the new bases. In mid August only four auxiliary mine-sweepers were ready at Brest, while those earmarked for the Loire and Gironde were still fitting out.[64] The setting up of 44th Minesweeper Flotilla at La Rochelle had to be postponed until November 1940 for lack of suitable vessels but, happily for the Kriegsmarine, under the armistice agreement the French navy operated two minesweeper groups which first cleared the French minefield in the Gironde and then British-laid mines, and so relieved German minesweepers of the burden.[65]

Protection of the coast and ports against enemy mining operations and submarines became ever more urgent once the German U-boat arm began to use the new bases to replenish. On 7 July 1940 *U30* became the first German U-boat to make fast along the Atlantic coast at Lorient. Almost at the same time the RAF had begun laying mines in the approach channels to the ports of Brest, Lorient, St-Nazaire and La Rochelle.[66] On 24 August Brest harbour was closed for the first time on suspicion of having been mined.[67] Shortly afterwards, a tug and a fishing trawler sank off Lorient after hitting mines. In September 1940 British submarines succeeded in sinking two prizes sent in by the German merchant raiders *Orion* and *Atlantis* close to the French coast, and on 24 September the German catapult ship *Ostmark* was sunk by the British submarine *Tuna* southwest of St-Nazaire. The day before Skl mentioned in their war diary that security along inshore waters must be considered 'as not present'.[68] In Berlin, the loss of the important catapult ship, which was to have been used to launch long-range reconnaissance aircraft from Brest, was acknowledged as a severe blow. At that time the Kriegsmarine had already been in control of the Atlantic coast for two months.

The setting-up of the naval bases

Even as fighting continued in France, Admiral Raeder was already speaking of Brest as being the new main base for German U-boats.[69] Two days later Group West declared the port as a 'Base of the 1st Order' and required it to be expanded as quickly as possible.[70] An organisational plan drawn up by the Naval Command Office at the beginning of July 1940 for

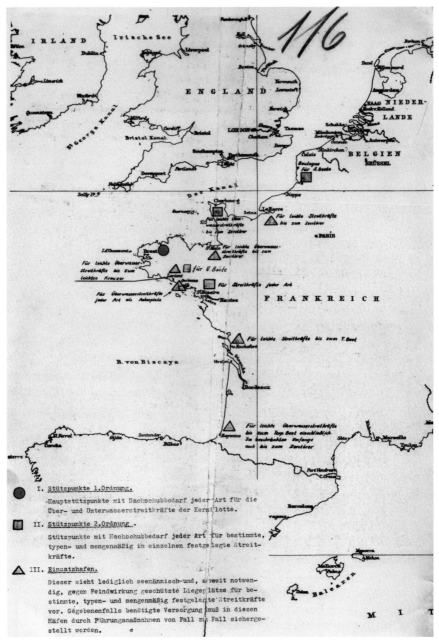

Bases on the French coast projected by the Naval Command Office, July 1940, showing Brest as the main base. The squares are second-order bases and the triangles are operational bases mainly for minor warships up to destroyer size, but offering protected anchorages for any kind of ship (St-Nazaire). (Bundesarchiv-Militärarchiv, Freiburg, RM 45 IV 747)

The naval arsenal at Lorient, August 1940. (Author collection)

the new bases in France identified Brest as a base of the first order, while Lorient and St-Nazaire were planned as second-order bases. St-Nazaire was to be the port for naval vessels of all kinds, and Lorient as a U-boat base, since no dry dock large enough existed at Lorient to take fleet units.[71] The Main Office for Warship Construction (*Hauptamt Kriegsschiffbau*), whose duty it was to fit out the harbours, reported a few days later that it would be impossible to find the necessary staff to man the new bases, operational ports and fitting-out centres and asked Skl to limit the requests for staff made by the Naval Command Office for France 'to a minimum' and if necessary even give up on Brest.[72] This demand poured cold water on the great expectations Skl had for the new main base, and it now saw itself in a situation in which the war against shipping in the Atlantic would have to be operated directly from its 'own' coast.

Reports from Brest also cast gloom over the initial joy at the supposed gain. According to a report by the Commanding Admiral France, Karlgeorg Schuster, at the end of July 1940 Brest had only one serviceable dry dock, the one in the merchant harbour, with its cranes only capable of taking light loads; it was not large enough to take a battleship.[73] It was impossible to estimate when repair work at the other dock installations would be completed. In the whole arsenal there was not a single crane which worked. Only the workshops could be used without restriction: as he saw it, the French workers were amply equipped to perform simple repairs. In his report Admiral Schuster came to the conclusion that it would be months before Brest could be made into an efficient base.

At Lorient, however, conditions were far more favourable. Repairs to the large dry dock there were expected to finish at the end of August. At St-Nazaire all kinds of ship repair could be performed at the undamaged private shipyards, leading Schuster to suggest that St-Nazaire rather than Brest should become premier base.[74] This prompted a discussion amongst naval planners as to the most suitable port to develop in the build-up of German naval bases until autumn 1940. Following the reports from France, Skl doubted that Brest was suitable as a first-order base because it lay within range of British aircraft.[75] Therefore in mid August it was decided to prioritise St-Nazaire farther south, while Lorient continued to be considered as the new main base for U-boats. The Naval Commander Brittany expressed his reservations about St-Nazaire as it was a very

U37 in dry dock at Lorient, August 1940. (Bundesarchiv, 101II-MW-1032-11A/Mannewitz)

difficult port for large ships to enter, but at OKM the final decision had been made.

In order make a final decision regarding the ongoing question of bases for fleet units, at the beginning of October a group from the Hauptamt-Kriegsschiffbau under its head, Konteradmiral Fuchs, arrived on the Biscay coast together with a delegation from Skl.[76] After looking over St-Nazaire, the leader of the Skl group reported to Berlin that, contrary to expectations, the port was only 'to a limited extent' suitable for receiving battleships or heavy cruisers.[77] With the exception of the Normandy Locks, a ship drawing over 8m (26ft) could not enter at all, which thus ruled out St-Nazaire as the principal base.[78] Next day the Skl delegation arrived at Brest. As a result of the delegation's report it was concluded in Berlin that the destruction to the harbour installations there had been overstated.[79] It was also believed that the greater danger of air attack to Brest as opposed to St-Nazaire could be reduced by improving preparations for the air defence system. Therefore, on 9 October, almost four months after German forces had occupied the French Atlantic coast, Raeder finally settled for Brest as the principal base for the Geman Fleet.[80] The report submitted by the Hauptamt Kriegsschiffbau Commission reinforced his decision.[81] Subsequently, at Brest a berth for a battleship at Flotilla Quay in the warship harbour and two places in the neighbouring large dry docks became available. These could only take ships up to the size of *Scharnhorst* and *Gneisenau*, so any repair to the *Bismarck* or *Tirpitz* would of necessity require a stay in the Normandy Lock at St-Nazaire. The main criticism was directed towards the lack of working cranes within the arsenal, or an efficient floating crane.

Whilst the development of the fleet base at Brest proceeded only slowly, a quite different situation prevailed at Lorient. The Kriegsmarine had set up a U-boat repair facility there on 15 August, which in October 1940 had a labour force of 650 German and 2,500 French dockyard workers, with capacity for repairing ten U-boats.[82] The dockyards director for France had recognised the special role of Lorient early on and in September ordered that the base was to be used only for the repair of U-boats, and arranged to retain the motor minesweepers needed to keep the approach routes free.[83] All other vessels had to divert to Brest or St-Nazaire.

The German naval yards in France

Once the decision had been taken in favour of Brest as the main base, on 28 October 1940 Hauptamt Kriegsschiffbau issued the order for a new dockyard organisation in France.[84] Three new naval yards at Brest, Lorient and St-Nazaire were to be ready by 15 November. While the yard at Lorient was to increase its repair capacity to thirty U-boats as soon as possible, at Brest arrangements were to be made for the repair of either a

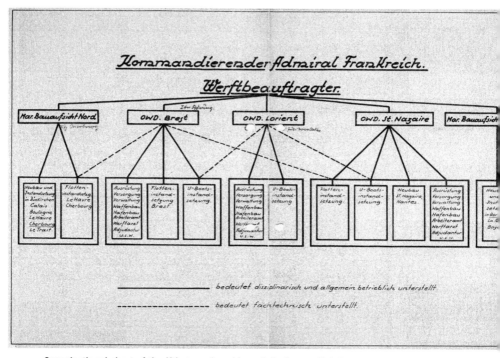

Organisational chart of the Kriegsmarine shipyards in France, October 1940. (Bundesarchiv-Militärarchiv, Freiburg)

single battleship or two cruisers or several destroyers. By 1 April 1941 a repair facility for thirty U-boats was also to be created at St-Nazaire. Of the three new dockyards, Lorient was to be responsible for all U-boat repair and restoration work along the Biscay coast, while Brest would do the same for fleet units. U-boat repairs were also planned for Brest, but the expansion of the fleet station had priority to the extent that the U-boat base would not be ready until 1 July 1941. In order to unburden the new yards of other repairs, it was proposed to pass smaller warships and auxiliaries requiring attention to the private French shipbuilding sector. Thus in December 1940 two boats of 2nd R-boat Flotilla and the tender *Brommy* were laid up for six weeks under repair at the French Forges de l'Ouest yard at St-Nazaire.[85] Other shipyards used by the Kriegsmarine in France were the Forges & Chantiers de la Mediterranée at Le Havre, the Compagnie Nantaise at Nantes and the Gironde yard at Bordeaux.

The general service structure in the new Kriegsmarine yards was based on the 'Shipyard Service Regulations' of the Kriegsmarine shipyard at Wilhelmshaven.[86] According to these, a Kriegsmarine yard was to be subdivided into various departments. The general service and

The Kriegsmarine shipyard at Brest. To the right is the former French
main building used by the German senior shipyard director, October
1940. (Author collection)

commercial department came under the central division (Z) controlled
by the senior shipyard director with his staff, amongst them the head of
the yard air defence (Z4), the head of the yard police (Z5) and from
1942 a leader for military training of yard employees (Z1). Besides the
equipment (chandlery) (I) and gunnery departments (II), the ship
construction (III) and engineering department (IV) were the two largest
and most important. Other areas of operations were the provinces of
harbour construction (V), torpedo and navigation (VI), signalling
equipment (VIII), supply (IX), the personnel office (A), administration
(V) and the yard senior medical officer (D). The chandlery department
arranged for replacement parts for naval units in the yard, as well as

anchorages, including towing and berthing of vessels and pilotage. The personnel office was responsible for accommodation, rations, uniforms and the social care of the German workforce and also for the employment, pay and care of French workers. The administration sector was responsible for the various arsenals in the yard and for the regular replacement of used materials. This structure changed often during the period of the occupation. For example, in 1942 the torpedo department (VI) was separated out to build the new Torpedo-arsenal Atlantik. In February 1943 after the setting up of Naval Construction Directorate France, the harbour construction department (V) built its new offices.

The Kriegsmarine shipyard provided the personnel for the new naval yards in France. By the end of 1940 it had sent a first contingent of 300 engineering and 100 ship construction staff for fleet repairs and another 180 engineering and 120 shipbuilding staff for U-boat repairs on the Biscay coast. A further 2,000 men to set up the U-boat repair facilities at Brest and St-Nazaire were foreseen for the spring and summer of 1941 respectively. Amongst these employees were, for example, specialists such as welders, electrical fitters and boilermakers. Special work such as large turntables was farmed out to French workshops. In the view of the Wilhelmshaven yard managers, the demand for 2,700 skilled workers far outstripped its possibilities. Its workforce at that time was about four thousand, of whom 700 were responsible for fixed installations such as the foundry and the boilerhouses. This left only 3,300 men free for detachment to France. However, the yard employed only 725 men in engine and machinery building, while according to plan they had to send 870 such men to France, and make available another 325 men for U-boat construction at Wilhelmshaven, a shortfall of 470 men in this area alone. If they were ordered to do it, the yard directors considered that the Wilhelmshaven yard would no longer be able to undertake any kind of shipbuilding or repair work. Despite the objections from Wilhelmshaven, the head of Hauptamt Kriegs-schiffbau, Admiral Fuchs, insisted, and set a deadline of 12 November 1940 for the transfer.[87] The insufficient number of skilled workers and engineers for U-boat repairs was to be made good by training at the French yards and the conscription of engineers from the private shipbuilding industry.[88]

The same situation prevailed for the workers. Thus at Lorient, for example, workers were installed from eleven different German under-takings, amongst them 345 men from the AG Weser yard at Bremen, forty-nine from Deutsche Werft Hamburg, seventy-one from the Deschimag Seebeckwerft, and work groups from Hagenuk Kiel, Krupp Kiel, Germaniawerft Kiel, AEG and Siemens.[89] These workers were paid

Arrival of German shipyard workers at their Brest barracks, end of 1940. (Archiv Heinrich Stamen, Bremen)

at the rates prevailing in Germany with a detached duty abroad supplement.[90] If the duty exceeded three months the men were given a green uniform as service clothing. The costs of lodging, food and medical care in the bases was borne by the Kriegsmarine.

That the creation of a working dockyard organisation in the occupied area was becoming ever more urgent is demonstrated by the complaints from the German naval commanders. At the end of November 1940 the Dockyards Director France had had to inform the naval commanders that, on account of the need for personnel for the increased construction of U-boats in the Reich, there were no staff available for construction supervision in France, and the existing staff levels were to be cut by a third.[91] In particular, these reductions affected supervision of work on minesweepers and patrol boats, which in future would have to be done

KRIEGSMARINEWERFT, Brest

DEMANDE POUR BREST

Ouvriers toutes professions et manœuvres

Les libérés de l'armée et de la marine bénéficieront de conditions spéciales qui leur seront données au bureau d'embauche

KRIEGSMARINEWERFT, BREST

Inspecteur LINDEMANN, bâtiment de la Majorité

Chambre 73 - Arsenal de Brest

Offer of jobs by the Kriegsmarine shipyard Brest published in the daily newspaper La Dépêche, July 1940 – workers of all kinds were sought. (Archives Municipales, Brest)

by the crews, while the few construction supervisors still available were limited to making spot checks. Already at the beginning of August 1940 Arnauld de la Perière had complained to Schuster, Commanding Admiral France, that the lack of German ship- and engine-building officials was causing 'irresponsible' delays in the conversion of the important new auxiliaries.[92]

A month before, the creation of the new coastal protection units had been compromised when the engineer officer responsible on the staff of Sea Defence Brittany had suddenly been ordered away. The Kapitän-leutnant in question had originally only been in charge of the lorries belonging to the naval artillery units at Brest, but then the equipping of auxiliary warships devolved upon him. In the view of the Naval Commander Brittany it was the personal involvement of this young officer alone which had resulted in having five of the eight vessels of the Brest harbour protection flotilla operational at this time. This officer's expertise was required to conclude work on other vessels in the French arsenal, since otherwise judgement of technical questions would remain the province of a French dockyard engineer, and the German naval centres at Brest did not want to leave themselves relying on his opinion about the seaworthiness of a German warship.[93]

Nevertheless, the technical knowledge of the French engineers and workers became increasingly important for the Kriegsmarine. In the two naval arsenals the dry docks and fuel tanks had been destroyed by the French navy before the evacuation of the ports, but most of the workers, the technical bosses and the administration officers had remained behind. Although the French had wrecked some of the machines, most workshops were still serviceable and the German harbour authorities set about a rapid restoration of the French installations. Thus the naval arsenal at Brest was up and running once more by 4 July 1940.

The French workers first had to clear the workshops and repair the tooling machines; later they helped with repairs to the other dockyard installations and the salving of ships sunk in the naval arsenal waters. This was also the case in the French naval arsenal at Lorient where co-operation with the French naval arsenal management had gone on 'without friction' according to a report of the German port commander.[94] The Hauptamt Kriegsschiffbau reported in September 1940 that the French naval arsenal at Brest had been busy converting and repairing several German harbour craft and auxiliaries and making repairs to German warships.[95] The French complement was about 1,800 men who – according to the report – showed themselves to be 'willing' and worked seven hours per day 'at the French tempo'. There was also not a single case of sabotage to report. From the point of view of the Hauptamt the capacities of the French workshops extended to all kinds of repairs to

French shipyard workers installing a flak position on a German auxiliary
vessel, 1940. (Bundesarchiv, 101II-MW-2210-09/Schöppe)

German fleet units except engine repairs at Brest where the necessary test
stands were absent. The French navy had always performed this work in
the naval engineering factory at Indret in the interior. Besides the French
naval arsenal at Brest, recourse was also had to the workshops of the
French private yard Dubigeon in the mercantile harbour, which also did
conversions and repairs to German auxiliary warships. This yard showed
itself to be 'speedy' and 'willing' according to the report and no acts of
sabotage were reported.

   In this co-operation with the French arsenals, incidents did occur. The
head of the French shipbuilding concern at Brest, Ingénieur Général
Roquebert, refused to renovate the salvaged French destroyer *Cyclone* for
the Kriegsmarine because, in his view, the work was of a purely military
nature. He was arrested and later released into the unoccupied zone. At
Lorient the head of the French arsenal prevented the employment of
French workers aboard the first German U-boats to put in.[96] Minor
repairs to the boats therefore had to be carried out either by the crews or
by the first German workers to arrive from the Wilhelmshaven shipyard.

   Gradually, the German workshops worked up. While the U-boat repair
facility at Lorient made its first small repairs to U-boats in August 1940,
in September the Kriegsmarine arsenal at Brest began converting the
German freighter *Rostock*, found at Lorient in June, into a *Sperrbrecher*
– a ship packed with barrels and corks to make it unsinkable – which

sailed about three hundred yards ahead of a U-boat as anti-mine protection. In October repairs were carried out to the engines of the merchant raider *Widder*. For reasons of secrecy, no French workers were allowed aboard and only those repairs were done which did not compromise the disguise of this freighter converted into a warship.[97]

U31 on the slipway at Lorient, August 1940. (Bundesarchiv, 101II-MW-3695-20/Schlemmer)

2

Brest as the Main Base for the German Fleet

After the decision had been taken to use Brest as the main base, on 14 October 1940 Grossadmiral Raeder explained the German naval planners' new strategy to Hitler.[1] In future its centre of gravity would be the surface forces. Battleships and cruisers would undertake 'long range operations in the North Atlantic', and as well as attacks on enemy convoys, would afford protection to German blockade runners returning home, or prizes putting into France.[2] In parallel, light naval forces would operate in the Channel and North Sea against British coastal traffic in order to cause the greatest possible disruption to the Royal Navy. Despite the warnings of the Commander Group West, Generaladmiral Alfred Saalwächter, who considered the planned breakout of heavy units through the Denmark Strait too dangerous, and saw the presence of more than three large units at Brest as indefensible because of the high risk of air attack on the base, Skl pressed ahead with their new strategy.[3] At this point the German planners were hoping for a further improvement in the strategic outlet situation consequent on the entry of Spain into the war on the German side; in the opinion of the admirals the conquest of Gibraltar and the use of Spanish ports would offer considerable advantages.[4]

In line with this new strategy, on the night of 1 November 1940 the heavy cruiser *Admiral Scheer* passed unnoticed through the Denmark Strait heading on a long cruise which brought her into the Indian Ocean; she sank seventeen ships of 113,233 gross tons and returned to Kiel at the end of March 1941.[5] The heavy cruiser *Admiral Hipper* also broke out through the Denmark Strait in December 1940 but this operation had to be cut short owing to engine trouble and the cruiser put into Brest.[6] These breakouts by German cruisers, unnoticed by the British, appeared to confirm the Skl in its new strategy. It was noted with satisfaction in the war diary that the operation of the *Admiral Hipper* had been 'a training manual example of the diversionary effect' and the widespread diversion of British naval forces in the search for the cruiser had had a positive effect on the operations of the *Admiral Scheer* in the South Atlantic.[7]

For Brest, however, the arrival of the cruiser was the moment of truth. Was the base in a position to repair her and protect her against the RAF? On 4 January 1941 *Admiral Hipper* was photographed by a British reconnaissance aircraft while in dry dock, as a result of which the base was the subject of 175 air attacks over the next few days, although the cruiser was not seriously damaged.[8]

On 1 February 1941 *Hipper* sailed for a new operation in the Atlantic. West of Gibraltar she found the unescorted convoy SLS 64 and sank seven British merchant ships of 32,806 gross tons.[9] Upon her return on 14 February, whilst entering dry dock in the mercantile harbour at Brest, the

The heavy cruiser *Admiral Hipper* in dry dock at Brest: British aerial photo, January 1941. (Imperial War Museum)

cruiser damaged a propeller after contact with a sunken barge in the harbour basin.[10] Because a repair was not possible at Brest, and in any case the Kriegsmarinewerft kept no spare propellers, a new one had to be brought from Kiel. This delay interfered with the Skl plan to send out *Admiral Hipper*, after refuelling and taking on more ammunition, in support of Operation *Berlin* by the battleships *Scharnhorst* and *Gneisenau*.

The reports from Brest at the time of the repair to the cruiser were an important indication of the efficiency of the new Kriegsmarine yard. Thus the commander of the *Hipper* described the repair facility at Brest as 'only for emergencies' and the base infrastructure as 'inadequate' for a fleet unit. In his opinion, the base did not have enough tugs, nor did the available tug crews have the necessary skills.[11] Even Schuster as Commanding Admiral France had remarked at the end of December 1940 that there were not enough tugs at Brest to handle two battleships or two heavy cruisers at the same time. Neither the air-raid warning system nor the flak was up to the standard found at German ports. It was decided to make use of the waiting time for the new propeller in overhauling the cruiser's rangefinding optics, but even this was not possible at Brest, and the equipment had to be dismantled and sent by train to Zeiss at Jena.[12]

Criticism of the circumstances prevailing at Brest was not new. In December 1940 the commander of a torpedo boat had complained to OKM about the yard.[13] The boat had entered on 23 December 1940 for repairs to the portside condenser pump, an electrical motor and the mine rails. The work should have taken only until the end of the month but the repairs to the pump needed repeated referrals to the boat's engine-room personnel. Initially, no crane had been available to remove the defective machine parts. When the boat finally left the yard at the end of December, neither the electric motor nor the mine rails had been attended to.

The senior yard director at the Kriegsmarine Yard Brest, Stobwasser, explained away the delays, citing the usual lack of cranes and tugs.[14] Furthermore, at the same time the destroyer *Richard Beitzen* had been in the yard, so that extra workers could not be spared for the torpedo boat. Accordingly, the commander of the latter had been informed upon arrival that repairs to machinery had to be carried out with such tools as were available aboard his boat. Defective engine parts were repaired in the workshops of the French naval arsenal. Pointing out that there were twenty other vessels in the yard besides the torpedo boat, Stobwasser emphasised that as far as the Kriegsmarine Yard Brest was concerned, everything had been done that could have been done at the time, especially since in this situation only a single foreman had been available. If one recalls that at the same time the Skl was planning operations by its battleships in the Atlantic, the question must be asked how the Kriegsmarine Yard Brest could have repaired a warship of such size if it could not guarantee repairs to a small torpedo boat and a destroyer, not to mention the smaller craft.

Further indications regarding the situation at Brest can be inferred from a report by the commander of *Richard Beitzen* submitted in January 1941. Machinery had to be repaired aboard the destroyer, but the yard did not have the necessary machine tools. Nearly all repairs, therefore, had to be carried out aboard the destroyer, or in the workshops of the French arsenal. Major turned work could not be handled. The yard also had no distillate for the destroyer's high pressure superheated steam machinery, so this had to be brought from Germany. This meant that the necessary tests and refining processes on the distillate could not be performed. The ship's officers thus concluded in their report that both the number of available German yard workers, and the level of their technical knowledge, could only be considered 'adequate', and assessed their working materials as 'very primitive'.[15]

Despite the fact that at the end of December 1940 Raeder had ordered that Brest must be expanded with as much as urgency as the background of the planned fleet operations in the Atlantic demanded, the cruiser *Hipper* reported at the end of February 1941 that the Kriegsmarine Yard Brest was not in a position, either from the point of view of personnel or materials, to handle the engine overhaul of several large ships or even the complete lay-up of a single large ship.[16] At the time the two battleships *Scharnhorst* and *Gneisenau* were already in the North Atlantic.

For a better estimation of the situation at the bases, in February 1941 No. 2 Fleet Admiral, Konteradmiral Werner Siemens, made a personal visit to the Atlantic coast. In his report he stated that Brest had a considerable anti-aircraft and coastal defence of eighteen heavy and thirteen light flak batteries and six coastal batteries, but only one of the two great dry docks in the warship harbour was operational.[17] Berths for large ships were available at Flotilla Quay in the warship harbour, at buoys in the roadstead there, and at buoys in the south of the Bight of Brest. The situation at the yard was more difficult. Although half of the machine tools requested from Germany had arrived, and the German yard personnel were in a position to do minor work, Siemens was obliged to mention that the number of German yard workers present did not extend to repairing a battleship. Even the repairs to *Hipper* had only been achieved by taking all the German personnel off other work. To emphasise the point, Siemens warned that 'if a large warship went there for a full overhaul ... it would bring all work on other warships and auxiliaries practically to a standstill.'[18]

Another problem was the continuing shortage of cranes. The one functioning floating crane had a lifting capacity of only 15 tonnes. A 100-tonne floating crane was on its way from Bordeaux but would have to be

A tug passing the great swing bridge over the Brest arsenal, 1941.
(Author collection)

reassembled after its arrival. As a reserve the Kriegsmarine had chartered two salvage cranes from the private French salvage company Neptune. There was also no protected area for fuel storage at Brest, since the French navy had destroyed all the tank compounds before abandoning the port. Refuelling came from three tankers which were highly vulnerable to air attack because of their size. One of these, the *J A Essberger*, had been sunk in an air attack on 4 February 1941, but meanwhile refloated. The base had no air-raid bunkers for the crews of ships at the envisaged berths.

Despite all these drawbacks, the two battleships *Scharnhorst* and *Gneisenau* put into Brest on 22 March 1941. An engine breakdown aboard *Scharnhorst* had forced the fleet commander to cut short the operation. Whilst *Gneisenau* went into the one functioning dry dock in the warship harbour, *Scharnhorst* made fast at Flotilla Quay. Apart from the repairs to the engine, an exchange of all boiler superheaters was needed and the fitting of banks of torpedo tubes.[19] As was to be expected, problems soon arose. The Kriegsmarine yard was missing important machine tools while the pump installation at the dry dock occupied by *Gneisenau* was out of action.[20] When the dock was finally pumped dry on 4 April, an unexploded bomb was discovered below the stem of the ship and she had to leave dry dock again. Moored at a buoy in the warship harbour on the

British air attack on Brest. The battleships *Scharnhorst* and *Gneisenau* are in the two dry docks at the left edge of the photo. (Imperial War Museum)

morning of 6 April, she was torpedoed in a surprise attack by British torpedo bombers. Brest did not have anti-torpedo nets against air attack.

Skl declared the torpedoing of the important ship to be an unlucky break and emphasised that, in view of the 'decisive operational and strategic significance of the French Atlantic coast', Brest would remain the fleet base, no matter what.[21]

In an air raid on the night of 11 April the RAF inflicted heavy damage on *Gneisenau*. The battleship, back in dry dock, was hit by four heavy bombs which killed seventy-five of the crew, including a large number of cadets who had just shipped aboard. The forward switching and computing centre for the ship's flak, the forward electric compass installation, the galley and bakery, as well as large areas of the accommodation deck, were seriously damaged. Amongst the dead were all the ship's cooks and, as all the galleys had been destroyed, the hundreds of crewmen had to be fed from field kitchens. This incident called the base into question for the first time at Skl and consideration was given to whether the battleships should remain there.[22] Raeder, however, held the circumstances at Brest to be on a level with those at Kiel and Wilhelmshaven and merely asked for an increase in the air defences, while ruling out any relocation of the ships.[23]

Burial of the *Gneisenau* crewmen who fell in the bombing raid at Brest,
11 April 1941. (Luc Braeuer collection, Batz sur Mer)

After the damage to *Gneisenau* there were new problems at the shipyard. For lightering the ship only a single oil barge with little capacity was available.[24] Some engine parts could not be repaired on site and had to be sent to Krupp at Essen, together with five connecting shafts from the starboard propeller shaft.[25] The crew had to remove the engine parts themselves.

Aboard *Scharnhorst* the Kriegsmarine Yard Brest had meanwhile begun work removing tubing, fittings and boiler covers to retube the superheaters.[26] As had been done previously for the minor vessels, recourse was had to the workshops of the French naval arsenal for repairs.[27] Although this work was deliberately carried out at a slow pace, in the opinion of the *Scharnhorst*'s commander, Kapitän zur See Kurt Caesar Hoffmann, it was 'better than anything that the yards at Kiel and Wilhelmshaven could have been able to do at this time.'[28] In order to give the Kriegsmarine yard a clear run repairing the two battleships, Skl decided not to send any more heavy units into Brest, nor U-boats for repair.[29] For the scheduled Operation *Rheinübung* involving the battleship *Bismarck* and heavy cruiser *Prinz Eugen*, it was decreed that Brest should only be entered if no major repairs were needed or the enemy presence or the condition of the ships made any alternative impossible.[30]

The repairs to *Scharnhorst* were completed in May 1941. The battleship was to go next to St-Nazaire to dock in the Normandy Lock there but these plans were overshadowed by the *Bismarck* event.[31] The idea had been that *Bismarck* and *Prinz Eugen* should join forces with the other two battleships in the successful Operation *Berlin*. Operation *Rheinübung* became a disaster from the time when the two ships were intercepted in the Denmark Strait by a British force of battlecruisers and cruisers. Although the British battlecruiser *Hood* was sunk, the *Bismarck* received three hits, resulting in her losing speed and trailing an oil slick. The fleet commander, Admiral Günther Lütjens, decided to head for St-Nazaire.[32] Group West told him to make for Brest because St-Nazaire would be impossible because of poor weather.[33] *Bismarck* never arrived. She went down on 27 May 1941 a few hundred sea miles west of Brest, after a battle with a numerically superior British naval force. Only *Prinz Eugen* was able to flee to the new base. The cruiser had been released by *Bismarck* on the night of 25 May to operate independently against enemy shipping in the Atlantic but was forced to head for Brest on account of engine trouble.[34]

After her arrival there on 1 June she went straight into dry dock in the mercantile harbour, where she was immediately covered over with camouflage netting against British air reconnaissance. RAF Bomber Command had decided previously to halt its air attacks on Brest in favour of concentrating on targets in Germany until reports were received of renewed movements by the German battleships at Brest.[35] After a reconnaissance aircraft identified *Prinz Eugen* in dock at the mercantile harbour, the air attacks were resumed.

The blow was bound to come eventually, and on 1 July 1941 a bomb hit the cruiser, destroying the radio amplifier and compass rooms, the gunnery switching centre and the bridge. This ship too was now out of commission, and Skl gave thought for the first time to the tactical value of this, in their opinion, 'most important Atlantic naval base'.[36] The bomb hits on *Gneisenau* and *Prinz Eugen* cost 140 lives, prompting the Brest naval centres to arrange quarters away from the danger area for those crew members not immediately needed. The men were found lodgings at hotels at Tréboul near Douarnenez in the south and Roscoff in the north of Brittany. Later the Kriegsmarine erected three barracks near the port, the so-called 'fleet camps', from where the crews would be transported back and forth by lorry or bus, and later by train, to their ships.

In order to protect the three valuable ships against further damage, the Kriegsmarine decided to introduce a gigantic air-raid protection programme on 17 April 1941.[37] The Luftwaffe experts recommended the use of artificial fog to prevent pinpoint bombing. This required five hundred smoke-making machines. In order to make orientation from the air as difficult as possible, easily identified buildings such as the French naval academy, the oil tank compound above the warship harbour and the large engineering workshop in the shipyard terrain were painted in a dark

Protective measures after the first bomb hits: the battleship *Gneisenau* under camouflage netting in dry dock at the Brest naval base, April 1941. (Author collection)

colour. To camouflage the two great dry docks in the warship harbour alone, an extra 15,000m² (18,000 sq yds) of netting had to be procured to add to the stock already on hand.

These figures are an indication of the battle for materials which the Kriegsmarine would have to fight over the next few months to protect their ships at Brest. It was planned to lay artificial smoke over a field 5km (3 miles) by 12km (7 miles), which over a period of fifteen minutes would rise to a height of 150m (500ft) and last for six hours. In order to extend it out over the Bight, boats of the harbour protection flotilla, tugs from the Kriegsmarine yard and other Kriegsmarine craft were turned into floating smoke-makers. These were replaced at the earliest opportunity by forty motor vessels which the Commandant, Naval Defences Brittany, Kapitän zur See Gustav Kieseritzky, impounded in the surrounding ports. Similar air defence measures had already been taken at Lorient in October 1940, but they had been rejected on the grounds of the high requirement in men and materials and the building of U-boat bunkers began instead. Obviously the same could not be done for major warships.

In the end the planned smokescreen needed 800 smoke-making

Decoy to attract British airmen in the Brest roadstead, December 1941.
(ECPAD, Ivry-sur-Seine)

machines and 550 men to man them. Another 200 men were required to
man the smoke-boats. Moreover the Kriegsmarine Yard Brest had to be
able to refill 800 pressurised bottles daily for the smoke apparatus. To
mislead British pilots, a decoy the size of a cruiser was built, using the
hull of the old French armoured cruiser *Gueydon* and two old French
naval yachts from the ships' cemetery at Landevennec.[38] The upper works
such as the battle mast, funnel and signal mast were tailored to resemble
those of the *Prinz Eugen*. The decoy was fitted out with flak and could be
towed to various positions in the roadstead.

The planned use of barrage balloons in addition to the smokescreen
came under criticism from the Luftwaffe.[39] Amongst the aircraft stationed
at Brest was the long-range reconnaissance squadron of the Fliegerführer
Atlantik (Flyer Command Atlantic), which flew missions in support of
the U-boat arm from the naval station at Poulmic. As the next such naval
station was at Hourtin near Bordeaux, there was no alternative landing
place if Brest was fogged in. In order not to endanger fighter aircraft
operating from the Brest-Nord and Brest-Süd airfields, the Luftwaffe
requested that barrage balloons should only be flown by day in good
visibility and at no higher altitude than 500m (1,640ft). Under these
conditions Kieseritzky considered barrage balloons would serve no useful
purpose and demanded instead that the war planes operate from
somewhere else, since it was more important to protect the battleships
than fly reconnaissance for U-boats.[40] On 5 July 1941 Kieseritzky even
advocated that the tower of the St Martin church at Brest be demolished
since in his opinion it could be used as a navigational aid for enemy
aircraft and could neither be smoked over nor camouflaged.[41] He argued
that 'minor civilian damage ... must be taken into account since the

'A harbour making smoke' – original caption to a propaganda photo
about the hiding of a naval base behind a smokescreen, a barrage
balloon overhead, undated. (Author collection)

purpose is to avoid very great military damage.'[42] Similar thoughts had
been expressed a few days before about the American memorial to the US
troops who fell during the landings at Brest in 1917. This obelisk and the
Portzic lighthouse were in a line, halfway along which were the dry docks
with the battleships. Accordingly, the obelisk was blown up on 4 July.

Against a background of increasing threat from the air, camouflage
measures were taken in bases along the Biscay coast. At Lorient only the
fish dock at Keroman, where Organisation Todt was building the new U-
boat bunkers, was fitted out with smoke defences, while at St-Nazaire
detachments of the Reich Work Service (RAD) camouflaged the area
surrounding the Normandy Lock, the great halls of the Penhoët shipyard,
the excavation trench for the new U-boat bunker and other noticeable
buildings in the harbour and shipyard grounds. At Brest the senior shipyard
director's camouflage company used no less than 1,000 tonnes of camouflage
paint, 200,000 rush mats, 50,000m^2 (60,000 sq yds) of chicken wire, 500m^3
(18,000 cu ft) of scaffolding poles and 300m^3 (10,000 cu ft) of timber.[43]

First, bright areas easily recognised from the air were earthed over, then
the two battleships given a coat of camouflage paint and their upper
works draped with camouflage nets. To break up the contours of
Scharnhorst at the quayside, camouflage mats on floats were placed ahead
and astern of the ship. Additional protection against bomb damage was

provided by armour plates on the decks. In Bertheaume Bay, west of the warship harbour, the Kriegsmarine built a decoy installation illuminated at night to lure British pilots away from their real target. The flak protection was increased so that with thirty-four heavy and twenty-two light flak batteries, Brest was better defended than Wilhelmshaven.[44]

Despite these measures, after completion of the repairs to *Scharnhorst*, the fleet commander declined to have the two battleships docked together. The danger was too great of losing the newly operational *Scharnhorst* to air attack. Group West suggested that the ship should move down to St-Nazaire, and on 18 July 1941 the battleship was reported ready to sail. Despite the misgivings of the fleet commander the final repairs were carried out at Brest to avoid having to enter dry dock at St-Nazaire. For full restoration of operational readiness the battleship was to go first to La Pallice for gunnery practice with the heavy armament and to work up the newly installed batteries of torpedo tubes. To conceal her departure from the RAF, thought was given to erecting a mock-up of the ship in the dry dock, but this would have taken too much time and thus after *Scharnhorst* sailed on the afternoon of 21 July a German tanker was put there instead.[45] RAF air reconnaissance noticed the absence of *Scharnhorst* very quickly, and on the afternoon of 24 July when Bomber Command launched its first daylight attack on Brest, fifteen of their bombers followed the Biscay coast south and discovered *Scharnhorst* at the La Pallice mole.[46] This exposed position compromised the ship. Although flak accounted for twelve of the fifteen attackers, the formation managed to hit the battleship with five bombs.[47] Thus Operation *Südwind*, the transfer of *Scharnhorst* to La Pallice, proved to be an error of judgement. Even on the day she had departed from Brest, Skl had expressed reservations about having her berth at the La Pallice mole because of the difficulty of protecting the anchorage against air attack.[48] There were no dock facilities there for large warships. Thus on the evening of 24 July *Scharnhorst* headed back to Brest. The air attack had shown that German fleet units could not escape the danger from the air merely by moving farther south down the coast.

Scharnhorst arrived on 25 July with a heavy list. On the way, British torpedo aircraft made an attempt to sink the ship but were driven off by her flak. The flooding caused comprehensive damage to cabling. After an initial inspection, Kriegsmarine Yard Brest estimated that the repairs would take four months. This was increased to eight months shortly afterwards when the full damage to the cabling was assessed.

This meant that all three major warships at Brest were now non-operational. The anti-shipping war with heavy units planned by the Skl had thus come to nothing because they had no more major warships to send out. The heavy cruiser *Lützow* had been torpedoed and seriously damaged by a British submarine whilst attempting to break out into the North Atlantic on 13 June 1941 and the heavy cruisers *Admiral Hipper* and *Admiral Scheer* were both being overhauled in the yards. The new battleship *Tirpitz* was still working up.

It was in any case questionable if any further breakouts into the Atlantic would have been possible, given increased British monitoring of the exit routes, assisted by new radar technology. Moreover, the fact that after the sinking of the *Bismarck* the Royal Navy had succeeded in rolling up the network of supply ships in the Atlantic by deciphering the German naval codes leads one to doubt the chances of further success by German surface units in the Atlantic.

Despite the unceasing efforts of the RAF, the Kriegsmarine yard at Brest had the ships ready to sail by December 1941. In order to achieve this, besides calling on yard workers from the Biscay bases, the Kriegsmarine had brought in workers from German home yards even when, for example, that meant delaying the completion of twelve new minesweepers at Rickmers shipyard, Bremerhaven, by more than two months.[49] The battleships had priority. The effect of the withdrawal of workers from the Biscay bases became apparent in the area of U-boat repairs. Admiral Dönitz recalled that there was a shortage of 800 workers, which meant that U-boats spent longer periods under repair, so that the blockade of Brest also affected the U-boat war.[50]

In an air attack on 18 December 1941, the RAF succeeded in inflicting

Prinz Eugen at gunnery practice from the flotilla quay anchorage, Brest, 1941. (Author collection)

a breach of the outer hull of *Gneisenau*, but flooding was minor and the damage was quickly repaired. In a situation report to Hitler one month earlier, Raeder had set out the SkI's new plans for the operational use of the repaired ships. According to this, the high risk of air attacks made any further stay at Brest undesirable, and after a brief anti-shipping sortie in the North Atlantic the ships would return by the Iceland route.[51] When Raeder remarked as an aside that the *Prinz Eugen* might be sent back to Germany alone through the English Channel, Hitler interrupted him to ask if it would not be possible to bring the entire Brest squadron back that way. When on 29 December 1941 Raeder reported the readiness of the ships to sail, Hitler ordered their return through the Channel in order that they should be available as soon as possible for the defence of Norway.[52] Should this not be possible, Hitler ordered that the ships should be decommissioned at Brest in order that their guns and crews could be used to reinforce the Norwegian coastal defences.

After comprehensive preparations, the Commanding Officer Battleships issued the order to attempt the Channel Dash on the evening of 11 February 1942. Operation *Cerberus* began at the end of a British air raid when the three ships left the base under a smokescreen and headed northeast for the Channel after reaching the open sea. The German ships were not spotted from the air until around midday. Despite being fired upon by the Dover battery and coming under attack from British air and naval forces, the Channel Dash succeeded. *Cerberus* was a tactical victory, even though both battleships sustained mine damage and had to enter the yards upon their return to Germany. On 27 February *Gneisenau* was the target of a heavy air attack, which so badly damaged her that she had to be decommissioned.

On Hitler's orders *Scharnhorst* sailed in October 1942 for the Arctic Circle to protect the Norwegian coast. In a questionable operation against an Allied convoy off the North Cape, on 26 December 1943 she was intercepted by British naval forces and sunk with most of her crew. The major German surface units played no further important role in the naval war. The last battleship, *Tirpitz*, was capsized on 12 November 1944 by air attack in Norwegian inshore waters, more than 1,200 of the ship's company losing their lives. The heavy cruisers were used in the humanitarian evacuation of East Prussia in the spring of 1945 and saw some action bombarding Soviet ground forces.

For Britain, the withdrawal of the German squadron from Brest was a success, despite the humiliation of the Channel Dash. On 17 February 1942 Churchill stated in the House of Commons that the three German ships had represented a serious danger to British supply routes.[53] In order to counter this danger, the Royal Air Force had been asked by the Admiralty to subject the German ships to unceasing air attacks. Until

Battleship *Scharnhorst* during the Channel Dash to Germany, 12 February 1942. (Bundesarchiv, 101II-MW-3695-20/Schlemmer)

their departure the RAF flew a total of 3,299 air raids against the French port.[54] This cost 235 French citizens their lives and about four thousand were injured.[55] At the same time the other ports were the target of no more than a few dozen attacks in which only Lorient in July and November 1941 suffered serious damage.[56]

As regards the fleet base on the Atlantic coast, yearned for by the Germans for so long, the Commander-in-Chief of the Kriegsmarine, Grossadmiral Raeder, stated his opinion after the war:

> Unfortunately it turned out that the possibilities of defending Brest against Allied air attacks did not meet the requirement to the extent that the ships were damaged repeatedly and extensive repairs became necessary. Moving the battleship *Scharnhorst* to La Pallice on the Biscay coast did not change anything. It was self-evident that the two battleships as a group were one of the most important targets for the British. As a result German anti-aircraft defences had to be installed. Insofar as this fell within the ambit of the navy, it was done by setting up numerous flak batteries, equipped with smoke-making machines and camouflage. However, cover from our own fighters was inadequate. Precisely here again it was shown how right it would have been to sacrifice the attack on Russia and use the weight of the Luftwaffe primarily for the struggle against our main enemy Britain.[57]

By withdrawing the heavy ships from Brest, the German naval planners finally handed the struggle for the sea lanes to the U-boats.

3
German U-Boats in the Atlantic

On the day war broke out, the Commanding Officer U-boats, Admiral Karl Dönitz, requested an increase in the number of vessels at his disposal from sixty U-boats, of which only half were suitable for Atlantic operations, to a fleet of three hundred with which he considered he could force Britain to its knees.[1] The first U-boat successes, amongst them the sinking of the battleship *Royal Oak* by Günther Prien inside the Home Fleet base at Scapa Flow, seemed to confirm Dönitz in his belief, and elevated the U-boat arm to becoming a favourite theme of Nazi propaganda, which led to its achieving legendary status over the course of the war.

The capture of the ports on the French Atlantic coast provided U-boats with a clear prolongation of their operational periods in the North Atlantic, the main operational area at that time. From then on, no longer did they have to pass around the north of Britain for access to their Norwegian or German ports to refuel or reload torpedoes. Admiral Raeder wanted Brest to be made into the new main base of the U-boat arm.[2] Of key importance was its location in immediate proximity to the British convoy routes from Africa and North America, which made it so interesting in the eyes of the German naval strategists. On 27 June 1940 Dönitz went to the Atlantic coast in person to gain his own first-hand impression of the

The commander of the U-boat arm, Karl Dönitz, as Commander-in-Chief of the Kriegsmarine, c.1943. (Author collection)

Re-arming a German U-boat with torpedoes at Lorient, August 1940.
(Author collection)

captured ports.[3] Even before the armistice negotiations, he had a train waiting at Wilhelmshaven, with torpedoes, spare parts and the corresponding personnel, which would set off for the Atlantic coast once the announcement was made that the armistice had been signed.[4]

The destruction wrought at the Brest naval arsenal convinced Dönitz to opt for the port of Lorient much farther south, against the wishes of Raeder.[5] Previously, on 25 June, Group West had urged the recommissioning of the French state shipyard there and the setting up of a German base for armaments and equipment.[6] Even the Naval Commander Brittany, Arnauld de la Perière, formerly a U-boat commander in the Great War, had recommended the port to Skl as being better suited as a U-boat base.[7] At Lorient, the naval centres had known of a mine-free channel into the port since the arrival of German troops, the French naval arsenal was free for navigation and, according to the new port commander, the French arsenal directorate was 'ready to co-operate'.[8] The lesser danger of air attack compared to Brest also spoke for Lorient. Moreover, at nearby St-Nazaire the Wehrmacht had been able to secure large reserves of fuel for a first replenishment of German U-boats.

On his first visit to the Atlantic coast Dönitz proved to be a man of action. He proposed that experienced shipyard managers be commandeered at once for the Atlantic coast and left an officer of his staff behind at Lorient who, as the 'U-Office Bretagne', would deal with the

Attack on a British merchant ship in the North Atlantic, 1941.
(Author collection)

first questions of supplies at Lorient. On 28 June 1940 Korvettenkapitän
Patzig reported the new U-boat base as a going concern.[9] Dönitz foresaw
four phases to follow.[10] First, U-boats would only use French ports for
fuel, provisions and to reload torpedoes. The second stage would see the
introduction of repair facilities for short lay-up times of from ten to
fourteen days. Then Dönitz would relocate his command centre to the
Atlantic coast, and fourth, provisions would be made for longer lay-up
periods in the yards.

On 2 July 1940 the torpedo train, under the direction of Kapitän zur
See Clamor von Trotha, arrived at Brest from Wilhelmshaven, and was
redirected to Lorient where two officers and thirty-six men of U-Office
Brittany spent the remainder of the month setting up a compound with
fifty-three torpedoes which would be taken to the U-boats by lighters.[11]
Cranes for the shipping of torpedoes were plentiful in the naval arsenal
and the fish dock.

Although the French navy tank compound at Lorient had been
destroyed before the port was abandoned, the Kriegsmarine solved this
problem before the end of July 1940 by sending to the base for U-boat
resupply 1,500m^3 (330,000 gallons) of fuel spread over 387 barrels, sixty-
four railway tank-wagons, one oil tanker and the prize tanker *Krossfonn*.[12]

The first U-boat to put into Lorient was *U30*, which berthed on 7 July 1940. Using the French Atlantic coast extended the operational period of U-boats by a whole week compared with the initial phase of the war. The increase in the number of enemy ships sunk from July to October was attributable to Dönitz's new base at Lorient.[13]

On 15 August 1940 the Lorient U-boat repair yard was inaugurated as the first Kriegsmarine yard in occupied France.[14] Additionally the Kriegsmarine yard at Wilhelmshaven had transferred the outsourcing of its West Yard to Lorient.[15] Two months later, three new Kriegsmarine yards were set up at Brest, Lorient and St-Nazaire.[16]

The German yard directors at Lorient occupied the Gabriel Pavilion, former seat of the French naval prefect, in the former French naval arsenal. For U-boat crews, a barracks for six hundred men was built on the east bank of the Scorff river, the former French port barracks on the inner harbour being made available to them for accommodation. After a short stay in Paris, in November 1940 the Commanding Officer U-boats (BdU) removed to Lorient and together with his staff occupied a villa at Kernevel, nicknamed the 'Little Sardine Mansion', which had belonged previously to a French canning manufacturer and was opposite the Keroman U-boat base, then under construction. From here, Dönitz controlled the operations of German U-boats until the spring of 1942 and would go down to the various ports to greet incoming boats.

In June 1941 Lorient became the base of 2nd U-boat Flotilla, and in January 1942 10th U-boat Flotilla was reformed there. The existing flotilla staffs were transferred to the Biscay coast by train: personnel, tools, provisions and spare parts. A report by the former flotilla commander of 7th U-boat Flotilla, Korvettenkapitän Sohler, gave his first impressions of the new base as follows:

At first many of those employed at St-Nazaire were found lodgings in an old school in the town centre which had already been used by the advance party in order to set up the necessary installations. Although a significant part of the shipyard kept going with its former French workforce, German personnel were needed to handle the technically much more complicated U-boat repairs. This could be quite a problem especially bearing in mind that many Germans spoke no French and a large number of the French workers understood no German. To cap it all, the reserve parts came from far distant places such as Kiel, and the French bases were not only at the end of a long supply chain but the shipyard was in the precarious position of not knowing when the deliveries would probably arrive.[17]

Until the inauguration of the first berths in bunkers, U-boats used the available port installations. At Lorient these were primarily the three

Accommodation barracks in the new U-boat base at Lorient, 1940.
(Author collection)

repaired dry docks of the former French naval arsenal where there was room for eight U-boats. A raised platform for fishing boats in the Keroman fish dock could also be used for repairs. U-boats were towed out of the water over a ramp to occupy one of six berths arranged in a star formation. The Kriegsmarine had reinforced the weight-bearing capacity

The 'Little Sardine Mansion' at Kernevel, near Lorient in 2011. From November 1940 it was the seat of the commander of the U-boats; now it is in the possession of the French navy. (Martin Kaule)

Dining hall of 2nd U-boat Flotilla, Lorient: on the walls the history of the submarine, 1941. (Author collection)

of the raised slipway and used it for repairs from mid August 1940. For protection against air attack two of these six berths were provided with tall, pointed-roof concrete shelters later known as 'cathedral bunkers'. By 15 January 1941 Lorient had a repair capacity for thirty U-boats which meant that up to fifteen boats could be handled at the same time in a two- to three-week period for a front overhaul.[18]

At this time only two boats ran into Brest. On 22 August 1940 *U65* made fast in the Tourville dry dock at the centre of the naval arsenal under the gaze of the interested civilian population and left on 28 August. The second boat, *U29*, arrived in Brest on 31 October for a short visit to the yard and to replenish. Because it had been designated initially as a fleet base, not until June 1941 did Brest become a U-boat base and home port to 1st U-boat Flotilla, whose personnel used the former French naval academy above the warship harbour. In September 1941 9th U-boat Flotilla was reformed at Brest, their quarters being in the new hospital building in the town centre.

On 14 April 1941 Raeder had ruled that on account of the continual British air attacks on the battleships blockaded in Brest, no U-boat repairs were to be carried out there until the U-boat bunker was completed, although he had no objection to a small repair section in the backwaters of the naval arsenal.[19] U-boats there were protected against aerial detection by high cliffs on either side of the arsenal stream, as well as

Type II U-boat on the reinforced trawler repair berth at Lorient, August
1940, later given the protection of a cathedral bunker. (Author collection)

The Saltzwedel Barracks, quarters of 2nd U-boat Flotilla, Lorient, 1942.
(Author collection)

being hidden under camouflage netting. Only *U204* was lightly damaged in these narrows (nicknamed *Wolfsschlucht* after Hitler's military headquarters) during an air attack on the night of 7 July 1941.[20] Once the U-boat bunker in the warship harbour was ready, all repairs were transferred there. Only the underground French navy torpedo store in the backwaters of the naval arsenal continued in use, the torpedoes being brought to the bunker by rail or lighter.

In March 1941 it was decided to set up another U-boat base at La

German U-boats under camouflage netting in the backwaters of the Brest arsenal, April 1941. (Author collection)

Pallice, which had until then been the alternative base for Italian submarines stationed at Bordeaux. The German armament and equipment station in the former French naval base at Rochefort set up the new Kriegsmarine yard at La Pallice. Its capacity for repairs was at first limited to three berths on the north side of the harbour basin and the dry docks in the harbour. At the same time work was begun on a U-boat bunker on the eastern side of the harbour basin. La Pallice became home to 3rd U-boat Flotilla which took over the base on 27 October 1941 and whose staff occupied a former French barracks. The first boat of the flotilla, *U82*, entered the new base on 19 November 1941. Other boats followed in December and in the same month shipyard personnel from the Bremer Werft AG Weser arrived. Until then a repair team of about fifty men from the Kriegsmarine Yard Wilhelmshaven had carried out small repairs to U-boats. The workers were housed in a compound of huts at Châtelaillon, about 30km (20 miles) south of La Rochelle, and transported to the shipyard by bus, later by train. The departmental head and foremen, in common with the other bases, came from the Kriegsmarine Yard Wilhelmshaven.

The fifth and last German U-boat base on the Atlantic coast was set up at Bordeaux in the summer of 1941. The port on the Gironde had been the seat of the BETASOM base for Italian submarines which used the basin of the mercantile harbour. This base had been created under the command of Admiral Parona in August 1940 to support the Kriegs-

Italian submarine of the BETASOM base in the mercantile harbour dry dock, Bordeaux, 1940. (Bundesarchiv, 101II-MW-2198-05A/Engelmann)

marine in the fight against the British supply routes. Italian boats operated mainly in the South Atlantic. Kriegsmarine Yard Bordeaux had its problems. A shortage of personnel had obliged the Kriegsmarine to approach the Hamburg private yard of Blohm & Voss to request that they make available supervisors and workers. Even though the employee numbers there had been seriously drained by the increasing conscription of young workers into the Wehrmacht, Blohm & Voss believed that by adjusting the repair schedules they could make do with fewer workers than the Kriegsmarine. To realise their idea, the management of Blohm & Voss had first taken a close look at La Pallice. The Kriegsmarine feared that a takeover might cause too much unrest in an operation already up and running, and instead therefore offered the yard at Bordeaux which was still under development.

At the end of October 1942 Blohm & Voss took over the yard's repairs and a section of the gunnery shop. Despite the shortage of skilled labour, the firm had set itself the goal of at least meeting the time ratio for repairs set by Dönitz, of two yard- to three sea-days, if not improving on it. Military control of the repairs was undertaken by a small Kriegsmarine liaison office staffed by two naval works surveyors for ship and machinery construction and an engineer officer for the guns. The repairs sector began work at the beginning of 1943. For Blohm & Voss, taking over Bordeaux seems to have been good business. The Kriegsmarine paid all wages and disbursements up to 31 December 1942 and also the travel costs of the workers sent by Blohm & Voss to Bordeaux. Moreover, the Kriegsmarine made the workshop installations of the bunker available without charge, and was responsible for procuring materials, tools and fuel. Blohm & Voss handled the piecework and hourly rates. The German workers at the Bordeaux yard were housed in two compounds at Bouscat and Blanquefort. Although it had been hoped to recruit French labour – the Kriegsmarine Yard Lorient had estimated a requirement of 1,348 men, and Blohm & Voss up to 1,500 French workers – getting them was difficult because Bordeaux had already been scoured for candidates for labour in Germany and no skilled workers were to be found anywhere.

Bordeaux became the base of 12th U-boat Flotilla, whose first boat, *U178*, arrived on 9 January 1943. Up until the disbanding of the flotilla in the summer of 1944, the yard was never used to full capacity, so repair work was undertaken for other flotillas. In September 1943 Blohm & Voss took over the maintenance of artillery and hand weapons for the Kriegsmarine units from Royan to the Spanish border. Co-operation between the Kriegsmarine and Blohm & Voss at Bordeaux was a model for other bases. In March 1943 the management of Deutsche Werft made enquiries of Blohm & Voss at Bordeaux in connection with their taking over the repair yards at Toulon should the occasion arise, and Deschimag Bremen took over the U-boat repair sector of the Kriegsmarine yard at Brest in 1943.

Building the U-boat bunkers

When the French Atlantic bases were first used by the U-boat arm, the reception, repair and fitting out of U-boats took place in the open. U-boats were camouflaged with netting, but this did not protect against bombs. Because the new bases lay within range of British aircraft, on 25 October 1940 Hitler asked the BdU what protection he considered essential at the new bases. In response, Dönitz requested concrete bunkers on the lines of the U-boat shelters in Flanders in the First World War.[21] These pens would also house workshops, so that all work on the boats could proceed under protection from air attack.

Organisation Todt (OT) was asked to undertake the building work. On 16 November 1940 its head, Dr Fritz Todt, met with representatives of the Commanding Admiral France, Wolfgang Schuster, and the head of the Skl Office Group for U-boats, Konteradmiral Werner Siemens, and agreed on the sites where the bunkers were to be constructed at Brest, Lorient and St-Nazaire.[22] At Brest, a former naval air station on the west side of the warship harbour was chosen, and at Lorient an open space behind the Keroman fish dock. At St-Nazaire the bunker was to be built immediately by the town on the north side of the harbour basin. All three

U-boat bunker under construction at Lorient, August 1941. (Bundesarchiv, 101II-MW-4019-14A/Tölle [Tröller])

locations were near large shipyards whose capacity could be used to repair U-boats.

The Kriegsmarine Planning Office and the OT Operations Staff oversaw the bunker construction at Lorient. OKM just informed the planning office how many pens they required for the future U-boat bases, the basis for the calculations being the relationship of forty days in port to sixty days at sea per boat as laid down by Dönitz. Thus twenty pens could accommodate around two flotillas, corresponding to a total strength of fifty boats.

For the construction work, as much attention as possible was paid to the available routes for transportation. Thus at Brest the site could only be accessed by a narrow road on the bank of the

Excavation work to enlarge the U-boat bunker at La Pallice, October 1942. (Bundesarchiv, 101II-MW-6863-23/Tölle [Tröller])

The harbour of St-Nazaire before the Second World War; the German U-boat bunker was built on the left-hand side. (Author collection)

river and the harbour railway in the arsenal, making many journeys by water necessary. At St-Nazaire, on the other hand, the bunker was at the edge of the harbour, which was convenient for the transport of building materials, and even for the building work itself by use of the harbour basin. Thus the first three pens were ready on 30 July 1941 after only four months' work. The achievement in terms of transportation was enormous, of course: for the two bunkers Keroman I and Keroman II at Lorient, sixty thousand wagonloads of building materials were needed, most of it coming to the Atlantic coast from Germany, including the prefabricated ceiling supports and reinforcing irons.

Alongside large German construction companies at the bunker building sites, such as Holzmann at Lorient or Berger at Brest, various other German and French sub-contractors were active, as for example the Parisian building firm of Campenon Bernard at Brest.[23] The Berlin construction firm Julius Berger, which had been commissioned by OT to carry out the work, founded a work community known as 'Bergtcamp' at Brest.[24] Campenon Bernard had been involved in building the dry docks at Brest for the French navy pre-war, and their equipment and materials were still there. OT transferred the building contract to these firms and with the assistance of the senior building managers monitored the quality of the work. The chief of the OT head office, Xaver Dorsch, recollected that there was no cause for complaint in their collaboration with French firms: 'In general OT had very good experiences with the French building firms used. The legendary ability of the French to improvise was confirmed here 100 per cent. It could not be avoided that even secret plans

—— ON EMBAUCHE ——

ENTREPRISE DE TRAVAUX MARITIMES - BERGTCAMP
PORTE CAFARELLI - ARSENAL DE BREST

Manœuvres .... 6 fr. »» l'heure	Mineurs ...... 6 fr. 30 à 6 fr. 50	Charpent. bois 7 fr. 20 à 7 fr. 50
Maçons-cimentiers 7 fr. 20	Mécaniciens ... 7 fr. 20 à 8 fr. »»	Charpentiers monteurs
Ferrailleurs de 6 f. 30 à 7 f. »»		fer .... 7 fr. 20 à 7 fr. 50

CONDUCTEURS DE TRAVAUX — CHEFS DE CHANTIER
CHEFS D'ÉQUIPES

Hourly rates for Bergtcamp construction work advertised in the Brest
newspaper *La Dépêche*. (Archives Municipales, Brest)

had to pass through French hands, and some were even drawn up by them.
Hitler approved this because the operation was more important to him
than secrecy.'[25]

At the beginning of the period of German occupation, the U-boat
bunkers were the biggest building operations on the Atlantic coast.
According to Dorsch, at the bunker building sites of Brest, Lorient and
St-Nazaire alone, about 45,000 workers were employed.[26] Only one in five
of these was German. Thus at Brest, for example, besides many French,
Belgians and Dutch, there were also Italians, Greeks, Spanish, Portuguese,
and Russians who had fled to France after the October revolution.[27] What
attracted most of them was a secure paying job at the OT sites. Amongst
them was the 18-year-old Belgian, Frans van Dooren, who reported as a
volunteer to the St-Nazaire site in August 1941:

I went of my own free will to St-Nazaire, and for various reasons.
Primarily because there was no work in Belgium at that time. I was the
oldest son of a family with three children, and my father had died of
cancer in May 1941. Therefore against my will I had become the
family's breadwinner. We did not have enough money to buy food. Food
was in short supply anyway, and the prices on the black market put it
out of reach. I also feared being sent to work in Germany. There were
enough rumours about that sort of thing. So I went to St-Nazaire where
an uncle of mine had already been working several months. Once I got
there I was taken on by a German firm and given a shovel. Soon I was
offered the opportunity to work a cement mixer, cement pump, com-
pressor, etc. By doing that I got double rate, 80 pfennigs an hour, a good
wage in those days. The money was sent to my mother in Belgium, and
she got it regularly and always correct. Personally I only got pocket
money of 200 francs a week, enough to buy something extra and go to
a cinema or cafe.[28]

Workers at the Atlantic bunker sites were paid according to the OT tariff
for foreign employees with various categories depending on the country of

Sketch of the U-boat bunker installations at Keroman near Lorient, c.1943. (Wilhelm Fahrmbacher & Walter Matthiae, *Lorient*, Weissenburg 1956)

origin.[29] Most of the men were accommodated in OT's own camps or in private lodgings. Only the 'Red Spanish', Republicans interned in France who had fought against Franco in the Spanish civil war, were kept under strict watch in barracks and taken to and from work by the French police. OT was quite willing to have them on the workforce because apart from feeding them, nothing had to be paid to the French authorities. For the other workers as volunteers on the building sites there was the opportunity to earn a good wage. The fact that working for the OT protected a worker against being sent forcibly to Germany to work may have influenced the decision of many Frenchmen. It is of interest to note that French workers and the French building industry showed themselves to be much more willing than was the similar case in Norway where the German occupiers found very few workers willing to help building U-boat bunkers and later had recourse to Soviet PoWs.

Hitler had approved the building plans for the U-boat bunkers on 23 December 1940 during an inspection of the coastal batteries at Cap Gris Nez.[30] Whilst a large tidal bunker with twelve places was to be built at Brest, dry bunkers were planned for Lorient in the immediate vicinity of the Keroman fish dock. The bunker installations at Keroman were built on a rocky tableland and consisted of two great buildings facing each other (Keroman I and II) with a total of twelve pens into which U-boats would be pushed on a rail-mounted cradle. Once the armoured doors were closed the boats could be repaired dry, standing freely. Previously they would have left the water for a bunkered slipway from where they would be shunted on a cradle to the selected pen. This procedure took about an hour and was considerably faster than the usual method of entering a dry dock which took up to four hours. The buildings were constructed by the German firms Philip Holzmann and Siemens Bau Union. Technical fittings such as the slipway, docking chassis and mobile stage came from the firm MAN which previously had made the new dock gates for the dry docks at the French naval arsenal, and later the gates for the two dry docks in the tidal bunker Keroman III. This latter had five wet pens so that when the Keroman installation was completed twenty-five U-boats at a time could be repaired, safe from air attack.

Another smaller fitting-out bunker with two wet pens, the Scorff bunker, rose inside the French naval arsenal on the east bank of the Scorff river. The crane installations and armoured doors of the Keroman bunker were manufactured by the Gutehoffnungshütte at Oberhausen, and the electrical gear came from Siemens-Schuckert. At Keroman I, barracks for a thousand shipyard employees were built, equipped with air-conditioning, heating, ventilation system, canteen, food depot, clothing store and a cinema. This was a complete 'shipyard under concrete'. Only toilets and kitchens had not been planned for; this oversight was made up for later when air raids destroyed the facilities located in barracks near the bunkers.

Except for the two special dry bunkers at Keroman, the other wet bunkers were all built to the same principle. They had a loading passage with a railway track the whole breadth of the bunker separating the workshop area from the tidal pens/dry docks, so that material could be delivered into the bunker by road or rail. Initially, a pen was completed into which the workers could retire upon the air-raid alarm being given. The first such pens were mostly dry docks since the Kriegsmarine was anxious to get its U-boats out of the open-air dry docks of the French naval arsenals. Some of these pens were already in use before the building complex was finished. Thus at Brest the first dry pen was operational a whole eight months before the end of the building work.

Once OT had completed the outer shell of the bunker, the port construction office took over the internal fitting-out work. Besides the various workshops of the ship and engineering construction departments, at the rear of the bunker offices were installed U-boat flotilla offices, a torpedo workshop, sick bay, telephone exchange, stores and a weapons workshop. From 1942 the bunkers were equipped with anti-tank and MG positions at the entrances, plus observation cupolas and mortars on the roof to protect against surprise enemy attacks. In the immediate vicinity, large bunkered stores for torpedoes and fuel oil reserves were created; the only French navy underground torpedo storage galleries were located at Brest. For storing its torpedoes in France protected against air attack, in

Extension of the U-boat bunker at La Pallice, 1942: the *Melan-Träger*
(prefabricated steel frames) can be seen through the open roof.
(Bundesarchiv, 101II-MW-2849-03/Scherl)

1941 the Kriegsmarine built the new torpedo magazine 'Pilz' at Houilles,
northwest of Paris, in which the torpedo departments of the individual
bases were gathered together. In the galleries of a former mushroom-
growing concern, 7m (23ft) underground, was an area of 65,000m^2 (78,000
sq yds) for the preparation, maintenance and overhaul of the torpedoes
needed for the Atlantic coast.

Concrete roofs 3.5m (11ft 6in) thick gave the U-boat bunkers complete
protection against all types of bombs known at the time. The inner
resistance of the roofing was provided by steel carrier-frames known as
Melan-Träger, prefabricated in Germany, and assembled on site at the
Atlantic coast between the completed side walls. In the spaces between
the frames, curved-head iron rods were installed for reinforcement and
finally cement poured over the roof. On account of increased bomb size,
in 1942 consideration was given to reinforcing the roofs, which received a
further 30cm (1ft) concrete layer, over which a second bunker roof of 1.9m
(6ft 3in) to 3.8m (11ft 6in) thickness was applied. In its interior, pre-
stressed concrete supports transferred the burden of the second ceiling to
the side walls. Upon this second ceiling, or on those parts of the bunker
which could not take the weight of the second ceiling because of the
weakness of their foundations, a *Fangrost* was erected, consisting of 1.5m
(5ft)-high reinforced concrete beams. These were laid crosswise on

reinforced concrete beams 3.8m (11ft 6in) high. The purpose of the *Fangrost* ribs was to explode a bomb above the roof proper and deflect the blast over the open sides of the bunker. In order to avoid having near-

Kapitänleutnant Rudolf Franzius leaving the Brest U-boat bunker, 1943. (Bundesarchiv, 101II-MW-6059-10/Hasert)

misses close to the walls, the bunker was given a 'projecting collar', in which the ceiling overlapped the walls by 4m (13ft).

To protect the foundations, OT built in a 2m (6ft 6in)-thick concrete 'crash slab' for a breadth of 10m (33ft) around the bunker. From 1943 this was used as a foundation for the construction of the so-called circum-vallation, set up at the rear of the bunker for annexes, with walls and ceilings 2m (6ft 6in) to 3.5m (11ft 6in) thick. These would accommodate facilities such as toilets, kitchens, provisions stores and other workplaces, such as firing positions and bunkers for short-range protection against commando raids, all of which had been overlooked in the original plans. The entrances on the shore side were protected by armoured revolving gates driven by electric motors. Pedestrian access was provided by two sliding doors. In case of emergency the gates could be shut by hand wheel.

On the waterfront the dry docks under water were protected by gates which could be raised, but the wet pens were unprotected below the waterline. Nets were set in front of the bunkers to protect against tor-pedoes and midget submarines. Initially, the entrance area between the waterline and bunker ceiling was open. In order to provide protection against bomb splinters and blast, the entrances were at first covered with armour plating mounted on floats, these being replaced later by lifting shutters.

The Brest U-boat bunker was inaugurated on 13 May 1942. At first it provided twelve places in two wet boxes and eight dry docks. By additions in the west and east the bunker eventually had five wet boxes and ten dry docks, thus berths for twenty boats, the required number of protected berths for two U-boat flotillas. In the autumn of 1942 and April 1943 the ceiling was reinforced; in the summer of 1943 a *Fangrost* was built on the roof. Between July and October 1943 the landward side of the bunker received a circumvallation. Extension work on the east side of the bunker to take the new Type XXI U-boats proceeded no further than excavating the trench for the foundations.[31]

At St-Nazaire three dry docks were ready at the end of June 1942 after a four-month period of construction. These were the first bunkered berths on the Biscay coast. The first section had three dry docks and four wet pens, a further five dry docks and two wet pens being added in the course of the year so that in the end the bunker also had the required twenty berths.

The building of the U-boat bunker at La Pallice followed a different route. By including harbour installations – the workshop area was set up on the quay and the bunkered pens built into the harbour basin – little lifting was required, thus shortening the construction time. The first dry docks were ready by October 1941, the other pens the following month. When on 19 November *U82* became the first U-boat to enter the new bunker, this had two wet pens and five dry docks, a capacity for nine U-boats. In April 1942 work began to extend the bunker southwards by three more pens. This made comprehensive excavations necessary because the harbour basin had to be widened for the addition. The former quay wall was left in place to serve as a mole between the old and new bunker region. By the time that the work to create one wet pen and two dry docks finished in the spring of 1943, 230,000m³ (8 million cu ft) of earth and limestone had to be removed. The bunker then had capacity for thirteen U-boats.

By the end of 1942 the number of berths in France which were protected against bomb attacks had risen from thirty-four to seventy, half of them being dry docks. Only at Bordeaux were there no protected berths at this time, for which reason, as at La Pallice, the bunker was built directly into the backwater basin of the mercantile harbour. The first pens were ready by the beginning of January 1943, and the bunker was inaugurated with the arrival of *U178* on 17 January 1943. It had four wet pens and seven dry docks. Because Type XIV U-tankers were to operate from Bordeaux, the wet pens were 20m (66ft) wider than at other bases. To supply these U-tankers and also the Type IX D2 long-range East Asian or monsoon boats, which had a larger fuel capacity than the standard Type VII boats, the base was equipped with a large 4,000m³ (900,000 gallon) fuel oil bunker. Another bunkered power station was built at the northwest corner of the bunker.

Two Type IX and one Type VIIc U-boat in the large Keroman III wet pen, *c.*1943. (Bundesarchiv, 146-1975-014-33/Adrian)

The bunkers were called upon very quickly to prove their effectiveness. On 21 October 1942 at Lorient, a surprise daylight attack on Keroman by the US air force killed forty-six, including one German naval rating and seven, mostly French, workers, and injured 138.[32] The *Tauchtopf* building – in which escapes from depth were practised using breathing apparatus – and the provisional boilerhouse were badly damaged. Serious fire damage occurred in the workshops and halls. A hit on the roof of Keroman I made hardly any impression, however. The maximum depth of any damage to the ceiling was 55cm (22in). In another heavy air attack on 18 November 1942, only the building site was involved. No air-raid alarm had been given, so the workers had not been able to get to shelter. Sixteen were killed and twenty-seven injured. Later, the OT workers would stream into the U-boat bunker when the alarm was given, where their presence interfered to a considerable extent with repair work. In his summary of the year 1942, the senior shipyard director of the Kriegsmarine Yard Lorient reported that air attacks had killed four German employees; the death toll amongst other personnel, principally French civilians, had been around 370.

In 1941 the British had concentrated their attentions for too long on the German surface force at Brest and had thus more or less lost sight of the U-boat arm and its bunkers. Once the heavy units had left Brest, Bomber Command sought other targets. Not until Allied ship losses rose again in the second half of 1942 did the First Sea Lord ask for the resumption of air attacks against the U-boat bases. The new directive on 14 January 1943 for Bomber Command envisaged area bombing of the French ports, in order to destroy the entire surroundings of the base, and thus cut off the U-boats from their workshops and all other supply services.[33] The order of attack was Lorient, St-Nazaire, Brest and La Pallice. The U-boat bunkers withstood the attacks undamaged, while the surrounding towns were reduced to rubble and ashes. At Lorient 60 per cent of the buildings were destroyed and another 20 per cent made uninhabitable. Life in the city was no longer possible: water, gas and electricity were cut off, and on 3 February 1943 the prefect of the department of Morbihan obtained German agreement for evacuation of the population. The department of Seine et Marne took over responsibility for the ruined town, which was declared a forbidden zone on 17 February 1943. Entry was only permitted to holders of a German work and residence permit.

As a result of the bombing, the Kriegsmarine decided to remove the less important installations and accommodation to areas outside the bases. Each evening, workers and German military left the ports in buses and trains in order, for example, to spend the night at safe Hennebont, north of Lorient, while those who remained behind inhabited the air-raid

German soldiers in the ruins of Lorient, February 1943.
(Author collection)

shelters and bunkers of Keroman. The air attacks failed to achieve their actual purpose of destroying the U-boat yards. No U-boat was lost and no major delays occurred in the repair service. Although elements of the French labour force did not report for work out of fear of the bombing – according to a report by the OT senior directors at St-Nazaire 735 workers were absent there from January 1943 – U-boat repairs were only compromised to a minor extent.[34]

Because of damage in the naval arsenal at Lorient and to the St-Nazaire yards, repairs to surface vessels had to be referred elsewhere. The Penhoët yard at Nantes, less threatened by air attack and where the port was planned to become a base for German supply ships, was bombed by US aircraft on 16 and 23 September 1943. The harbour installations and the centre of the city, before then spared air raids, were badly damaged. Until this time Nantes had not been bombed by the Allies and the population had considered itself safe. Thus on the afternoon of 16 September 1943 many people paid no attention to the American bomber formations in the skies over the city and did not seek cover, despite the air-raid alarms. Compared to Lorient and St-Nazaire the death toll was high, 1,463 citizens of Nantes losing their lives.

After the near-destruction of the towns of Lorient and St-Nazaire in the spring of 1943, without having achieved anything notable by way of a military victory, the British decided not to proceed with the planned

Lager Lemp (Camp Lemp), a retreat for 2nd U-boat Flotilla men north
of Lorient, 1943. (Author collection)

bombing of Brest and La Pallice. Even so, by reason of the increasing
Allied air attacks on French lines of communication and particularly the
railways, German building activity was held back. The planned expansion
of the U-boat bunkers gave way to the building up of the Atlantic Wall,
and proceeded no further than initial studies, such as the excavation of a
building trench at Brest, or the erection of the first walls for Keroman IV
at Lorient.

The bombing of the French ports was 'the most ineffective and tragic
episode' in the history of Bomber Command, for it had done nothing to
impair U-boat operational readiness.[35] Now they had cause to regret
bitterly their failure to attack the German U-boat bunkers during the first
stages of construction, and later the British admitted it as a grave error:

> When they began to excavate deep trenches behind the seawall defences,
> in the initial building phase we had had a very good chance of inflicting
> severe destruction and flooding by bombing ... In view of our generally
> decreasing losses at sea, the shortage of bombs, the concentration of the
> Air Ministry on Germany and the Admiralty on the *Scharnhorst* and
> *Gneisenau*, very little was done to prevent the building work.[36]

By the time that the Royal Air Force obtained the newly developed 5.4-
tonne Tallboy bomb in 1944, specially designed to go through strong

fortifications such as the metres-thick ceilings of the U-boat bunkers, the strategic value was already sharply reduced by the war situation, so that in precision attacks it provided more of a late satisfaction for the RAF than any military benefit.

Shipyard operations

When a U-boat returned from an Atlantic patrol, boat and crew could expect a scheduled shipyard lay-up. All movements could be observed by the French yard workers. Edmond Calvès, then under instruction at the gunnery workshop of the French naval arsenal at Brest, reported the arrival of a German U-boat at the arsenal:

> They tied up alongside the gunnery jetty, right in front of our work-shop. Small white pennants would flutter from the half-extended periscope mast indicating the tonnage of the ships they had sunk. A welcoming committee awaited them, including a row of *Blitzmädchen*, female employees of the Kriegsmarine, some officers, behind them a military band playing martial music. We heard the music so often that we all soon knew it by heart.[37]

After the official welcome by the flotilla commander and the presentation of a floral tribute for the officers, the boat would go into the U-boat bunker. Once the US air force attacks began, even the reception ceremony would take place in the bunker. After berthing there would first be a

U123 being greeted at Lorient, 1941. (Author collection)

Repairs to *U333* in the dry dock of the La Pallice U-boat bunker, 1942.
(Bundesarchiv, 101II-MW-6861-21/Tölle [Tröller])

shipyard conference while the crew cleared out the boat and handed over the unused torpedoes or fuel to the relevant yard authority. The chief engineer of the boat would submit his damage reports, the necessary repairs would be discussed, and a timetable established for the work.

In order to get the boats operational again as soon as possible, Dönitz told the yards that once the timetable was set they had to keep to it. The priority was always the next boat in line to be got ready, even if it meant that all available personnel had to be concentrated on this boat around the clock. If the necessary spare parts did not arrive in time they would be taken from another boat in order to keep to the deadline.[38] If there was only wear-and-tear damage to be attended to, the lay-up time could be terminated at the two-week stage. At the beginning of the Battle of the Atlantic 1941/42, a Type VIIc U-boat would lay up in the base for an average of four weeks, and this was only prolonged to five weeks by the increase in air attacks. Larger boats such as the Type IX required correspondingly longer periods of lay-up.

The basic repairs were to sea damage on the casing, corrosion damage in the regions exposed to seawater, leaks in the dive tanks and fuel bunkers, and the overhaul of hatches, hydroplanes and rudders, vents, valves and levers.[39] In the narrow engine room the diesels would be reduced to their components and all important parts habitually exposed to wear, such as connecting rods, cylinder liners, cylinder heads, pistons and couplings checked over in the workshop.

Initially, the Atlantic bases were only expected to carry out repairs, while a full overhaul would be done at the original shipyard. In mid 1942 the BdU ordered that the front yards would also perform full overhauls. In this area the diesels presented the greatest challenge. To take out the diesels the upper casing and fuel tank above the motors had to be removed in order to expose the diesel mounting hatch. To open this hatch several hundred rivets had to be bored open and after the bedplate screws were released the heavy diesel could be lifted free of the boat.

During the lay-up the electrical workshop handled the overhaul or exchange of batteries, transformers, switches and relays, and the torpedo department the servicing of the torpedo tubes and fire-control installation. Once the work was concluded the boat would be checked for operational readiness. After the diesels had passed muster on the test stand, the first trim trials would follow and then a shipyard test under the supervision of the flotilla engineer. Once any loose ends were seen to, the boat would be declared ready to leave the yard and passed back to the crew.[40] Next it would be loaded with fuel, provisions and torpedoes and then degaussed. Shortly before sailing, fresh foods would be shipped, and a final trim test made with a full load. After the official departure and reaching the 200m (650ft) contour, a deep dive would be performed to 170m (560ft) to test for leaks in the pressure hull. Finally, the commander would open the envelope containing his orders, and then head for his new operational area.

4

The Significance of French Collaboration

With their occupation of the French ports in the summer of 1940, the Kriegsmarine had also obtained possession of the French naval shipyards at Cherbourg, Brest and Lorient. Until the Kriegsmarine could build its

Gateway to the Lorient naval arsenal, 1941. (Author collection)

own yards, French infrastructure had to be used right away for the shipping war in the Atlantic. Although the French navy had destroyed the gates of the dry docks before evacuating the ports, the workshops remained intact.

At Brest and Lorient the German service centres made contact with the French directors, whose leaders had no instructions as to what to do next. At Brest they decided to accept any non-military work in order to keep their workers engaged at least for the time being and to take over responsibility for the workforce. On 15 June 1940 the front page of the Brest daily newspaper called upon all French dockyard personnel willing to work to report to the main gate of the naval arsenal.[1] A few days later, on 4 July, the naval arsenal resumed work. The French workers were forbidden, however, to remain away from their workshops or offices without good reason. At Lorient the French national shipyard also resumed work.

The German harbour commandant gave the naval arsenal directors the task of repairing the damaged shipyard installations, and reported to the Naval Commander Bretagne that the collaboration was going 'smoothly'.[2] The Kriegsmarine gave the arsenal the task of overhauling several fishing trawlers in order – according to the report of the harbour commandant – 'to get the shipyard working normally so that time can be gained to investigate the total practical workings of the shipyard.'

The further employment of French naval shipyard workers was approved by the French Admiralty at Vichy at the beginning of August 1940.[3] As many workers as possible were to return to work at the shipyards to prevent unemployment and the drifting away of skilled labour over time. For this reason, the French Admiralty ordered the continuation of projects already afloat in order to clear the stocks and dry docks of new ships as quickly as possible. Furthermore, under the terms of the armistice treaty, the ships which the French navy had scuttled in June 1940 were to be raised.

At Brest the senior French officer, the head of the French commissariat, was ordered by Vichy to prioritise projects which required a large number of personnel, amongst them repairs to the large dry docks and the further construction of the new French sailors' home in the city centre.[4] Accordingly, in December 1940 workers at the French naval arsenal repaired the gates of the two large dry docks in the warship harbour, and the French shipbuilding workshops built two new gates for the two docks inside the arsenal.[5] Working for the Kriegsmarine, the French workshops were also involved in converting former French fishing vessels into German auxiliary warships. Industries Navales completed steel oil-spill deflectors for the newly set-up destroyer anchorages along the south mole of the warship harbour in December 1940.[6] The French workshops were

Salvage work in the Brest naval arsenal, 1941. (Bundesarchiv, 101II-MW-
2238-05/Kunze [Kuntzel])

even used for the first repairs to German warships. Thus the completion of machinery repairs to the destroyer *Richard Beitzen* in January 1941 had only been possible with recourse to the workshops of the French arsenal.[7]

Although the director of official group shipyards at Hauptamt Kriegs-schiffbau had laid down in July 1940 that, because of the risk of sabotage, no repairs should be performed to German warships in French shipyard installations, the slow trickle of workers arriving at the Atlantic coast from the Reich left the German naval centres with no other choice.[8] Thus, for example, by February 1941 only 470 German workers had arrived at Brest, whereas the complement of the French naval arsenal was an impressive 6,349 Frenchmen.[9] Lorient in July 1942 had a total of 2,160 German, 2,152 French – including 504 women – and seventy-two foreign workers.[10] A review by the senior yard director, Vizeadmiral Walter Matthiae, in July 1942 provided a breakdown of how the German and French workers were distributed within the individual shipyard departments. Thus in the U-boat repair sector French workers were mainly employed inside where they outnumbered Germans in the ratio 440:163, whereas outside only German workers were active with 887 men, the greater part of the German employee force. In the very much smaller surface-vessel repair sector, the work was mostly done by Germans, in the ratio 66:33. In general bunker business the French predominated 387:251; in the weapons sector the Germans in the ratio 333:300. The greater part of the French staff was to be found in the administrative and equipping centres, where the French outnumbered the Germans 482:49. In the adherents' office, 688 French, almost half of them women, worked alongside twenty-nine German employees. The workers and other staff of the French naval arsenals provided the Kriegsmarine with an enormous source of manpower serving German purposes – if not on board German warships, then at least in the workshops or aboard the no less important auxiliary warships.

Admiral François Darlan, Commander-in-Chief, French navy, c.1940. (US National Archives)

On 30 September 1940 the Commander-in-Chief of the French navy, Admiral Darlan, expressed the situation as follows regarding the collaboration of the French naval arsenals with the aims of the occupying power:

'It seems to me absolutely useless to decline German requests. To decline would only have as its consequence forcible measures and other grievous unpleasantness. ... The only realistic solution is to go along with the German requests from the outset and at the same time attempt to obtain from them such substantial valuable considerations as may be possible.'[11]

This instruction can be considered as the manifest for the collaboration of the French naval arsenals with the Kriegsmarine. It also shows the mental basis for Darlan's later policy, when as president of the Vichy government he would make concessions in an attempt to reach an accord with the German occupiers.[12] The directors of the French naval arsenals were instructed to make clear to their workers that hostile acts towards the occupying force would only have disadvantages for the future of France. Not every director went along with the new policy. At Brest the head of the French shipbuilding concern refused categorically to raise the scuttled French destroyer *Cyclone* for the Kriegsmarine.[13] The engineering officer was arrested and after a short spell of internment in Germany was released into Vichy.[14]

The employment of foreign workers at the Kriegsmarine yards in occupied France was the subject of a situation report to Hitler by the Kriegsmarine Commander-in-Chief on 4 February 1941. This was provoked by the powerful misgivings on the part of the German Abwehr about the use of French, Danish and Dutch workers at the important shipyards. Although Hitler shared their doubts, he had to give precedence to the employment of foreign workers, taking into account the manpower problem on the German side. Although Raeder found the situation 'very unpleasant', there was no alternative.[15] The so-called workers' question remained a problem throughout the entire war. The lack of skilled staff and the increase in repair work finally resulted in a notice from Raeder circulated on 23 September 1941 that all work that could somehow be put off, especially modifications, should be set aside and only such require-ments presented to the shipyards, 'which are absolutely necessary for the sea and fighting readiness of the ships.'[16] Work should be reduced to the least amount possible otherwise new ships or repairs to important ships would be compromised.

In the French Atlantic and Biscay bases whole phases were hived off to the French workshops, either because the Kriegsmarine yards did not have the necessary machinery, or lacked skilled staff for the work in question. Thus at Lorient all steel plating was rolled in the French arsenal because the Kriegsmarine had no rolling machines.[17] Repairs to the engines of *Scharnhorst* and *Gneisenau* at Brest were carried out by the French engineering workshops.[18] In December 1940 the head of the French shipbuilding division at Brest reported that his books were full with orders

Admiral Darlan and Grossadmiral Raeder after a meeting at Evry near Paris, 1942. (Erich Raeder, *Mein Leben*, Tübingen 1957)

from the occupying power.[19] In May 1941 the French shipbuilding division at Brest was working on a floating dock for the Kriegsmarine in parallel with anti-torpedo protection for the gates of the two large dry docks in the warship harbour. According to a report by the director general of the French national shipyards from Vichy, in September 1942 a total of about 16,000 French shipyard workers in the occupied zone were working almost exclusively for the occupying power.[20] Co-operation would continue to be significant, because the Kriegsmarine was continually in the process of reducing its own personnel and handing ever more work to the French workshops.

Although in August 1942 the representatives of the Commanding Admiral France, the German senior shipyard staff and the French Secretary of State for the Navy had agreed that, if possible, no French workers were to be employed aboard German warships, this did not affect the ancillary work of the French workshops.[21] The French Rear Admiral Germain Paul Jardel, liaison officer for the French Admiralty in Paris and senior commander of French navy forces stationed in the occupied zone, explained the collaboration with the Germans on 2 September 1942 as follows: 'We have a special interest in that the workers at our arsenals work, and that they work in the arsenals and not in Germany.'[22] A month before, the French navy had agreed to send skilled electrical workers from the naval arsenal at Cherbourg to La Pallice because the Kriegsmarine lacked skilled men there.[23] Despite its accord, however, the French Admiralty could not avoid having to make available workers at the French naval arsenals for 'employment in the Reich'. Thus in October 1942 almost a thousand men from the Brest and Lorient naval arsenals were sent to German shipyards at Hamburg and Wesermünde where they were employed as 'foreign workers' until the end of the war.[24] As they left, the families affected and others present at the railway stations openly protested against the Vichy government. The French politicians responsible, such as President Pierre Laval, were reviled, and the crowds were loudly critical of the French navy. As the trains pulled out, the workers who stayed behind sang the Communist song, the Internationale. In order to avoid future incidents of the kind, further detachments were made by the French navy in areas of the naval arsenals hidden from the public gaze.

From all of this one may infer that most workers in the naval arsenals were well aware that when all was said and done they were working for the occupying power. It could hardly have been anything else, for practically all activity in the ports was linked to the Germans. The fact that only a few workers were ready to speak out after the war about their supposed collaboration in the naval arsenals can be interpreted as an indication of their inner conflict. Only a few were prepared in retrospect to confess openly that in the final analysis their further employment in the French arsenals and private yards served the German occupiers. This attitude resulted from the post-war prominence of the French Reistance, which prevailed upon shipyard workers never to mention publicly their wartime role. They kept their lips sealed and after 1945 just kept on working.

A member of Organisation Todt giving instructions to a worker at a construction site on the Atlantic Wall, France, 1942. (Bundesarchiv, 101II-MW-2355-10/Kraupa; Tuskany; Duskamp)

Opposite: Aerial photo of the bunker installation at Keroman showing the building foundations for Keroman III (1) and the U-boat cradle on rails between Keroman I and II for the transfer of boats into the dry pens of bunkers I and II (2). Far left, channel to ramp for Type II U-boats, at the extreme edge of the photo is the turntable from where the boat would transfer into dry dock inside one of the two cathedral bunkers which can be seen either side of the ramp, October 1942. (Ullstein-Bilderdienst, Berlin)

For men in Brittany, a predominantly agricultural area, there was little alternative to applying for work on the building sites of the Atlantic Wall, this also being work for the occupying power. Thus for the mass of the French shipyard workers the judgement of the Brest historian Anne-Laure Le Boulanger is apposite, when in her study of the exploitation of the French workforce in Finistère during the German occupation she writes: 'If a man has to fill his own stomach and that of his children, the question of food becomes his primary concern but it does not prevent an inward rejection.'[25] Another important factor which the workers put forward as a justification of their activity was the fact that labour in the workshops was under French command, and thus they were not working directly for the Germans. The French historian Robert Frank, in considering the question of collaboration with the German occupier by large French industrial concerns, came to the conclusion that 'A large proportion of the workers were more inclined to work for Germany than in Germany'.[26]

Yet the work was not without its dangers. On 19 February 1942 four French workers lost their lives at the Brest arsenal in an explosion during welding work on the deck of a German warship.[27] The greatest threat to shipyard workers was from Allied air raids. When seven French yard workers died in air attacks on Brest on 3 and 5 April 1943, in posthumous recognition of their work the French shipbuilding authority declared them 'fallen for France'.[28]

Ultimately, it was the bombing which caused the Kriegsmarine to examine the significance of French collaboration more closely. When on 21 October 1942 in a surprise air attack on the bunker complex at Keroman thirty-two French were killed, the senior shipyard director at the Lorient yard, Vizeadmiral Walter Matthiae, considered the potential

consequences of all French workers ceasing work due to the number of casualties, or offering passive resistance.[29] The result of this investigation was a matter of concern for the German naval authorities: if the French left, all repairs on surface ships would come to a standstill, and U-boat repairs would be cut by up to 30 per cent.

At Lorient in March 1943 there was even a French division of the naval arsenal set up inside the bunker installation at Keroman where 357 French shipyard staff worked under the supervision of six

French shipyard worker, 1942. (Marineschule Mürwik/WGAZ)

French engineers and foremen; shortly beforehand another 100 workers at Keroman had become active for the German engineering and ship construction departments. Amongst other things the French workers installed pumps, carried out various welding jobs, took apart a ceiling crane and repaired a number of trawlers.[30] Over the long term the French group which had been set up at the request of the German administration was active in all departments at the Kriegsmarine yard. Administration informed the engineers what work was to be done, and allowed the French group full freedom as to how they went about it, except with regard to deadlines, which had to be met.

Although the relationship with the Germans was described as excellent, the French engineer Giraud mentioned in his report that the German side kept trying to give work to individual French staff members or work groups behind the back of the French engineers. Normally, the latter would look over the work to be done, and decide what they would take on and who would do it. In the workshops of the engineering and shipbuilding departments the French engineers could move about freely and control piecework by the use of time-cards. In both departments a French foreman oversaw the quality of the work done.

The French engineers were barred from entering the gunnery workshops. Here, French workers worked alongside German personnel or French employed directly by the Kriegsmarine. According to the French shipyard personnel, these men were paid a lump sum for ten hours work per day,

French naval tug from the Port Direction (DP) in the Brest naval arsenal, 1941. (Bibliothek für Zeitgeschichte, Stuttgart)

while the working hours of the French shipyard staff were controlled precisely by their own superiors. The French engineer officer gained the impression that the German administration did not care one way or another how the French workers were paid. Those French workers recruited from outside received a much higher wage than the French shipyard staff, and men with children even received a separation allowance.

In his report engineer Giraud stated that upon their arrival at Keroman, the French workers showed little enthusiasm for the work inside the bunkered complex, but after Allied bombing raids destroyed the French naval arsenal they had a quick change of heart. The only thing they missed was the arsenal canteen where in their opinion they received much better fare for lunch, plus a quarter-litre of wine. At Keroman all they got was a slice of bread and butter and one sausage. To raise morale, the French administration paid them the difference in value, and as compensation for having to work at Keroman every worker received one bonus unworked hour per day and a clothing allowance. Nevertheless, the rate paid was well below what those Frenchmen were paid who had volunteered at German recruiting offices, and some French navy shipyard workers took leave of absence in order to apply directly to the Kriegsmarine shipyard for employment. On the whole, however, the majority awaited their opportunity, settled in and got on with the job.

This attitude corresponded with that of the majority of the French,

Inspection of French fire brigade men by the Naval Commander, Western France, Admiral Eugen Lindau, Bordeaux, 1942. (Bundesarchiv, 101II-MW-6687-24/Andres)

who at the outset of the occupation came to an accommodation with Vichy.[31] In general, however, it may be that despite much praise from German service offices about the apparently trouble-free co-operation with the French shipyards and their employees, not all was quite so rosy as the impression they wished to give, as suggested in a report made in April 1943 by an agent of the French intelligence service about the shipyard Chantiers de Bretagne at Nantes: 'Taken as a whole nearly all the workers do not like the Germans and only put up with them because they have no alternative'.[32]

That the shipyard workers of the French naval arsenals at Lorient and Brest had scarcely any choice but to work for the German occupation force was due not least to the fact that they continued to be subordinate to their French military commanders, as even after the occupation by German troops the French arsenals had a military commander. At Brest the former French harbour commander was left in office by the German naval commander, while at Lorient the head of the shipbuilding workshops, and at Cherbourg the surgeon-in-chief of the naval hospital, retained command over French navy men who had remained behind, and thereby over the naval arsenals and their workers. Because at the beginning of the occupation Admiral Darlan had strictly refused to issue any official instructions to the French commandant at Brest, it was left up to this or that commander of any particular French marine unit to decide how he was going to act.

On 28 October 1940 the Chief of Staff, Commanding Admiral France took the following stance on the further employment of French naval personnel in the German bases:

> The accelerated commencement of operations of the French naval shipyards in the interests of prosecuting the U-boat war resulted in the French officers, who incidentally are without exception construction branch, not being watched or employed in a satisfactory manner. Orders for a reorganisation have been distributed to totally separate out these officers, who had made themselves available voluntarily, and there is no question of sending them off to Germany, based on reports in agreement from all service offices involved, since this would lead to serious interruption to the business of the yard. The Skl and BdU have stated that making the French construction branch officers into prisoners of war is bound to lead to disruption, which would very seriously impair U-boat operations. There exist therefore urgent grounds in the interests of the Reich to give these officers employment at least temporarily.[33]

A special kind of co-operation between the two navies took place at La Pallice. In the framework of the armistice agreement a French minesweeper unit was active which, after clearing the French mine-fields, took part in the hunt for British sea mines dropped by aircraft. When in the summer of 1941 Group West required that the French minesweeping unit be disbanded as an anti-espionage move initiated at Skl, its work was terminated and after a parting dinner with Kriegsmarine repre-sentatives they were released to North Africa.[34]

At Lorient in April 1943 the French navy was installing the net barrier in front of the Keroman bunker complex. Two French tugs stood ready while French navy men manned eight other tugs, two of them Kriegsmarine units, as well as several harbour vessels.[35] When on active service, French ratings wore naval uniform and were answerable

French and German naval ratings in conversation, Atlantic coast, 1940. (Bundesarchiv, 101II-MW-1079-18/Mendel)

to French commanders. At Brest they operated the cranes and dry docks and crewed tugs and lighters. The vessels had all-French crews under the French tricolour. They refuelled German ships, helped move German units in harbour and took charge of buoys and anchorages. According to an itemisation by the Naval Commander Western France, at Brest alone twenty-one of the twenty-six tugs at the Kriegsmarine yard were under French command.[36] Moreover, the French navy handled both floating cranes, eleven tankers, three buoy-layers and three Kriegsmarine yard water transporters. Within the shipyards the French naval divisions received their workload from the German senior yard directors. Besides their logistics activity, some French officers even took part in military work. In the spring of 1941 at the Brest harbour entrance, when the Germans laid a large net to prevent the ingress of enemy submarines, French naval personnel handled the large support buoys.[37]

In a memo dated November 1942 on the significance of French collaboration for German naval operations, the head of the central division of the senior shipyard staff France, Korvettenkapitän Wolfgang von Tirpitz, stated that the co-operation of the French navy went 'beyond the normal neutral playing along' of the private French shipbuilding industry.[38] He stated that the French naval arsenals at Brest, Lorient and

French naval gendarme searching a shipyard
employee, 1942. (ECPAD, Ivry-sur-Seine)

Cherbourg had placed their capacities 'unreservedly' at the disposal of the Kriegsmarine immediately the German occupation began and made it entirely possible 'to fully unfold the energies of the Kriegsmarine yards for the U-boat War.'[39] Tirpitz emphasised in his report that in the German naval bases in France almost 80 per cent of the tug services were provided by harbour tugs with French naval crews. If this co-operation were terminated, the various duties of the tugs such as hauling vessels, the opening and closing of net barriers, setting out buoys or conveying workers would be very much reduced in number and would lead to substantial delays in the shipyards and harbours. The same would be expected regarding ship repairs or in the materials compounds, where half the French personnel were to be found. Even the gunnery work at the Kriegsmarine yards was based essentially on French co-operation. At Lorient 60 per cent of the gunnery repairs were done by Germans, the rest in the French workshops. At Brest, work on German U-boat guns was performed mainly by French personnel with German supervision only.

Another important factor was protection of the military installations. It was the responsibility of the French naval gendarmerie to control all French persons entering or leaving at the gates of the Kriegsmarine yards, to guard all electrical plant and to body-search all French and non-German personnel. The work of the French security services had up to that point in time given no cause for complaint. Thus at Lorient a series of thefts of non-ferrous metals and in Brest systematic sabotage against the electricity works had been solved by the Gendarmerie Maritime. Equally important were the French naval fire brigades. They had fully proved their worth protecting shipyard installations and also during air raids, according to the relevant German air-raid precautions officers. Without them, the German fire brigade formations would have to have been increased by about 50 per cent.

The collaboration between the French navy and the German

Kriegsmarine continued even after the occupation of southern France in November 1942 and lasted until the Liberation in the summer of 1944. In 1943 in the naval arsenals at Cherbourg, Brest, Lorient and Toulon, 186 French officers, 3,069 naval servicemen, 909 officials, 2,313 employees and 25,753 workers were active for the Kriegsmarine.[40]

German everyday life at the bases

After the German forces had celebrated the signing of the armistice agreement with joy and relief in the summer of 1940, they set up as occupiers. The streets of the Atlantic and Biscay ports were strewn with military equipment from the French and British armies, and large quantities of materiel were in the depots of the French navy. Until the Wehrmacht crews took possession, it belonged to anybody, including the serving men at the Atlantic bases, as the example of a member of Marine Artillery Division 262, who was on a security detail in June 1940 in the Brest arsenal, reveals:

> One night ... we found the coffee roaster. Gas mask holders were converted into tins of coffee and found their way to our loved ones in the Homeland. Another occasion we discovered the French navy clothing store, a gigantic depot. Right at the top, cloth-bound, were bolts of the finest officers' uniform material. The off-duty watch was alerted and everyone got four metres of it. Next morning came the complaints by the French administration officials who at this time were still performing their duty. Obviously there was nothing to be found on us.[41]

The shipyard directors had to threaten court martials before the plundering in the darkest corners ceased.

On reading the memoirs of German soldiers at this time, one sees how many were fascinated by this previously unknown country, as they discovered French culture and cuisine. Private photo albums were filled with pictures of the sea. The naval propaganda division (West) published books with such titles as *Fought-over Coasts* or *Land on the Biscay Coast* as an initial introduction for soldiers to the regions, full of Nazi pretensions of might, but which emphasised primarily the good relationship between the German occupying force and the civilian population, be they Basque, Breton or the fishermen of the Channel coasts.

In the occupied territories, both the Reichsmark and the French franc were acceptable currencies for payment. The favourable rate of exchange set down in the armistice negotiations and the great variety of unrationed wares on offer made France seem a paradise on earth to many German soldiers. The German military administration attempted initially to limit

German Navy NCOs and ratings at Versailles, 1941. (Author collection)

A member of the Reich Work Service and a German naval rating at a
market hall in France, 1940. (Bundesarchiv, 101II-MW-0937-24A/Hasert)

the buying mania by a ban on the purchase of foodstuffs and the imposition of maximum weights on private postal parcels but these restrictions were lifted on Hitler's order.[42]

The infrastructure of a naval town was created at Brest, Lorient and St-Nazaire. Besides the local naval administration there was a naval hospital, the staffs of the naval commandants, naval defence commandants, a harbour commandant with harbour control post, the provisions office, clothing store and numerous other service centres.[43] The Kriegsmarine shipyards with their various departments had their own structure and were their own town within a town. Hotels and private dwellings were requisitioned for officers and female auxiliary staff.[44] For the most part, other ranks were housed in former French barracks or in requisitioned schools and other public buildings. The security vessels stationed in harbours such as the minesweeping and patrol (VP) flotillas had shore accommodation only for the flotilla staff; the crews lived on board their vessels.

With the setting up of the three Kriegsmarine yards at Brest, Lorient and St-Nazaire on 28 October 1940, a U-boat base with two U-boat flotillas was to be created at each.[45] Accommodation had to be found for the approximately 1,800 personnel of the flotillas and the two staffs. At Lorient a barrack compound for six hundred men was constructed on the east bank of the naval arsenal; U-boatmen also lodged in the former French harbour barracks and the city music school.[46] A rest and recuperation home was erected on the nearby Quiberon peninsula.

The U-boat Home at Lorient, 1941. (Author collection)

The sea resort of La Baule on a pre-war postcard. (Author collection)

At St-Nazaire the crews were first housed in a school and a town hostel. Later the U-boat flotillas removed to the bathing resort of La Baule 10km (6 miles) away, where several houses and hotels were requisitioned. Thus 6th U-boat Flotilla had over sixty-four small and large hotels or villas for

Camp Lemp for the rest and recuperation of 2nd U-boat Flotilla on the Scorff river at Caudan, north of Lorient, 1942. (Author collection)

Camp Lemp: U-boat crew bathing in the Scorff. (Author collection)

billeting, officers' mess, staff quarters, rest home and the commandant's residence.[47] At Bordeaux, 12th U-boat Flotilla was lodged in a barracks compound near the U-boat bunker, while 3rd U-boat Flotilla at La Rochelle used a former French barracks. At Brest, 1st U-boat Flotilla had its main residence in the former French naval academy overlooking the warship harbour, while 9th U-boat Flotilla resided in the no less impressive newly-built hospital at Brest. As air raids increased, more air-raid shelters were built near the accommodation. When the air-raid alarm sounded, 1st U-boat Flotilla at Brest used a gallery system connected by underground passages to the U-boat bunker below the naval academy.

The flotillas had dedicated rest and recreation retreats for crews returning from patrol. 1st U-boat Flotilla provided the *Hôtel des Bains* in the small bathing resort Trez Hir near Brest.[48] Near Lorient, *Lager Lemp* (Camp Lemp) was built close to a river, thus affording crews opportunities for swimming. Other similar establishments for U-boat men were hotels in the bathing resort Morgat on the Crozon peninsula, or the Quiberon peninsula. The officers had their own facilities as, for example, at Château Rosmorduc, near Logonna-Daoulas to the south of Brest, as mentioned by Buchheim in his book, or the Château Quillien near Brasparts.

At the bases many of the town facilities were shared by the German units stationed there. On the Brest city basketball field, for example, from March 1941 No. 2 platoon of the Naval War Correspondents' Division West practised there.[49] For smaller events, Gustav Kieseritzky,

German ratings in the garden of the naval prefecture, Brest, 1941. (Archiv Hans-Joachim Spallek, Lübeck)

Commandant of Sea Defence Brittany, requisitioned the city festival hall.[50] City stadia were used for sporting events between the units. In the summer, German theatre groups visited the coast, or the crews went together to the beach or on excursions into the surrounding countryside and to Paris. U-boat officers report in their memoirs of visits to popular locations such as the Moulin Rouge or the 'Sheherezade', while others took the BdU train between the Atlantic coast and Kiel and enjoyed longed-for leave in the homeland.

For those left behind the Wehrbetreuung (military welfare) established bookshops and military retreats: the French communes had to foot the bill. Thus on 14 October 1940 the District Commandant Brest required the city to provide various items of furniture and material for curtains and tablecloths for Soldatenheim ('soldiers' home') III.[51] Local cinemas were used for film releases. During the lay-up of battleships, presentations of Shakespeare's *A Midsummer Night's Dream* or self-written plays, such as *Between Shanghai and St Pauli*, were laid on in the Brest city theatre, in which crew members of the battleships participated.[52] Under the title *Gegen Engeland*, the Kriegsmarine published its own newspaper for its units in Brittany, and brothels were set up in the towns, these being regularly monitored by the German medical service.[53]

German servicemen at the base were controlled by their NCOs or officers, or the Feldgendarmerie (military police). Others went to remote hotels where many of the crews of the battleships were billeted during the

Brest lay-up. The diary entries of the *Gneisenau* administration officer, Kapitän zur See Ernst Bethmann, mentions such pleasant things as good food and comfortable lodgings away from the bombing, but also the dark side in the small ports of Roscoff or Tréboul. Apparently, due to sheer boredom there were occurrences of leave violations, drunkenness, outrages against the French civilian population and malicious damage. Retribution for the culprits was provided in the 'Fleet Camp' outside Brest, in which the battleship crews were lodged away from the population and subjected to military discipline.

Contacts with the civilian population were described by many former Kriegsmarine personnel in retrospect as reserved, which was not surprising considering the circumstances of German occupation, but also courteous: 'As regards contact with the French,' a former crewman of *Gneisenau* remarked, 'all I can say is that we never played the occupier, and the workers at the French arsenals thanked us for this constantly with loyal conduct.'[54] Whether the French conduct was honest sympathy or rather the fear of repression can no longer be determined almost seventy years after the war ended. All the same it seems clear that contacts between Germans and French at the beginning of the occupation were often reported as very correct, and probably for this reason many personal contacts developed which survived the war.

Increasingly, however, relationships changed with the radicalisation of the occupation as the French Resistance took violent measures, thus invoking reprisals by the German army of occupation. Sixty years after the end of the war, former German naval men from the first phase of the occupation reported relaxed visits to the markets for purchases, the occasional visit to a bar, a private appointment with a hairdresser, a call on a French tailor or conversations with French employees in the yards:

On the beach at La Baule, 1941. (Author collection)

What did I do after duty? Well, we had our bistros, and there were really plenty of them. What did I say earlier? Every third house was a cafe, and we were always surrounded by the French, even at the hairdresser ... When I was there in 1941/42, it was still very quiet at Brest. In the rest of Brittany as well. We made trips to Roscoff, Quimper via Douarnenez – financed with the surpluses from the canteen till – there were never any incidents. We knew that Brittany was pro-British, but that didn't stop us.[55]

Mariners aboard the VP-boats told of seaborne traders who often came up alongside in their boats and as at Brest offered to sell the crew vegetables, fresh fish or fruit. Helmut Obst, an armourer at the Lorient naval artillery supply office recounted carefree private wanderings in his free time:

German naval ratings and shipyard workers at the stall of a Breton woman, probably Lorient, 1941. (Bundesarchiv, 101II-MW-4025-14/Tölle [Tröller])

If possible on Saturdays I liked to go to the weekend market. Apart from buying fresh fruit the wide variety of goods on offer interested me. ... I was a regular customer at a French hairdresser. On Sundays I went to the cycling track at Lorient. I even went to a French boxing hall. For my girlfriend in Germany I bought perfume and good soap. On all these outings I was a German naval rating amongst pure Frenchmen. At no time did I ever feel uneasy. It was almost possible to forget that we were at war.[56]

These trips into the imagined normal world were made in uniform, as civilian dress was forbidden, and were in general limited to what little time there was free of duty. On religious feast-days German soldiers would occasionally attend French mass:

My comrades Gödde and Baston, both from Duisburg-Hamborn, were Catholic. The three of us went at Christmas and Easter to mass in a church at Brest. For the life of me I cannot remember which one it was. Naturally all the pews were occupied and both times we stood on the left side of the nave near the altar. But nobody gave us dirty looks.[57]

Officers' reminiscences often speak of outings by car into the countryside around Brest. Then they would eat oyster and lobster, enjoy the pleasant-nesses of an officer's life and try to escape the reality of the war. Kapitän

Commanders of 9th U-boat Flotilla with female company in the garden of
their quarters at Trez Hir near Brest, 1944. (Herbert A Werner, *Die
eisernen Särge*, Hamburg 1970)

Bethmann was amongst the officers of *Gneisenau*, who booked into a
hotel in the small bathing resort of Trez Hir in March 1941; he wrote of
it in his diary: 'Most of all we would have liked to have settled forever in
this oasis of deepest peace and longed-for forgetfulness. Everything
seemed like a beautiful dream compared to our "iron hotel" berthed at
the quayside in Brest.'[58] Later U-boat officers would often come to Trez
Hir in order to flee the war for a few hours.

In contrast to the officers, the ratings had contact with the civilian
population only in the nearest harbour bar, in the shipyard or on duty
errands. Most of the time they spent on board. Through not knowing
the French language, contact with women was limited to German female
employees of the Kriegsmarine yards and the female naval or signals
auxiliaries in the bases. Moreover, their superiors warned of the dangers
of contagious venereal diseases through unprotected sex with French
women, and of espionage. Nevertheless, contact with French girls was
not ruled out. The kind of establishment for officers like the 'Bar Royal'
as depicted in the film *Das Boot* seems to have existed in other bases.
The former U-boat commander Herbert A Werner recalled such a place
in Brest in which young French girls offered their services. Whether
special clubs for the officers or the rest homes for the crews, the purpose
of both was above all to enable them to unburden themselves of the
stresses and strains of wartime patrols, especially from 1943 when losses
rose ever higher.

On reading the post-war memoirs of U-boatmen, one gains the impression that the few contacts with the civilian population were completely friendly on both sides. Two examples from near Brest in the summer of 1944 demonstrate how strong the ties grew over the years. When, in the course of the fighting around the city on 7 August, the occupants of a farm in the small village of Gouesnou east of Brest became the victims of a German reprisal for an attack on a nearby searchlight post, the injured people at the farm came to the aid of two German naval artillerymen who had long been lodging in the vicinity.[59] In Locmaria-Plouzané to the west of Brest in August 1944, soldiers manning a searchlight position of Marine Flak Division 803 came to help the population and prevented German paratroopers from requisitioning a bicycle.[60]

German soldiers were regularly reminded by their officers to treat the French with respect. Heavy disciplinary penalties were in force for offences against the civilian population. Amongst small units stationed at one place, the officers would always attempt to find a compromise for minor offences. Thus a rating from 7th VP-boat Flotilla who forgot to pay the bill when leaving a village bar returned next day with a bunch of flowers, and in the presence of an NCO made atonement to the landlady for his omission. Whether the relationship between the French and the Germans really was of a friendly nature is doubtful but even so 9th U-boat Flotilla invited its French domestic servants and their families to a dinner at Brest.

A change in the relationship between Germans and French came about with the commencement of the Russian campaign in the summer of 1941. The Communist party called upon its members to engage in action against the occupying power. Up to this stage resistance had extended only as far as passing on intelligence information, and public protest. With the introduction of the Obligatory Work Service (STO) for the German war economy, the French Resistance movement grew in size and struck out increasingly, culminating in the fighting of the summer of 1944. The conditions for German soldiers changed correspondingly. Whereas previously they could take part in civilian life relatively untroubled, from mid 1941 Kriegsmarine men were ordered to go about in pairs, go ashore armed with a bayonet, and not frequent shady bars, dark corners and alleys.[61] When going ashore officers had to take their service pistol. Now additional protection for men with leave was provided and armed naval patrols from ships in harbour walked the streets.

5

Life under the German Occupation

In the summer of 1940 the Breton population were almost incredulous at the arrival of the Wehrmacht: 'The German soldiers on their vehicles appeared so big, so strong that we looked at them as if they were supernatural beings from another planet. They were like fabulous machines. They wanted to impress us. They had won. We were speechless and numb.'[1] Responsibility for security in the region was given to 5th Panzer Division, and its commanding officer, Generalleutnant Joachim Lemelsen, was appointed military commander in Brittany. The area of his command coincided with that of the new naval commander for Brittany, Admiral Lothar von Arnauld de la Perière, and stretched from the peninsula of St-Nazaire in the south to the bay of Mont Saint-Michel in the north.

The Franco-German armistice signed at Compiègne on 22 June 1940 divided France into two zones. The area in the north and west occupied by German troops embraced forty-nine departments with about 23 million inhabitants. Alsace-Lorraine came under direct German administration, and the coastal departments Nord and Pas de Calais fell into the ambit of the German military commander for Belgium and northern France. In the south lay unoccupied France, ruled from the former spa resort of Vichy. The government of Philippe Pétain had selected this spot because of its numerous hotels available to accommodate the ministries and administrative offices. Furthermore, the town which was to give the Vichy regime its name was close to the demarcation line between occupied and unoccupied France.

With the arrival of German troops the lives of the coastal inhabitants changed fundamentally. One of the first edicts of the German occupying power required the surrender of all firearms, including hunting rifles, and all slash and stab weapons, within a single day to the German Kommandanturen, the mayor's office, or the police or gendarmerie stations. From then on, possession of a weapon was a punishable offence. All radio sets had to be handed in, and the population was notified by announcements in newspapers that deliberate damage to military materials, including French and British, would incur punishment. Damaging German signals centres was punishable by the death penalty. The inhabitants of the coastal area were required to register and until July 1941 were issued with special identity cards. Holiday excursions to the Atlantic were forbidden, and telephone calls were limited.

Finally, on 20 October 1941 the Germans set up a forbidden zone 10–20km (6–10 miles) broad extending along the entire French coast from Hendaye on the Spanish border to the Belgian frontier in the north. Warning signs were erected along its length and it could only be entered by persons in possession of a pass issued by the German Kommandanturen. Offenders against this regulation were threatened with imprisonment or large fines. Control of the regulation was difficult, however, mainly because of the many foreign workers at the regularly changing construction offices of Organisation Todt.

In the towns, public life gradually resumed. Newspapers reported the daily exchange rate of the Reichsmark against the French franc and shops reopened. In the view of the prefects of the department of Morbihan, above all it was the traders who profited from the new masters. Thus a report in November 1940 about the behaviour of local inhabitants towards the occupation troops stated that 'The people present a correct but definite reserve. The only ones who are really giving them a welcome are the traders, for whom they are good business.'[2]

The supervision of the French administration and local press was handled by the German Kommandanturen, who were themselves subordinate to the German military commander in France with headquarters in Paris. By the end of August 1940 the German military administration had set up a system of forty-six field and 129 regional Kommandanturen. The field Kommandanturen oversaw the administrative level of the department and operated from the equivalent centre of the French prefecture. Besides a military command staff they had a war administrative staff covering the areas of interior administration, commercial economy, food and farming, employment and road traffic. The administrative group responsible for the department of Finistère, Felkommandantur 752 at Quimper, for example, was made up of fifteen German officials. These were either reservists or officials who had been called up as war administrators for their professional knowledge and were distinguished from regular soldiers by insignia on their uniforms.[3]

At first the German occupation meant deep cuts in industry in the coastal areas. Before the Germans arrived, workers at the national shipyards had been discharged, and at the St-Nazaire private shipyards it remained uncertain how many workers would be needed and what building projects would proceed. Against this background, with no

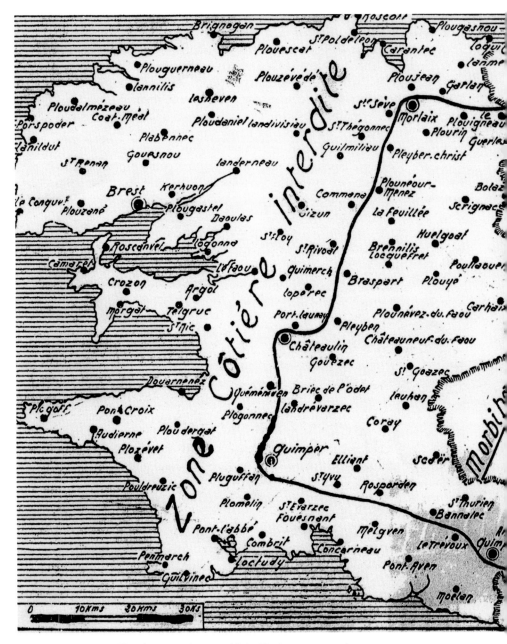

The prohibited Finistère coastal zone published in the newspaper *La Dépêche*, 1941. (Archives Municipales, Brest)

alternatives available for the skilled workers of the shipbuilding industry in Brittany, many workers answered the call of the occupying power to report back to their places of work. It was therefore primarily anxiety for their families which led these men voluntarily to serve the occupying Germans.

Besides the shipyards, farming and fishing had been the two main sources of income for Bretons before the outbreak of war. At the

Luftwaffe soldier on the passenger ship *Crozon*, Brest, 1941.
(Author collection)

Control of French fishermen by the crew of a German harbour protection
vessel. (Bundesarchiv, 101II-MW-2460-05/Vorländer)

beginning of the German occupation, the fisheries were subject
immediately to strict regulations. On 9 July 1940 the German Naval
Commander Brittany enforced a curfew on all seaborne movements
between dusk and dawn for reasons of coastal security.[4] On 11 November
1940 a notice appeared in the Brest newspaper *La Dépêche* stating that
any boat attempting to leave harbour before nine in the morning, or enter
harbour after seven in the evening, would come under fire from the coastal
batteries.[5] Although coastal fishing was resumed later as a source of food,
French fishermen always ran the risk of attack by British aircraft or
German U-boats. The Germans, for their part, also feared that during
their activity fishermen could report the departure of German U-boats,
smuggle in enemy agents, or evacuate shot-down RAF crews. Fishing on
the seas and coasts was again prohibited in January 1941 by order of the
Kriegsmarine, but then permitted once more as a food source under the
condition that fishing vessels exhibited a yellow triangle below the French
national flag for recognition purposes.

In the course of the occupation there were frequent incidents in which
fishermen lost their lives as, for example, on 22 October 1942 when
German sentries fired on a fishing boat in the Bay of Trez Hir. French
fishing boats were known to rescue shot-down Luftwaffe crews or German
shipwrecked sailors. Occasionally, some fishing boats were given German

Announcement of a nightly curfew for the citizens of Brest, newspaper *La Dépêche*, September 1941. (Archives Municipales, Brest)

contracts to fish for the occupation force. At sea, French fishing vessels were regularly searched by German VP-boats or vessels of the German customs service.[6]

In the towns the nightly curfew, the enforced blackout and routine inspection of identity documents became synonymous with the German occupation. Whoever was on the streets during curfew was living dangerously. In the early morning of 26 July 1940 a worker from the Brest mercantile harbour was shot dead after failing to heed an order to stop by a German patrol.[7]

Above all, the British aerial bombing which began in the summer of 1940 set the tone for people in the Breton coastal towns. Even if at the beginning it had been only single bomber aircraft or uncoordinated night attacks by small formations, which in general caused only minor damage, the situation soon changed. The French officer, Lt Cdr Jean Philippon, might have been able to express regret in December 1940 that the German

Aftermath of the British air raid on Brest, 24 July 1941. (Archiv Hans-Joachim Spallek, Lübeck)

cruiser *Admiral Hipper* could 'lie as peacefully in the naval arsenal as if she were at Wilhelmshaven', but that changed with the arrival of the two German battleships in the spring of 1941 when Brest became one of the important targets of RAF Bomber Command. Three hundred air raids made Brest one of the most bombed cities in France during the Second World War.

As with the German cities, the French civilian population was initially totally unprotected against these attacks. In 1940, Lorient had over thirty reinforced air-raid shelters and a number of anti-splinter trenches, but the construction of bombproof air-raid bunkers was not begun until May 1941. Gustave Mansion, head of the French air-raid protection service, recalled that during the first air-raid alarm of 8 August 1940 in Lorient, people went out on the street to watch.[8] Later they understood the new situation: 'On the alarm being given we went down to our cellar with two neighbours. Often the alarm would come at dinner time in the evening. Then we would go down with plates, cutlery and pots and eat by candlelight when the power was lost.'[9] In cellars at Brest during the first bombing raids a hymn of praise was composed to the RAF: 'Ah! Quel plaisir on a, d'entendre la DCA, quand les avios survolent nos remplais. Nos coeurs en les voyant redeviennent confiants. Vole à tire d'aile, reviens vers nous chaque soir, vole et sur tes ailes, porte nous l'espoir.'

German air raid bunker at Lorient, 1942. (Author collection)

Français :

Quand nos avions viennent :

Mettez-vous à l'abri !

Exigez le droit de vous abriter !

Nous ne voulons pas tuer de Français !

This British leaflet warning the French civilian population about bombing raids, Brest 1941 reads: 'Frenchmen: When our aircraft come: Take cover! Demand the right of shelter! We do not want to kill French people!' (Archives Municipales, Brest)

Despite the draconian penalties for doing so, shot-down British airmen were hidden by the population and returned to Britain with the help of the Resistance or Breton fishing boats, or if they were apprehended, applauded in the streets. On 30 December 1940 about two thousand people attended the burial of a shot-down British bomber crew at the Lanester cemetery, near where many workers at the Lorient naval arsenal lived.[10]

The clearly expressed pro-British attitude of the townspeople was put to the test by the increasing number of British bombing raids on the French ports. On 24 July 1941 Brest was the testing ground for a British daylight raid from high altitude, the idea being to destroy both battleships there. The outcome was that twelve bombers were shot down, and forty-nine crew lost their lives, *Gneisenau* being undamaged. Although the operation was to a limited extent successful in the damage inflicted on *Scharnhorst* at La Pallice, the citizens of Brest paid the price for this, the heaviest raid to date: eighty-four townspeople were killed and serious damage was done to the city centre. The long casualty lists changed the mood of the inhabitants appreciably against the British, as the prefects of the department of Finistère reported.[11] It was their proximity to the harbour which proved so calamitous for residential areas. In order to destroy the German battleships a variety of attack methods were tried from the air, from daylight attacks to bombs with special armour-piercing properties in December 1941, and then a beam to help get British bombers nearer their target. All failed.

Like Brest, from the summer of 1940 Lorient was repeatedly the target of British air attacks, but French engineer officer Le Puth reported not a

Interior of an air-raid bunker of 2nd U-boat Flotilla, Lorient, 1942. (Author collection)

single bomb hit on the building site of the Keroman U-boat bunkers. The main target of the attacks was the French arsenal with its workshops which, as at Brest, were very close to the city centre. From May 1941 at Lorient work was begun on deep air-raid bunkers in the central squares to protect the population, while at Brest the natural position of the city on a steeply inclined rocky plateau was used to build deep air-raid galleries which, from the summer of 1943, could accommodate up to twenty thousand people, approximately the entire population of the central area of the city. For the inhabitants of the Recouvrance district on the western side of the arsenal, an entrance to a railway tunnel ran underneath the area. This could be used as a shelter during air attacks, but it was anything but comfortable as Léontine Drapier-Cadec, an inhabitant of the district, recalled: 'In the bunker it was always cold, both summer and winter. The tunnel was open-ended with a permanent icy draught. Water dripped from the high ceiling and lapped around one's ankles. It was also dark and you had to make sure that your feet did not get trapped under the railway track.'[12] Galleries were also constructed for German soldiers, and roomy air-raid shelters built as close as possible to their quarters. Some of these in the U-boat barracks were so comfortable that when the alarm went off the men simply changed beds and slept on under the protection of metre-thick concrete ceilings, as recalled by witnesses of the time, while the air-raid protection for the civilian population contained just a couple of rough-hewn benches.

After the German battleships sailed from Brest, the air attacks stopped and Bomber Command concentrated on targets in Germany. In the autumn of 1942, however, the bombing of French towns was resumed with renewed ferocity. The increasing successes of the German U-boat arm were the reason for this, particularly off the coast of the United States, which had entered the war in December 1941 after the bombing of Pearl Harbor on the 7th and the declaration of war by Germany and Italy on the 11th. The main base of the U-boats in France at Lorient was the target of the first daylight raid by the US air force on 21 October 1942, in which forty-six people lost their lives and 136 were injured. Because the U-boats were sheltered by the mighty walls and ceilings of the U-boat bunkers, the Allied air force command decided on the strategy of surface bombing against the French ports. The aim of this policy was to raze to the ground the entire infrastructure around the German bunkers.

Gustave Mansion, who lived in Lorient at the time, recalled the beginning of the Allied air offensive against his town:

When the sirens sounded at 2355 hrs on 14 January 1943, it was the 317th air raid alarm since the war began. Nobody anticipated what was to come. One could hear distinctly the humming of a large formation at altitude. Twenty minutes later the whole town was illuminated by the flare bombs they dropped. Despite the heavy German flak the Allied aircraft dropped down to about 2,000 metres [6,500ft] and approached in waves of twenty machines, one after another. The flak and the explosions could be heard 50 kilometres [30 miles] away.[13]

For five weeks Lorient was the target of Allied air attacks. The beleaguered population had no comprehension of their purpose. Although they had been warned in leaflets and by the BBC to leave the town, only a few did so. Laurent Georget takes up the story of the following attacks:

> On the afternoon of 23 January 1943 for some time we watched a long row of Flying Fortresses flying high above us. Then forty of them detached from the formation and flew directly for the inner town area. Panic broke out and everybody ran for the bunker below Place Bison. I got to the bottom without touching the steps.[14]

If hundreds of townspeople had left in the autumn of 1942, at the beginning of 1943 there was a real exodus. On 16 January around twenty thousand people turned their backs on their home town and found somewhere else to settle in the surrounding countryside. The official evacuation of the town took place between 3 and 10 February 1943. Another forty thousand had to leave their houses, amongst them Paul Fontaine:

> On the morning of 7 February we followed the convoy so as to escape this glowing oven, it did not matter to where, one fled because there was no more hope: nothing existed any more, everything was destroyed, the streets were unrecognisable without facades, no shape, everything was burning and one's only aim was not to be buried beneath the collapsing walls.[15]

The Germans declared the city a prohibited area which in future could only be entered with a special German pass. Only members of the civilian air-raid defence and the fire brigades remained behind. Fireman Xavier Allainguillaume was in the bunker below Place Alsace-Lorraine on 7 February 1943 when he experienced another air raid on the ruined town: 'When the sirens sounded the all clear we left the bunker to see a Dante-like spectacle. All the houses around the Place Alsace-Lorraine were on fire, and those in the surrounding streets, a real funeral pyre.'[16]

When the last bombs fell on 17 February 1943, Lorient had ceased to exist. The Allies had sent more than 1,800 aircraft to bomb the town in eight heavy raids and had dropped 4,000 tonnes of bombs, equivalent to one bomb per square metre. More attacks with HE bombs followed on 6 March, 16 April and 17 May 1943. Of five thousand buildings, 3,500 had been totally destroyed, and the remainder were uninhabitable. Lorient had been turned into a ghost town. Only the German U-boat bunkers remained intact. Not a single German U-boat had been damaged. The German flak shot down thirty-four machines and 217 Allied airmen lost their lives bombing Lorient. The population had comparatively few

German workers' camp at Hennebont near Lorient, looking from the gate
to the community hall, 1942. (Wilhelm Fahrmbacher & Walter Matthiae,
Lorient, Weissenburg 1956)

casualties considering the scale of the devastation. Between 1940 and 1943 about 252 people were killed in Allied air attacks on Lorient. Between November 1942 and April 1943 Brest was also the target of five heavy air raids which claimed a total of 111 lives. In the city 163 buildings were destroyed and 431 damaged.

The heavy air raids forced the population of the towns out into the country. From Brest alone about nine thousand people were evacuated into the departments of Sarthe and Loir et Cher in the interior. Often the men stayed back in the towns alone, or took the train or cycled to work. German shipyard workers, OT men and the U-boat crews were accommodated safely in barrack compounds beyond the ports from where they were brought to the bases in the mornings by buses and trains. OT put up concrete bunkers of several storeys near the German quarters where naval men could take cover when the air raid alarm sounded. Such installations were built at Brest behind the new hospital, quarters of 9th U-boat Flotilla, at Lorient in the courtyard of the French harbour barracks and at La Rochelle on the barracks terrain of 3rd U-boat Flotilla. At St-Nazaire and Bordeaux, too, air-raid bunkers were built inside the barrack compounds of the U-boat flotillas. It was these bunkers which dominated the skyline of the port towns when the war ended.

In constructing air-raid protection, but also in many other areas of the

Building work at the Brest-Nord airfield, 1941. (Author collection)

German shipyards, local enterprise was brought in to assist. In general, it can be said that most firms in the region were active for the German occupying forces one way or another. The construction of the U-boat bunkers, the building of the Atlantic Wall and supporting the German troops demanded a large number of workers. The head of the French Inscription Maritime at Brest stated in a report dated March 1942: 'Everybody who wants to work can find a job, whether it be in the fishing industry, the harbour works or building trade, but above all in the building of air-raid bunkers.'[17]

The task of recruiting of a hundred French workers for the Railway Board North at Brest in September 1942 shows how deep the links were between local businesses and their German occupiers.[18] Nearly all the firms approached by the city administration at the urging of the Feldkommandantur declared that they were not in a position to make available the personnel requested, since they were already working for German service centres. The building firm Renvoisé stated that it had been working for the Kriegsmarine since August 1940 and did not have the staff for the work required, which included repairing the rail network of the national rail organisation SNCF in areas near Rennes, Lorient and Brest, although the sixteen lorries and about twenty employees that were available were now on the way.[19] The building firm Le Bras employed 418 workers on an OT project at the eastern mole of the mercantile harbour, while another firm had its entire labour force working at the Poulmic

French female employees in a Kriegsmarine factory, France, 1942.
(Bundesarchiv, 101II-MW-6863-11/Tölle [Tröller])

Luftwaffe base.[20] The shipbuilding concern Gourio, and the Dubigeon shipyard in the mercantile harbour, were working for the Kriegsmarine and other smaller enterprises were also active for the German occupiers.[21] Thus builders put up structures for the Kriegsmarine at Brest and at the Poulmic and Ploujean airfields, and smaller firms fitted out the new chart room in the U-boat bunker at Brest.[22] French building concerns were the ones which profited from the contracts of the occupying force, but other branches of industry also had dealings with the occupiers. A Brest shoe factory, for example, made boots for the German naval clothing depot.[23]

The labour force at the French state yards provided the greater part of the workers in German service. At Lorient alone, 4,300 Frenchmen worked at the Kriegsmarine yard, which employed thirty-three officers, 137 officials, 600 other ranks, 415 staff and 4,000 German shipyard workers.[24] According to information supplied by Otto Feuerhahn, a former senior official in the shipbuilding section of the Kriegsmarine yard at Brest, there were 2,500 French workers, while a former foreman there recalled that there were only 450 Germans.[25]

Inside the French naval arsenals, apart from the shipbuilding sector, many other divisions were active on behalf of the occupying force, since the Kriegsmarine had taken over most installations, together with the French personnel. Thus the clothing workshops of the French naval commissariat also turned out off-the-peg uniforms for Kriegsmarine officers.[26] French personnel managed the various supply establishments, such as bakeries and abattoirs, the flour mill, the freezers, wine cellars, transformer stations and other institutions inside the naval arsenals. The local German administration simply co-opted the bakers, slaughterers, compound administrators and the female personnel and also contributed a percentage of their pay.[27] The greater part of this, however, was listed as an occupation charge to be settled by the French state. The French naval commissariat also made available to the Kriegsmarine a cook, two cleaning ladies and twenty workers for the various local German naval administrative offices, but the Kriegsmarine recruited workers from amongst the populace for its own accommodation, so that in February 1942 it required from the Brest city administration eleven cleaning ladies and a stoker for the naval guesthouse, and in March 1943, sixteen cleaning ladies for the house used by the Kriegsmarine staff in the inner city.[28]

That not all workers and employees of these firms were delighted at working for the Germans is shown by a complaint in January 1941 from the commandant, Naval Defence Bretagne, to the local Kommandantur at Brest. The naval commandant requested that the French police oversee the conversion work on the guesthouse and staff house, because he did not think that the work was progressing as fast as it should.[29] Protracting the

The French submarine *Africaine* (*UF1*) in June 1940 on the slipway at Le Trait. It was worked on for the Kriegsmarine from 1941 as *UF1* but the will of the French yard workers to finish the boat was lacking and when the Germans left in 1944 she had still not been completed. (Author collection)

completion of German contracts or getting them done slowly was a common form of resistance. Thus the partially-built French submarine *Africaine*, captured in the summer of 1940 at Le Trait on the Seine and taken on by the Germans as *UF1* from May 1941, was subjected by the French yard workers to so many delays that when the Germans left France in 1944 it was still not in commission.

Nevertheless, the German delegation for industry attached to the Franco-German Armistice Commission reported on the French yards on 31 December 1942: 'The French authorities and shipyard workers work impeccably and quickly at fitting out and preparing the vessels for sea, no acts of sabotage have occurred.'[30] Although there were many demonstrations and attacks against the occupying power in occupied France, most French people held out until the summer of 1944, nursing a kind of inner detachment. At Lorient, naval Captain Charrier noted, 'The main worry of the workers at the Lorient naval arsenal is surviving from day to day. Only a few have joined active Resistance groups but in this way they represent the thinking of the greater part of the French population.'[31]

From the beginning of the occupation there were individual groups which attempted to harm the occupiers by acts of sabotage or espionage. The murder of the German naval administration assistant, Alfons Moser, on 23 August 1941 at the Paris Metro station Barbès is seen as the first

French Resistance graffiti on the walls of a public convenience, France, 1941. (Bundesarchiv, 101II-251-0980-27A/Gretschel)

armed act of resistance in France, but the background to the death of a German naval artillery rating, shot dead by unknown perpetrators whilst on sentry duty on the night of 13 August 1940 in the grounds of the Golf Hotel at Royan, remains unclear.[32] On 1 October 1940, in the naval arsenal at Brest, bricks were thrown at two German officers from the bridge spanning the area.[33] These two examples show that even in the summer of 1940 German occupation troops had to be aware that attacks against them were possible. Nevertheless, in the early part of the occupation they were rare.

As in all parts of France, in Brittany there were inhabitants who came to an arrangement with the Germans. Most Bretons were anything but pro-German and preferred passive resistance, which for many citizens such as Léontine Drapier-Cadec of Brest consisted of simply not noticing them: 'To pay them too much attention flattered them ... Our dignity existed in ignoring them.'[34] On 1 January 1941 the prefect for the department of Morbihan stated of the attitude of the populace: 'Apart from the traders the population has little contact with the occupying soldiers and it seems that people want it that way as much as possible: therefore in football matches involving German teams nobody turns up to watch.'[35]

All the same the first signs of resistance appeared early on. German announcements were torn down and in some places, such as a public convenience at Brest, slogans such as 'Down with Hitler' and 'Death to Hitler' were daubed.[36] In January 1941 the slogan 'Long live de Gaulle and Pétain, we will get the Boche' appeared on a wall of the former French naval prefecture at Brest which the Kriegsmarine used as an officers' mess.[37] The cross of Lorraine, as a symbol of Free France, began to be seen more frequently on the walls of houses. The French police made every attempt to remove these graffiti before German patrols saw them.

Occasionally, there were open protests. In July 1940 at Brest a German flag was removed from German quarters.[38] One month later, the German Feldgendarmerie handed over to the custody of the city police a young man who had made 'an improper gesture' to the sentry in front of the local Kommandantur.[39] In December 1940 a passer-by shouted, 'Long live de Gaulle!' in front of the same building.[40] A month before, on 11 November 1940 in celebration of Armistice Day 1918, the memorial at Brest was decorated with wreaths in the British colours. As a punishment the town had to provide citizen sentries at the memorial for eight days.[41] On 24 July 1941 in the port of Les Sables d'Olonne a large crowd gathered on the quayside and openly showed sympathy for a British bomber crew shot down over La Pallice.[42] At Brest, despite the high casualties they had suffered in the British air raids on the harbour, the civilian population placed flowers on the graves of shot-down British airmen.[43] French, British and US flags were discovered on the grave of a British pilot at

The graves of British airmen adorned with floral tributes, Brest cemetery,
1941. (Author collection)

Crozon in November 1942.[44] On 20 May 1941 almost three thousand
people attempted to protest against the Vichy regime's policy of
collaboration.[45] The protest march was prevented by French and German
police. A few days before a number of citizens had obeyed a call by de
Gaulle and visited the First World War memorial on Joan of Arc day.

The first resistance to contracts issued by the occupying authority
occurred in February 1941, when workers at the former French naval
ammunition establishment of Saint-Nicolas, eastern Brest, refused to
manufacture shells for French guns captured by the Wehrmacht.[46] The
relevant German Feldkommandantur intervened, provoking a second
refusal. Orders were then given to draw up a list of the workers who were
on strike and the work then went ahead for fear of the reprisals. In
October 1941 workers at the Brest naval arsenal laid down their tools in
protest against the shooting of French hostages after the assassination of
the German Feldkommandant at Nantes.[47] On 15 July 1942 unknown
saboteurs cut the drive belts of machines in the naval arsenal. The
punishment awarded by the French naval commandant was answered by
a one-hour strike.[48]

It was principally in the cafes and bars in the French ports that
altercations between French and Germans occurred, under the influence
of alcohol. On 6 April 1941 German naval ratings and French civilians

brawled in a cafe near the market halls of the St Martin district in Brest, and on 27 April fighting broke out between French and German soldiers in the Rue Traverse.[49] A Kriegsmarine NCO drew his pistol and fired at one of the Frenchmen involved in a brawl in the Brasserie de la Marine on 10 August 1941.[50] A Kriegsmarine Kapitänleutnant was knocked down on 12 September 1941 in Lorient under cover of darkness, by a person unknown.[51] Alongside these incidents, the Abwehr sub-office Brest reported in August 1941 that the telephone cables of Marine Flak Division 704 had been cut through near Lorient. Four children were discovered sabotaging a cable at Plouhinec near Carnac. On 10 August 1941, on the Île de Croix, drunken French guests at an inn attempted to relieve two German soldiers of their sidearms. For the German Abwehr, these examples were a significant indication that 'particularly in Brittany, resistance to the occupation forces is increasing, and will stiffen foreseeably if the campaign in the East turns into a lengthy one.'[52]

The cutting of cables and brawls in guesthouses were just the beginning. Following the attack on the Soviet Union in June 1941, the Communist Resistance groups, which had previously been largely silent as a result of the Hitler–Stalin Pact, were the ones who became particularly active against the German occupiers. Already, in April 1941

Announcement of death sentences passed on the five named persons at a court martial for taking part in a Communist demonstration aimed against the German Wehrmacht. The sentences were carried out by firing squad. (Author collection)

during an air-raid alarm in Brest, a German sentry at the Kriegsmarine yard had been fired at.[53] After similar incidents occurred on other nights, on 12 September the District Kommandantur Brest imposed a three-week curfew on the civilian population.[54] On 18 October at Lorient a lorry of Marine Flak Division 705 was fired on and the driver wounded. These events culminated in the murder of the Nantes Feldkommandant on 20 October 1941. At Bordeaux the following day a war administrative official also fell victim.

The occupying force reacted with great harshness. Previously, in August 1941 after the murder of Alfons Moser in Paris, two French Communists had been shot and all French persons arrested by German service centres declared hostages on the orders of the military commander, General Otto von Stülpnagel. Now, as a reprisal, Stülpnagel ordered the immediate execution of fifty hostages for the two assassinations. The Vichy government attempted in vain to have the death sentences lifted. The head of state Pétain and President Darlan appealed to the population to lay down their arms and accept the 1940 armistice. The shooting of the hostages on 22 and 24 October 1941 came as a shock to the French. Answering terror with counter-terror resulted in an even greater rejection of their occupying masters. French politicians such as the minister for industrial production, François Lehideux, warned of an escalation of violence: 'The hostage-policy is madness, it is a policy without end: each execution summons up a fresh murder, and the murder is followed by more executions. We find ourselves in a devil's circle.'[55] After more killings at the beginning of December 1941, von Stülpnagel ordered a hundred hostages, amongst them Communists and French Jews, to be shot in Paris at Mont-Valérien.

In the Atlantic bases, the attitude of the occupying force towards the assassins became ever more unyielding. When on 12 November 1941 the crew of a naval flak searchlight were fired upon with a pistol by a person unknown at the Brest-Süd airfield, Frenchmen found in a ditch during a search of the terrain were shot on sight. Finally, the cafes which German soldiers liked to frequent increasingly became the target of bomb attacks. In an explosion in a cafe in Brest city centre on the night of 15 February 1942, five German naval ratings and five Frenchmen were wounded.[56] On 1 May two explosive devices were set off in front of two German Soldatenheim at Quimper and Concarneau.[57] One month later a bomb went off at a cafe in the Brest suburb of Lambézellec, and on 9 September 1942 another in the cellar of a cafe in the centre of Brest.[58]

The Kommandantur reacted by closing suspected bars and imposing a curfew on the civilian population; the mayors were forced to post civilian guards for the protection of German quarters. In the spring of 1943 in Brest a series of bomb explosions directed towards the occupation troops occurred. The first went off in front of a cinema and two Kriegsmarine quarters, the last two at the staff office of Marine Flak Division 805 and the local Kommandantur.[59] The Resistance, which had previously been limited to passive protest strikes or conducted under cover of darkness, had now transformed itself into an open offensive against the German occupying power.

The Feldkommandanturen were responsible for the protection of military installations and combating internal unrest. For the maintenance of security and order in occupied France the military commander had been given a total of 105 rifle battalions in August 1940. Most of these units, composed primarily of older men poorly equipped with only captured weapons, were used to guard prisoners of war, the remainder being of insufficient numbers to control all the departments in the occupied territory. Even after they had all been given French rifles in May 1941, they were still not well armed, for in most cases they were only issued with between five and ten rounds.[60] After the Russian campaign began, some of these battalions went to the eastern front, leaving many important installations and railway connections unprotected from autumn 1941, while the number of attacks by Communist Resistance groups rose. Because of the lack of German security forces, Stülpnagel focused his efforts on maintaining particular strong points, so that in some French regions only patrols were carried out, and increasing calls were made on the French police.[61]

Sabotage or technical defect? The main magazine at the Brest arsenal on fire, 8 August 1941. (Author collection)

Acts of sabotage inside the complex structure of the shipyards are difficult to identify because it is often unclear whether an accident, technical defect or sabotage was the cause. Although some French workers were employed inside U-boat bunkers, they did not normally work on the boats themselves. The deck of a U-boat in a bunker was kept under constant guard, in order to prevent unauthorised access to the interior.[62] So proveable acts of sabotage were those directed against auxiliary installations and machinery which were easier to access. The first major act of sabotage in Brest noted in the Skl war diary occurred on 3 September 1942. A diesel generator in the U-boat bunker was damaged while several attempts, not all successful, were made against the electrical transformer installation inside the French naval arsenal, but also one inside the heavily guarded U-boat bunker.[63] Until then the main target had been the easily cut drive belts of machinery.[64] An attack with an explosive was made against *U663* in January 1943, but the boat was not damaged.[65] On 29 April 1943 three explosive devices went off in the power station at the French arsenal, and on 31 August 1943 a machine was damaged by an explosion in the workshops there.[66] At the same time a number of bombs directed at German installations were set off in the city centre. The investigation by the French police revealed that the explosives came from French building firms working for the Germans at the Atlantic Wall.[67] On 5 January 1944 a bomb went off in the power plant at the French arsenal at Lorient, destroying the facility which distilled water for U-boat batteries.

Other Resistance acts in the arsenal were much less observable. For example, members of a Communist Resistance cell obtained work with a French metal firm which appraised metal scrap. At the firm's collection point they loaded certain railway wagons used to transport the metal above the authorised weight limit, or tampered with the brakes.[68] In another case, French workers flooded storage rooms by destroying immersed water piping at the former French naval academy, which was being used by 1st U-boat Flotilla and the commandant of Naval Defence Bretagne.[69] At St-Nazaire a wooden board was found in the diesel air intake mast of *U264* and wooden props in the pump connections aboard *U773*, but how they got there is not recorded. Some technical incidents were caused by the negligence or inadequate training of German yard workers.[70] At Lorient it often happened that a boat leaving on patrol had to turn back because the injection pumps for the diesel aggregate were blocked up. Sabotage was suspected initially, but finally investigations revealed that these boats had been in the Scorff bunker at the naval arsenal and had undergone a standing test of the diesels and trim trials at the same time. The harbour slick settled in the fuel tanks and later collected in the diesel injection pumps. On a 3rd U-boat Flotilla boat from La

Tugs guiding a Type IX U-boat at Lorient, c.1942. (Author collection)

Pallice the diesels seized up during a trial voyage by the yard. The investigation here revealed that before sailing the blind flange which released cooling water into the connecting pipes between the cylinders had been left off.[71] It was not known if this was an oversight by German or French yard workers.

In general, however, the German naval centres were very satisfied with the work of French yard personnel. In a review, the head of the U-boat repair operation at Brest particularly praised the French dock personnel for the way they handled the difficult task of dry docking U-boats with their sensitive hydrophonic and depth-sounding equipment.[72] The German centres overwhelmingly attributed such excellent co-operation to the attitude of the French Admiral Jardel, responsible for command of the French naval units in the occupied sector. In the opinion of the German liaison officers at Vichy and in Paris, it was:

> due to his personality that in the entire occupied region no act of sabotage or espionage had harmed German-French naval co-operation, but that all naval commanders and the two Commanding Admirals always reported that the French auxiliary naval service had worked blamelessly and dynamically even after the Normandy Invasion and until the end [sic!].[73]

All the same there were some incidents. On 11 February 1942, when French tugs were assisting the heavy cruiser *Prinz Eugen* to sail for the Channel Dash, the tow line broke and wrapped around the propeller of the leading tug. Then the rear tug tangled in a torpedo net and afterwards also in the tow line. It is not known if these manoeuvres were intended by the tug crews to delay the departure of the German battleship squadron. The same question arose when a U-boat was slightly damaged at St-Nazaire through incorrect operation of the swing-bridge.[74] They were charged with sabotage and appeared at a court martial of the Naval Commander Western France, but the outcome is not recorded.

Because of their work in especially sensitive areas, the yard employees and French navy members were of special interest to the French Resistance. Although those employed in the German yards could only move freely with special passes or metal tags, and non-local workers were vetted by the French naval gendarmerie or dockyard police before employment, it was very difficult for the Abwehr to prevent their passing on to the Resistance what they knew about the shipyard. Already in September 1940 in occupied France a Resistance cell called 'Confrérie Notre-Dame', had been established, whose purpose was the passing of information to the military secret service of Free France. Led by Colonel Rémy, a network of informants was set up, to which, for example, Lt Cdr Jean Philippon belonged under the cover name 'Hilarion'; information was regularly transmitted to London regarding repairs to the German battleships. At Lorient the deputy leader of the French shipyard concern, Jacques Stosskopf, passed important information to the Allies about U-boat movements in the bunkers, including a report before Operation *Paukenschlag* in early 1942 off the US east coast, that the Kriegsmarine had pulled out the relevant charts from the French navy chart store at Lorient. Whereas Philippon escaped the Abwehr investigation by a transfer to Toulon, Stosskopf was arrested at Lorient for espionage on 21 February 1944, and executed later at Natzweiler concentration camp.

The difficulties the Germans had in keeping things secret is shown by the transfer of the battleship *Scharnhorst* to La Pallice in July 1941. The battleship commanders had classified all preparations for Operation *Südwind* as top secret, knowledge of which was to be limited to a very small circle, yet the officers in the entourage of Vizeadmiral Ciliax discovered on the day of planned departure that not only the German naval centres at La Pallice and Brest knew, but so did the French population.[75] At La Pallice the day and actual time of arrival was known, while in Brest the departure of *Scharnhorst* was being discussed openly by local bartenders. Since the crew of the battleship had not been informed of the operation, it was clear that a major breach of security had occurred in the shore bases, and an investigation was ordered.

A German minesweeper in a French shipyard at Nantes, March 1944.
(Bibliothek für Zeitgeschichte, Stuttgart)

Berlin was well aware of the numerous possibilities for spying in the French bases. When on 3 October 1941 the U-boat supply ship *Kota Pinang* was surprised and sunk off the Azores by the British cruiser *Kenya*, the cruiser using her guns to ward off *U129* sailing as escort, Skl blamed the loss on French informers, since the ship had been laid up in the harbour at Pauillac on the Gironde for conversion work and fitting out, and French workers had been aboard.[76] When the return of the battleships and cruiser from Brest by means of a Channel Dash was discussed at Führer HQ, Hitler thought that because of the 'good knowledge of the British through their spies' all further movements

Admiral Jean Philippon in a post-war photo as Commander, French Mediterranean Squadron. (Jean Philippon, *Le Blocus*, Paris 1967)

by the ships on exercises would inevitably lead to reinforced air attacks which would endanger the ships, and thus these should attempt the Channel Dash as soon as possible.[77]

Besides excellent examples such as Lt Cdr Philippon at Brest, or the French engineer officer Stosskopf at Lorient, various other Resistance groups were active in the ports. A report sent from Brest on 28 February 1943, for example provided precise details as to the formation and timetable of German U-boat escorts off the coast, contained a description of the U-boat net defence in the Goulet, and mentioned the degaussing of German U-boats in the mercantile harbour, a time at which surprise air attacks could be especially dangerous to unprotected boats, according to the informant.[78]

Another missive of 20 July 1943 reported the transfer of important machinery from the workshops at the French arsenal into the underground gallery system below Brest castle, and also supplied the exact number and kind of machines involved.[79] In order to obtain even more accurate information from the arsenal, in 1943 local Resistance leaders requested that the informants set up their own Resistance cell to be led by an engineer from the French harbour building office, five other engineers, eleven foremen and twenty-five workers from various sections of the shipyard, including the U-boat bunker.[80] Besides espionage, in the event of a German retreat the group was to prevent destruction in the arsenal.

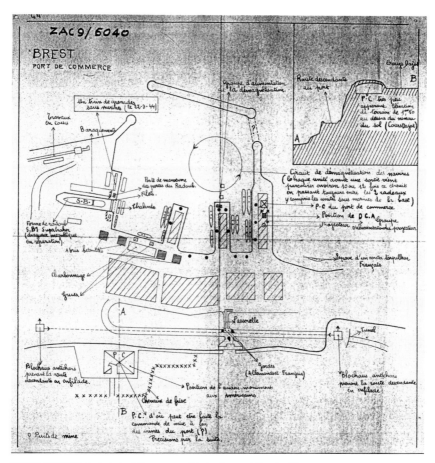

French Resistance sketch of the mercantile harbour at Brest with notes on the German installations, July 1944. (Service historique de la Marine, Brest)

The group reported U-boat movements in the U-boat bunker and identified the boats by reference to number, heraldic devices or paintings on the tower. Besides repairs, the Allies were informed by photo and sketch of the new *Schnorchel*, the gear of German minesweepers in current use, flamethrowers fitted to the masts of VP-boats as a defence against low-level air attack and the defensive installations at the arsenal.

The Germans were well aware of the dangers of espionage by French yard workers, but because of the lack of skilled German personnel they were not in a position to eject the French workers. In order to minimise the indications that a U-boat was about to sail, the crew were ordered to arrive in twos and threes, and the final refuelling and departure mostly occurred at night. Nevertheless, French informants could also calculate the sailing date of a U-boat down to a few days by its repair state.

Occasionally, the Resistance would also attempt to exert psychological pressure on the occupying force, as was exemplified by a German language leaflet found on 16 September 1941 in rooms at the Sperrwaffen-kommando Brest, in which the Communist parties of Germany and Austria urged soldiers and workers to foment strikes and commit acts of sabotage.[81] The leaflets were distributed around Brest by members of a Communist Resistance group.[82] Text in French requested that those finding the leaflets should pass it on to German soldiers.[83] That not all members of the occupation forces supported German policy in France is shown by the example of two German soldiers at Brest, who were seen by French police on the evening of 27 September 1942, tearing down a poster placed in a central city street announcing the deaths by firing squad of French Communist prisoners.[84]

It seems clear, however, that up to the beginning of 1943 the Resistance found only a weak response from the general population. With the introduction of the obligatory work service (STO) by the authorities, more and more young Frenchmen chose the road into the underground movement. By the end of 1943 action against the occupiers also increased. Finally, in the spring of 1944 the German Commander-in-Chief West issued an instruction to German troops stationed in France as to how they should act in the event of an attack by the Resistance. This edict found its way into the most remote corners of the Kriegsmarine, as its publication in a fleet order by the commander of the Hafenschutzflotille Gascogne at Bordeaux on 20 February 1944 shows. German troops were urged always to take a firearm with them when leaving their base or boat.[85] Should a group or a single soldier be attacked, fire was to be returned immediately whatever the risk to civilians: 'If the innocent are in any way affected, that is exclusively the fault of the terrorists!'[86] As well as arresting all civilians in the vicinity, without discrimination as to their social position or status, the houses from where the shooting occurred were to be burnt to the ground. Only when that had been achieved were their superiors to be notified of the occurrence and, according to the order issued to all soldiers, 'should a lack of resolve and softness at such occurrences come to light', severe punishment would ensue.

This example makes clear that, even at the end of the occupation, the Kriegsmarine was involved at least technically in the repression of the French population. Even at sea action became sterner. After French fishing vessels took ever less notice of German regulations, on the night of 13 May 1944 a fishing boat proceeding without lights off the Île de Croix was fired on by a VP-boat, while off Lorient another French fishing boat with lights not set was rammed and sunk.[87]

French militia leading away Resistance prisoners, July 1944.
(Bundesarchiv, 146-1989-107-24/Koll)

There is certain evidence of crimes by German naval personnel against the French population as a result of civilians involving themselves in the Allied military offensives in the summer of 1944. Thus, in connection with the fighting around fortified Brest on 7 August 1944, reprisals were taken in the small village of Gouesnou, east of Brest. According to French accounts, an officer of 9th U-boat Flotilla stationed at Brest ordered and carried out the shooting of the occupants of a nearby farm, the farmer and his wife, after an attack on a German searchlight position.[88] On the same day, forty-nine other people in the village were shot dead by an unknown German military unit.[89] This was the worst massacre by German troops in Brittany, together with other reprisals at Plouvien and St Pol de Léon on the northern coast. The commanding officer of 266 Infantry Division stationed in northern Brittany, Generalleutnant Karl Spang, eavesdropped by the British, told other German officers at the British prisoner-of-war institution at Trent Park that he had ordered his own troops to proceed 'with ruthless severity' and admitted to pronouncing numerous death sentences against the French Resistance.[90] Against this background, Spang feared being handed over to the French Resistance movement.

On 7 August 1944, 1st Battery, Light Naval Artillery Sub-Battalion 686, fighting as ground troops, burnt the small village of Segré near Angers to the ground, 'as ordered', after they were fired on by armed Resistance civilians during their advance.[91] The small community of La Chapelle sur Erdre to the northeast of Nantes barely escaped a similar fate. A Kriegsmarine equipment compound there had been plundered by the village people after the German sentries withdrew. Once the depot was reoccupied on 5 August 1944, on the orders of the Commanding Admiral Atlantic Coast it was announced that plundering would be halted by burning down the village should the inhabitants fail to return the stolen goods within a specified period of amnesty.[92] Only the liberation of the village on 6 August 1944 by US troops prevented the order being carried out.

The German military commander in France, Otto von Stülpnagel, had been associated from early on with the shooting of hostages, which was detrimental to the important collaboration with the French population. As he saw it, the purpose of the assassinations by the Resistance movement was simply

> to provoke harsh measures in response in order to stir up the population against the occupying power. They aim to foment strikes and passive resistance, for it has become important to them to prejudice the war potential of the occupied zone once the French worker ... had placed himself voluntarily at the disposal of the German war industry.[93]

The framing of the hostage edict and the execution of French prisoners as an answer to the murder of the German Feldkommandant at Nantes had been painful for him, and as a result of his doubts at the justification of the measures he had taken, he accepted the personal consequences and tendered his resignation on 15 February 1942. Nevertheless, in France his name will always be associated with the first shootings of hostages. His successor, Carl-Heinrich von Stülpnagel, fell victim in the aftermath of the 20 July 1944 plot. Otto von Stülpnagel was handed over to the French in 1946. Whilst on remand in the Paris Cherche-Midi jail he took his own life in February 1948.

6

Holding Out to the Bitter End

Ports become forts

On 14 December 1941 Hitler issued the order to build the so-called Atlantic Wall.[1] This gigantic undertaking along the European western coast was to extend from the Spanish border to Norway and with the help of bunkered gun and machine-gun positions prevent a major Allied landing.

The permeability of the German coastal defences at this time was demonstrated by the British commando raid against St-Nazaire in March 1942. The purpose of this attack was to do enough damage to the great Normandy dry dock to prevent its possible use by the German battleship *Tirpitz*. British forces succeeded in eluding the German coastal defences and a number of MTBs, and the old destroyer *Campbeltown*, converted into an explosives carrier, penetrated the harbour. The destroyer rammed the outer lock gate, and was eventually destroyed when its cargo exploded.[2] The subsequent fighting in the town and port area highlighted a further weak point of the German naval bases: because no army troops were stationed there, the Kriegsmarine alone had to defend them. Thus the surprise night attack had to be countered by the naval units based at St-Nazaire. Lacking house-to-house combat experience, their counter-measures progressed only slowly, and were initially so uncoordinated that the Commander-in-Chief West later felt compelled to complain at the wild shooting in the town.[3] Eventually the Anglo-Canadian force was out-numbered by the Germans and forced to surrender. The U-boat bunker was undamaged, but the Normandy Lock remained out of commission until the war ended.

An immediate consequence of the attack on St-Nazaire was the integration of the U-boat bases into the coastal defences.[4] In the ports additional guns were installed and additionally one battalion of infantry was stationed in every U-boat base to repel troop landings.

To obtain full control of the town districts along the waterfront, the

HMS *Campbeltown* after ramming the lock gates at St-Nazaire, March 1942. (Bundesarchiv, 101II-MW-3722-03/Kramer)

Kreiskommandatur of Brest had almost a thousand civilian inhabitants evacuated from the mercantile harbour in April 1942.[5] Restaurants and bars had to close, although established firms and traders in the port area were allowed in during the day. Access to the harbour required special approval, documents being checked by sentries at the entrance points. Another consequence of the British attack on St-Nazaire was the immediate transfer of the many naval staffs from the coast into the interior.[6] Thus Dönitz was obliged to abandon his chateau at Kernevel near Lorient for Paris. The rest homes for U-boatmen directly above the beaches were not abandoned, but Dönitz ordered their closure until further notice.

In order to protect against any more surprise attacks from the sea, surveillance of inshore waters was stepped up. For this purpose the harbour protection flotillas had to detach all seaworthy boats to the VP-boat flotillas.[7] In the spring of 1942 in the west there were almost two hundred of these VP-boats, although only eighty-six were operational.[8] This left the harbours themselves unprotected, since there were no substitutes for the boats they had been forced to release. At Brest in May 1942, for example, the harbour protection flotilla had only two boats operational instead of the usual twenty. The Kriegsmarine office at Bordeaux was in charge of requisitions but discovered in their search that

Grossadmiral Karl Dönitz inspecting naval crews at Brest, 1943.
(Author collection)

in France all suitable boats had already been assigned, apart from some old fishing cutters and unseaworthy craft.[9] This meant that from the summer of 1942 the harbour protection flotillas could only keep watch from a few of their waterborne stations.

The danger of air attacks was also increasing. On 2 March 1943 the Fliegerführer Atlantik informed Dönitz as the new Commander-in-Chief, Kriegsmarine, that his airborne units were no longer in a position to protect the channels into and out of the ports against enemy air attack once the Allies resumed air attacks on U-boat bases.[10] The heavy bombardment of Lorient and St-Nazaire forced the Kriegsmarine to withdraw all surface vessels from these bases and transfer them to smaller ports such as Concarneau or Benodet.[11] U-boat repairs under the metres of concrete bunker ceilings remained completely undisturbed by the bombing, although for a short while bottlenecks occurred in supplying the workshops due to the devastation in the two towns.

On the other hand, it became ever more dangerous for U-boats running into and out of the ports. The coastal waters were continually being mined by Allied aircraft. *U171* was sunk by one of these mines immediately outside Lorient on 9 September 1942, and *U526* was similarly lost there on 14 April 1943.[12] Off Brest at Pointe Saint-Mathieu a U-boat and escort were even attacked close inshore by Allied aircraft.

The Kriegsmarine reacted by
arming U-boats with extra flak
guns. If attacked they were not to
dive, but accept combat with the
aircraft and shoot it down – an idea
which did not work in practice.
Therefore, on 22 May 1943 the
'flak-trap', *U441*, left Brest and was
attacked two days later by a
Sunderland aircraft. Although the
flak crew shot down the aircraft,
the boat was so badly damaged that
it had to turn back to Brest. On the

Attack on *U118* by US aircraft, 12 February
1943. (US National Archives)

second such outing on 11 July 1943, *U441* came under attack by a number
of aircraft. Ten crewmen were killed and thirteen wounded, including all
the officers. The only officer on board to emerge unscathed was the
medical officer who brought the boat back into port. None of the
attacking aircraft was shot down. Because of the death toll it was decided
not to proceed with 'flak-trap' experiments. A special radar detection
device for U-boats, known as the 'Biscay cross' for its shape, which gave
early warning of the approach of aircraft, proved impracticable and was
soon discontinued.

At the same time, Allied radar technology had made major advances.
Thus in the spring of 1944 British aircraft detected a formation of S-boats
(fast motor torpedo boats) leaving Brest by night and bombed them.[13]
Since it was not possible to shake off the aircraft, the S-boats were forced
to put back into the bunker at Brest.[14]

In February and March 1944, after British aircraft began renewed
attacks on escorted U-boats outside Brest and St-Nazaire, Skl decided
not to escort U-boats far offshore, thus releasing the escorts to concentrate
on minesweeping in the exit channels.[15] This decision extended the
dangerous solo run of the U-boats out to sea by a whole day. In March
1944 Skl described this rightly as 'a retreat to the coast'.[16] During the
previous September, in the face of increasing British MTB attacks on
German coastal convoys, Group West had already determined that the
available units lacked the numbers to protect the convoys satisfactorily:

> The fact that enemy naval forces have lurked unmolested in our inshore
> waters for days ... highlights at a stroke our weakness in the air, at sea
> and in our coastal defence. It is neither possible to engage these vessels
> effectively nor to maintain a proper watch over the sea area. This
> strengthens the self-confidence of the enemy and provides him with the
> opportunity to probe the weakness of our own forces.[17]

Wrecked Canadian tank and burning landing craft, Dieppe beach, August 1942. (Bundesarchiv, 101I-291-1229-17A/Meyer; Wiltberger)

In view of this situation, ever more attention was paid to defending the coast. Skl had accepted in July 1942 that the main purpose of an Allied landing in the west would be to take out the U-boat bases.[18] In order to better protect these, on 13 August Hitler ordered that, besides reinforcing the existing installations, a defensive belt should be built around the ports.[19] Of the 15,000 bunkers planned for the spring of 1943, only 4,000 were to protect the U-boat bases ashore.

The Anglo-Canadian landings known as Operation Jubilee at Dieppe, in which on 19 August 1942 British commando units and Canadian infantry supported by tanks made an unsuccessful attack on the Channel port, nevertheless demonstrated to the German command staff that the Allies were not only capable of launching commando raids but that to a limited extent they could also land troops in a German-occupied port.[20] Even though the German troops stationed at Dieppe eventually succeeded in repulsing the landing attempt, the attack showed the urgency of erecting a rearward defence of the ports on the Atlantic coast, especially since long stretches of beach in proximity to important bases such as Brest and Lorient were favourable for landing operations. The announced expansion of the defence installations was then placed behind other projects of allegedly greater importance for the conduct of the war, such as extending the U-boat bunkers, fortifying the Channel Islands and bunkering the V-2 firing sites on the Channel coast, such that by the time of the Normandy landings only a few defensive sections had been completed.[21]

At the end of 1943, the German coastal defence installations in the west had so many large gaps that Rommel, whom Hitler had put in charge of the Atlantic Wall, had recourse to provisional measures: wooden stakes with French grenades, or tree trunks dug into the beaches, the so-called 'Rommel asparagus' which would impede Allied landing craft. Although some new anti-tank guns were delivered to the coastal defence, often they were not installed in the bunkers built for them, but mostly placed in a position where their field of fire was limited to the beach immediately outside the bunker. Long-range batteries were only to be found in the Pas de Calais, Norway, and near the important U-boat bases; other stretches had no protection at all. Thus the Atlantic Wall so highly praised by Nazi propaganda remained a patchwork.

Another problem was the shortage of armaments. Admiral Friedrich Ruge, attached to Army Group B as a consultant, recalled that troops in the later landing zones of the Allies in Normandy had ninety-two different weapons of the most widespread manufacture, for which no less than 252 kinds of ammunition were on hand.[22] Furthermore, the troops were convinced that the German positions were known to the Allies by their air reconnaissance or from French informants.

On 19 January 1944 the ports of Ijmuiden, Hook of Holland, Dunkirk, Boulogne, Le Havre, Cherbourg, St Malo, Brest, Lorient, St-Nazaire and the Nord and Süd bases on the Gironde estuary were all declared to be fortresses.[23] Amongst other things, this meant that in the case of an Allied landing they could resist for a period of at least fifty-six days, and so prevent the harbours being used. The quality of the troops was extremely variable. Thus according to the battle instructions of 3 February 1944, the complement of the fortress at Brest consisted of only 3,000 army troops who in the case of an alarm would call on 1,000 Organisation Todt workers and 12,000 naval men.[24] While the army troops who made up the permanent nucleus belonged to XXV Army Corps, and were to man the bunkers along the defensive line should the alarm be raised, the naval units made up the bulk of the defenders. Depending on their size, the various service offices – from the flotillas based at Brest to the military court of the Commanding Admiral Atlantic Coast down to the naval meteorologist staff – had to set up alarm units, whose equipment and composition was anything but uniform.[25] Thus 7th VP-boat Flotilla had a 53-man platoon armed with two 2cm flak, three light MGs and fifty-three rifles, while the degaussing centre could only offer ten men armed with four rifles.[26] This example makes the problems faced in defending a harbour clear, especially since the naval personnel had little experience in fighting ashore.

The defenders' lack of weapons and training were to be compensated for by the extended lines of defence. The company at Brest would have a fortified belt of 160 bunkers running from the Bay of Sainte-Anne in the west of the city, through the old forts of Montbarey and Kéranroux in the north, to the old city walls in the east. At the centre of this installation was the U-boat bunker developed into a home base. Two mobile army batteries and encampments of naval flak made up the fortress artillery. In addition, in the grounds of the former French naval academy above the warship harbour, in 1944 two further special bunkers were built, whose mortars could pound anywhere in the fortress territory, including the roadstead. Despite all this activity, the defensive state of the harbours in 1944 was not what had been planned in 1942, and so the main front lines still had large gaps.

The extent to which the Allies were informed about the German defensive measures is shown in a report dated 30 March 1944 from a French informer in Brest.[27] Besides the number of German warships lying

Map of fortified Brest with front line and defensive installations as an appendix to the battle instructions of the Commander-in Chief West, 8 March 1944. (Bundesarchiv-Militärarchiv, Freiburg, RH 19 IV 120)

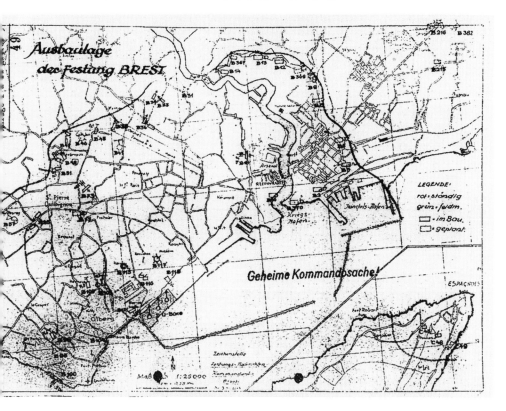

at Brest and their armament, the shape of their superstructures and speed, there were also accurate details of the harbour defences, the position of the anti-submarine net at the harbour entrance, other nets in the warship harbour, the smoke installations, the locations of flak guns and barrage balloons. The demolition chambers in the quays of the warship harbour and on the mole were also reported, together with the condition of the individual dry docks in the harbour. Even information about the present use and staffing of the U-boat bunker found its way into the report. Finally, its author mentioned that in the city a number of streets were sealed off with armour-protected walls and the entrances to the harbour secured against landing craft by the use of sunken twisted metal railway track. German fortification engineers had built well-camouflaged concrete command posts into the old city walls, which dated from the time of Vauban. According to the report, the discipline of the fortification troops was intact and acts of sabotage were unknown. The informer evaluated the morale of the U-boat officers as 'good', but only 'middling' for NCOs and ratings. The German naval offices were doing all they could by way of organisation to distract the men from the true situation.

In September 1943 Dönitz had attempted to prevent a falling-off of morale within the U-boat arm by means of his 'Edict against Addiction

Field Marshal Rommel with entourage inspecting obstacles on the foreshore, Channel coast, April 1944. (Bundesarchiv, 101I-719-0243-33/Jesse)

to Criticising and Grumbling'. Six months later – while the crews, faced with the rising losses of German U-boats, searched increasingly thoroughly for defects in their boats to prevent them having to sail – their commander, the BdU, spoke these heroic words aimed at raising morale: 'Despite their knowledge of the heavy losses, despite many hunts and stresses, the U-boatman does not allow it to get the better of him. Hard with himself and fate, hating the enemy, believing in his weapons and victory, he sails out time and again into the unequal struggle.'[28]

That this readiness for self-sacrifice sworn to by Dönitz was really present amongst the mass of U-boatmen is more than doubtful. The fact that they sailed despite everything probably had less to do with the cohesion of the crews so roundly praised by propaganda, than fear that to refuse to sail would result in a court martial for disobeying an order and cowardice in the face of the enemy. It might also be mentioned in passing that the ratio of officers and NCOs to ordinary ratings aboard a U-boat was much greater than on other naval vessels: a Type VIIc had four officers and nineteen NCOs, a total of twenty-three against twenty-seven ratings. The long voyages and the lack of privacy in the steel tube may have welded the crew together in many cases, so that many even spoke of themselves as 'family', but once the serious losses set in from 1943 onwards, doubts arose even in the U-boat arm.[29] French Resistance informers reported in July and September 1943 from Nantes and Marseilles of repeated anti-regime statements by German officers and men, and of a dwindling readiness to take a U-boat to sea.[30] Additionally, in the U-boat bases French workers were encouraged by the crews to work slower.[31]

Skl reacted against such sentiments with increased control and harshness. In order to counter the attempts of crews to delay sailing on the grounds of alleged technical deficiencies, 'Deep-dive Commissioners' were installed at the bases. These engineer officers, usually the base engineer, accompanied the boat on its last deep-dive trial before commencing the patrol, and then made his decision as to whether the boat was operational or not independent of the crew.[32] Furthermore, Dönitz also took the path of deterrence. In the case of the Lorient boat *U154*, its commander Oberleutnant zur See Oskar Kusch was denounced by his IWO for making statements criticising the regime. Kusch was arrested at Lorient on 20 January 1944 after the FdU West, Kapitän zur See Rösing, responsible for all questions relating to U-boat arm servicemen on the Western Front, initiated action against him for sedition.[33] On 26 January 1944 he was condemned to death by court martial at Kiel, the sentence being carried out by firing squad on 12 May 1944 after Dönitz had refused to commute it. Although the sentence and execution were not made public, the word soon got around within the Kriegsmarine and had its effect.

Another deterrent measure was detailing U-boat crews to attend executions.[34] To motivate the officers Dönitz swore to the hitting power of the 'miracle U-boats' such as the new Type XXI, and he succeeded, despite the signs of looming defeat, in reawakening hope, as Kapitänleutnant Hanns-Ferdinand Massmann remarked after such a speech: 'Something like a fundamental change of mood came about. So we can still have a go at them.'[35]

In the face of invasion

In the spring of 1944 the Kriegsmarine units on the Channel and Atlantic coasts were increasingly obliged to fight off enemy intrusions into the coastal stretches. Thus on the night of 26 April after a mining operation, 4th Torpedo-boat Flotilla stationed at St Malo ran into a strong British squadron consisting of a cruiser and several destroyers. The leading boat *T29* was sunk and *T27* damaged. In another action on the night of 29 April the torpedo boats sank the Canadian destroyer *Athabaskan*, but *T27* was damaged again and had to be abandoned. In this way the heavier German naval units at the Atlantic front were being decimated.

The US landings on Omaha Beach, June 1944. (US National Archives)

When the Allied landing fleet finally appeared off the coast of Normandy on the morning of 6 June 1944, the Kriegsmarine had little with which to oppose it. Besides a torpedo-boat flotilla and thirty-four S-boats, they had mainly minesweepers and VP-boats converted from steam trawlers to oppose the Allied landing fleet of seven battleships, two monitors, twenty-three cruisers, three gunboats, 105 destroyers and almost two thousand smaller warships and landing craft.[36] The most powerful German surface warships in the west, the three destroyers of 8th Destroyer Flotilla, were based in the Gironde, far from the invasion front. In view of its weakness in naval forces, the naval planners had arranged for minefields to be laid along the French coast to prevent Allied landings. In the case of an alarm, *Blitzsperren* – lightning minefields – of bottom mines and coastal mines were to be laid off the endangered coastal sectors.[37] On 6 June the notice given was too short, and even the permanent minefields were only partially in place.

From the outset, the few German surface forces had no chance against such an enormous opponent. Nevertheless, the S-boats stationed in the Channel and 5th Torpedo-boat Flotilla did attack. They sank the Norwegian destroyer *Svenner* off Sword Beach and four landing craft in Seine Bay, but ultimately these were only pinpricks. The senior naval commanders pinned greater hopes on the U-boats. On 6 June 1944 seventeen U-boats sailed from Brest, fourteen from St-Nazaire, four from La Pallice and one from Lorient. While some of these reached the Allied landing zones, the others formed a reconnaissance patrol line in the Bay of Biscay where the naval commanders feared more landings. Even the last of the large Kriegsmarine naval units in the west, the three destroyers in the Gironde, headed north. They were joined by the torpedo boat *T24* from Brest, but on 9 June were intercepted by a force of Allied destroyers off Île Vierge north of Brittany, two German destroyers being sunk and the two surviving ships fleeing to Brest, leaving the U-boats to take up the unequal struggle. In particular, those U-boats without a *Schnorchel*, exposed to the technical superiority of the enemy anti-submarine electronics, had virtually no chance of either inflicting heavy damage on Allied ships or preventing the landings of troops and materials from proceeding. Dönitz, on the other hand, expected self-sacrifice to the last man from his crews: 'Every enemy vessel serving the invasion, even if it lands only fifty infantry or a tank, is a target. It is to be attacked, even at the risk of losing your own vessel. ... The boat that inflicts casualties on the enemy during his invasion fulfils its highest duty and justifies its existence, even if in doing so it comes to grief.'[38]

The U-boat war had changed from a tonnage war to a duel. At Skl the head of the U-boat Command Division, Konteradmiral Eberhard Godt declared: 'One landing craft transport sunk in the invasion area ... is more

US landing craft off the Normandy coast, June 1944.
(Bildarchiv Preussischer Kulturbesitz, Berlin)

important today than a Liberty ship in the Atlantic.'[39] Of the thirty-six
U-boats which had put to sea, two were sunk on 8 June by a British
Liberator and *U740* went down next day. Four Brest boats were so badly
damaged by air attack in the Channel approaches that they were forced
to put back. Only U-boats fitted with a *Schnorchel* succeeded in reaching
the invasion front by 14 June, where they sank one frigate and a landing
ship, while six U-boats were lost within a few days to air attack or the
specialist U-boat hunter groups. By the end of June 1944 another wave
of U-boats sank a corvette and some freighters. Finally, on 27 August,
owing to the extent of the losses, Dönitz called a halt to the operations
in the Channel and sent the U-boats off to Norway. This decision
signalled the end of the usage of the French Atlantic and Biscay ports by
the German U-boat arm.

The final balance of U-boat operations in the Channel amounted to
seven escorts, three landing ships and thirteen freighters of 59,230 gross
tons sunk, a ratio of roughly one U-boat lost for every ship sunk. This
was an unsatisfactory outcome for the Germans, not least because these
sinkings had no effect on the Allied supply line. By 30 June 1944 180 troop
ships, 570 Liberty ships and 788 coastal motor ships, together with
hundreds of landing craft had unloaded men and materials on the French
coast.[40] The danger presented by the German torpedo boats and S-boats
in the Channel was eliminated by heavy bombing raids by the Allies on Le
Havre and Boulogne, particularly on 15 and 16 June 1944, when most of
these vessels were destroyed. At Le Havre alone, three torpedo boats, ten

Supplies coming ashore along a Mulberry harbour, Normandy, June 1944.
(Bildarchiv Preussischer Kulturbesitz, Berlin)

S-boats, seven minesweepers, eight VP-boats and numerous smaller warships were sunk. With this destruction, the Kriegsmarine at the Channel had de facto ceased to exist. The few units still available withdrew eastwards, and from then on the only German presence was S-boats coming from Dutch bases, and some explosive boats and one-man torpedoes inside the invasion waters.

Off the Brittany coast, Allied warships and aircraft had meanwhile begun to hunt for the remaining German escorts and departing U-boats. On 7 June off Brest, low-level aircraft attacked *U256* under escort by a minesweeper and damaged her so badly that upon reaching Brest she was decommissioned.[41] Even under cover of darkness it was no longer possible for German VP-boats to keep station unobserved off the ports, as the attack by Allied fighter bombers against a pair of VP-boats of 7th VP-boat Flotilla on the night of 5 July 1944 showed.[42] The same day, Allied destroyers embarked on Operation Dredger along the Atlantic coast, which had as its aim the systematic destruction of the German security vessels. On 5 July they sank VP-boat *V715*, on the night of 8 July near the Channel Islands the minesweepers *M4605* and *M4601*, and on the night of 15 July off Lorient the submarine-hunters *UJ1420* and *UJ1421*.[43] Group West then ordered that VP-boats were no longer to keep watch on station: the inshore waters were to be monitored by radar and coastal artillery units.[44] When Allied warships came inshore to send lamp signals

to the German signals station on the island of Ushant, the Commanding
Admiral Atlantic Coast, Vizeadmiral Ernst Schirlitz, noted in his war
diary, 'The enemy in this sea area feels himself totally safe.'[45] The
Kriegsmarine had nothing left with which to hinder Allied shipping
movements, and even their radar was gradually diminished by air attacks.

Meanwhile, the Germans prepared to defend the ports, French civilians
being co-opted to help. In July 1944 the inhabitants of the small village of
St Pierre-Quilbignon, west of Brest, were ordered by the commander of
the fortifications to excavate anti-tank ditches along the roads and byways
of the village for German troops.[46] Before the end of June Feldkommandantur 752 at Quimper had ordered the grouping of work units from
the French communities along the railway embankments in order to repair
stretches of the routes which had been destroyed by Allied air attacks and
the French Resistance.[47] Because railway traffic was at a standstill and
nearly all bridges over the Loire were down from Allied bombing, on 12
June the Kriegsmarine considered using German shipyard personnel
preparing to evacuate Brest, Lorient and St-Nazaire for the repairs.[48]

Konteradmiral Otto Kähler, Commandant, Naval Defence Bretagne,
intervened to prevent this, because at the time the Kriegsmarine yard at
Brest still had full order books. On 15 July the thousandth German
surface vessel went into dry dock there.[49] Besides nine U-boats there were
thirty-five other vessels, amongst them *Sperrbrecher* and tankers, various
VP-boats, harbour protection boats and minesweepers, in the yard.[50] To
conserve electrical power, minor repairs to minesweepers and VP-boats
were carried out in the bombproof U-boat bunker, which had its own
generator. In other Kriegsmarine workshops, on the other hand, work
had to be abandoned for lack of power. The first absences amongst the
French workforce began to be felt. Since the Allied invasion, 303 French
naval ratings, firemen and gendarmes had failed to return from leave or
absented themselves without leave from quarters.[51] Of the 6,000-strong
shipyard labour force, 250 could no longer be found.

The French naval commandant Jean Louis Negadelle reported in July
1944 that the railway connection from Brest to the south had been
interrupted since 10 June; to the east only a workers' train was operating
a shuttle service as far as Morlaix. All other public transport had come to
a halt after the German service centres had commandeered all the
available buses to bring back female auxiliary personnel and OT workers.
The telephone and telegraph network was no longer working and the post
office had shut down. Because the civilian population had been ordered
by the Germans to hand in all radio sets to the Kommandantur on 4 June,
people were cut off from all sources of information.[52] At Lorient the
situation was the same, according to a report by the director of the French
shipbuilding concern. All railway connections had been discontinued save

for a workers' train between Lorient and Quimper. Nevertheless, half the workers at the naval arsenal continued to report for work, on foot or by bicycle, the latter often undertaking journeys of 80km (50 miles).

In anticipation of the Allied invasion, Resistance activity had increased. Peter Charton, head of the engineering department of the Kriegsmarine Yard Lorient, noted in his diary in May 1944:

> The activity of the terrorists is becoming more violent, every couple of days another act of sabotage. The Auray–Lorient railway line is interrupted once or twice a week. The resulting absence of French workers and the late arrivals of the German shipyard company is a substantial shortfall in personnel. The spare parts compound of the ship repair department at Baud was attacked and partially destroyed. ... The military units are much too weak to offer the terrorists much opposition. Surprisingly, almost no acts of sabotage occur in the yard.[53]

On 16 April the BdU train was attacked and derailed at Quimper, and on 3 July a workers' bus from the Kriegsmarine Yard Lorient was fired on northeast of the town from an ambush, killing two German soldiers.[54]

The German occupying authority reacted to these attacks with increasing brutality.[55] Kriegsmarine men were used in the taking of reprisals. On 3 July a group from the Lézardrieux harbour commandant attacked a Resistance camp at Pontrieux. Two weeks later a fourteen-man strong Kriegsmarine 'hunting commando' and army troops sought out Resistance fighters, killing ten and taking eight prisoner.[56] On 3 August a group from 3rd Marine Flak Brigade stationed at Brest helped clean out a French Maquis camp near Chateaulin.[57]

Calm reigned in the ports. In July 1944, according to a French engineer, the Lorient arsenal was 'an oasis of peace and quiet'.[58] In the Kriegsmarine yard the interruption to road traffic was making itself noticeable. Coal and electrical power were scarce. Because of the increased danger of sabotage, Resistance attacks, and the introduction of Alarm Stage II following the Allied landings, more and more shipyard workers were being transferred from repair work to the alarm companies in order to guard residential compounds and depots, and protect worker transports.[59]

Meanwhile, Allied forces in Normandy had broken through. On 1 August 1944 American armoured divisions penetrated the German defensive front at Avranches. Between there and the Loire there were no German forces worth mentioning. Naval Group West had been ordered by Skl the day before to place all available naval ratings at the disposal of the army: about 3,600 men.[60] Skl knew that if US troops broke through into Brittany, it would mean 'the end of the military strategy' there.[61] That also went for the U-boat war. They therefore waged everything on one last card and lost.

After the breakthrough at Avranches, the American forces split. Whilst the bulk of their troops made for the Loire with the aim of getting to Paris, the US VIII Corps, under the command of General Troy Middleton, headed for the Atlantic coast. The intention was to capture the ports and as soon as possible turn them into an American supply base. For this purpose the US general had two fast motorised divisions. While the US 6th Armored Division was moving along the northern coast towards Brest, the 4th Armored Division headed for Lorient via Rennes. Because they expected major damage to the ports, the Americans were planning the construction of an artificial harbour in the Bay of Quiberon, south of Lorient.[62] Ninety days after the Normandy landings they calculated on a daily consignment of 7,000 tonnes of materials there, and another 5,300 tonnes at Brest.[63]

Guaranteeing certainty of supply was crucial for the Allied forces, as the landing beaches in Normandy were remote from major harbours. Initial supplies for the landed troops had been safely laid on by the use of artificial harbours near Arromanches and Omaha Beach. Although the Americans captured Cherbourg on 26 June 1944, its usefulness had been greatly reduced by German demolition work in advance of the surrender of the town. Thus the Allied line of supply continued to be dependent on unloading direct on to the beaches or by air drop, and from there in a time-consuming manner by lorry to the front. It was therefore urgent that other alternatives had to be set up for the advance eastwards into Europe.

While American tanks headed quickly for the coast, just as German panzers had done in 1940, the German defences were in disarray. On 2 August 1944, General Wilhelm Fahrmbacher, the commander of XXV Army Corps stationed in Brittany, ordered all German troops into the fortified areas. This order contradicted the regulation issued by the new Commander-in-Chief West, Feldmarschall Günther von Kluge, who had taken up his post on 2 July 1944 and ruled on 3 July that the positions in Brittany had to be held at all costs, and only 'in the face of superior pressure' was recourse to be had to the fortified areas. At this time XXV Army Corps had left its command post at Pontivy for Lorient, and Fahrmbacher's order could not be rescinded. Moreover, the German troops stationed in Brittany were not in a position to resist the American armour in open territory. Near Rennes a battle group did hold off the US 4th Armored Division for twenty-four hours before the Americans simply went around the city.

German troops withdrawing into the fortified enclaves gained a little more time because General Leonard Wood, the commanding officer, US 4th Armored Division, decided on Rennes, so that he could push on for the Loire instead of following his orders for Quiberon. It required an official countermanding order from Allied HQ before Wood turned his tanks back

General George S Patton, Commander-in-Chief US 3rd Army, 1944. (US National Archives)

towards Lorient. This incident is a good example of how much the American advance depended on the outlook of the various commanders. Whilst General George S Patton, the Commander-in-Chief of the US 3rd Army, had ordered his armour to advance towards Brest and Quiberon, the commander of US VIII Corps, Troy Middleton, decided on a slow advance across a broad front. The commanders of the armoured divisions backed Patton's idea. They crossed Brittany by the most direct route, advised by French Resistance scouts, with the streets echoing to the cheers of the local inhabitants. The American tanks would not stop until they came within range of the guns of the remaining German enclaves.

The Kriegsmarine had not been informed about the XXV Army Group order and Vizeadmiral Otto Kähler, Commandant, Naval Defence Bretagne, was thus surprised on the morning of 4 August 1944 by numerous reports from the coastal stations in the north regarding the imminent departures of their infantry. He ordered the coastal stations involved to make all necessary preparations to destroy the harbour installations, but harbourmasters and naval radar personnel were to remain at their posts for the time being. Towards midday, the harbourmaster at St Brieuc reported that the infantry had marched, and the Resistance had blocked the access road; he was still holding out in the harbour with 120 men. In view of the uncertainty of the situation, Köhler asked Group West for permission to allow the naval units to accompany the infantry on their withdrawal.[64] In Paris, the Commander-in-Chief, Group West, Admiral Theodor Krancke, gathered from the reports he was receiving that 'unholy confusion' reigned in Brittany.[65] 266 Infantry Division, originally intended for deployment on the Normandy front, was ordered back to the position from whence it had departed, but this had been partially destroyed when abandoned. Despite the Führer's order to hold well-established positions, after the order to retire, important installations within the fortified areas had been destroyed by the troops stationed there, such as the railway battery at Paimpol. Some of the

German troops in France pulling back, August 1944.
(Bundesarchiv, 101I-721-0373-05/Theobald)

American advance guard ran across retreating German units who lacked vehicles and were mostly proceeding on foot or in horse-drawn carts. Thus 266 Infantry Division was overwhelmed by the spearhead of the US 6th Armored Division while retracing its steps, and not many of the former managed to reach the fortified area at Brest.

All in all the picture was one of a totally disorganised German retreat. XXV Army Corps High Command ignored the orders from OKW to resist, and despite the orders of von Kluge to head for Brest, turned aside for Lorient which was nearer. The support services (*Tross*) entered Keroman on 3 August 1944 as Peter Charton, superintendent of superstructure at the Kriegsmarine Yard Lorient recalled:

> A colourful snake of automobiles and lorries with furniture, girls, etc, rolled through the streets. Supplies, Goliaths and other weapons had been left behind. KptzS Kals from the U-boat base stopped one of the vehicles and asked, 'What kind of circus is this?' The General-Kommando at once requisitioned half the bunker barracks, which our men had to evacuate. Naturally the same went for KII [U-boat bunker Keroman II]. The dry docks were occupied by vehicles and troops.[66]

On 4 August the first US tanks were sighted at some distance from St-Nazaire. The same day the naval bases St Brieuc, Paimpol, Lézardrieux, Morlaix and Benodet, and the islands Bréhat and Sein were evacuated and the harbour installations blown up. At midday on 7 August a searchlight battery of III Marine Flak Brigade at Milizac, north of Brest, reported ten armoured cars with soldiers 'in khaki uniform'.[67] The naval flak opened fire at them and the battle for the German base began the same day.

The battle of Brest

On 5 August 1944 in a multi-paged telex to the Commander-in-Chief West, the Wehrmacht Command Staff reiterated the principles for defending the fortified enclaves.[68] These were to be held at all costs, in order to gain time for countermeasures and to tie down enemy forces. The land front would be reinforced by a system of staggered positions and, if possible, in a 15km (9 mile)-wide 'destruction zone' surrounding these, every infrastructure which might be of use to the enemy was to be eliminated. The civilian population had to be evacuated. Despite the order given in 1942 to expand the harbours, many defensive installations on the

The U-boat bunker after the fighting around fortified Brest, September 1944. (Archives Municipales, Brest)

A German *Vorposten*-boat off the French Atlantic coast, 1944. (Wilhelm
Fahrmbacher & Walter Matthiae, *Lorient*, Weissenburg 1956)

land side had been sacrificed for more important building projects, so the
belt surrounding the fortification had large gaps in it.

At Brest and Lorient the tall structures surrounding the city had not
been included in the defences, and some of the earlier flak positions lay
outside the fortified area designated later. At Brest the so-called main front
line, a system of anti-tank trenches, minefields, tank obstacles and several
gun, MG and accommodation bunkers ran along the edge of the city. At
its eastern end the main front line was the seventeenth-century former city
wall. Generally speaking, it was more a provisional fortified area than a
real one. Army telephonist Erich Kuby noted in his diary:

> It is incomprehensible that no underground connection has been made
> between the fortification installations in the rock to the U-boat pens,
> not even bombproof cable boxes have been provided. Therefore we lay
> our cables under the railway track and on terrain which we must accept
> with absolute certainty will be the aiming point for aerial bombing.[69]

Already in April 1944 the civilian population had been required to leave
sections of the enclave. In June, whole blocks of houses in the
Recouvrance district on the western side of the arsenal had been
requisitioned by the regional kommandantur and pulled down so as to
give a free field of fire to the army battery built into the old city wall.[70]

Although on 20 February 1944 the Kreiskommandant had ordered the evacuation of all sectors of the population not immediately necessary for running the base, there were still almost fifty thousand people in Brest in February 1944.

After Oberst Hans von der Mosel had declined the American offer to accept the surrender of the fortifications commander, from 8 August 1944 Brest lay under siege for almost two months. The Kriegsmarine units, the shipyard workers' alarm company and the remnants of 266 Infantry Division and the permanent fortifications staff occupied the hurriedly dug infantry trenches outside the city. The backbone of the defence was 2nd Parachute Division; these paratroopers had been sent to Brittany to rest after operations in Greece and on the Eastern Front in the summer of 1944, and had withdrawn to Brest after skirmishes with American troops. The commander, Generalleutnant Bernhard Ramcke, would later take command of the enclave. Besides the alarm units, in the first few days the Kriegsmarine made available to the enclave commander another 161 men, including 100 from 1st U-boat Flotilla.[71] Although the army officers noticed in the sailors a strong readiness to fight, they lacked training for the field and their armament was poor.[72]

While the defenders dug in around the fortification, in the harbour the larger ships were decommissioned and their weapons and crews sent ashore to stiffen the main battle line. The Kriegsmarine arsenal built makeshift chassis for the former shipboard guns and manufactured entrenching tools and infantry obstacles.[73] Because the US armoured division halted outside Brest was not suitable for engaging an extensively fortified city, the tanks merely bombarded it while waiting for artillery and infantry. In the end the Americans required three infantry divisions to storm the fortress.

In the U-boat bunkers the yard personnel attempted to get the thirteen remaining U-boats ready to sail. On 5 August the Brest bunker was the target of a precision attack by the RAF. Four heavy Tallboy bombs hit the ceiling at a not yet reinforced spot and penetrated it. The U-boats beneath the opening were only slightly damaged. These hits panicked the French workers, and the German shipyard managers decided that all remaining French personnel should be released the same day. The German workers succeeded in getting all but two U-boats ready for sea. These boats evacuated some of the yard company to the harbours of La Pallice and Bordeaux which were still open. Thus *U309* on 7 August and *U963* on 12 August transferred eighty workers to La Pallice, *U953* some of the crew of *U415*, sunk at Brest after hitting a mine, together with fifteen shipyard workers, while *U766* evacuated four members of the Brest field agency of the security police and SD in France plus fourteen other passengers out of fortified Brest.[74]

After the last French people had left the city, the American attack on Brest began on 25 August 1944. Fighter bombers made pinpoint attacks against the German naval units still afloat in the bay and harbour. Erich Kuby watched it all going on from the bank:

> Some of our ships were still afloat on the mirror-calm waters. They lay quietly, and from a blue sky the bombers dived down like silver-shiny hawks spewing fire. The sea around the ships boiled with the bursts of fire which failed to reach their target: the ships went up in flames. Some ran across the blue mirror like large baskets of fire, others trailed long columns of smoke, perhaps in the hope of reaching the beach. Boats were let down. No return fire came from our side.[75]

The British battleship *Warspite* shelled the German enclave from seaward, while US artillery took the German positions under fire from surrounding high structures. It was mainly the flak batteries with their unarmoured guns which were picked off one by one from the air. A massive bombing raid on the afternoon of 3 September inflicted great damage on the city and the German defensive positions, and reduced the flak to only twenty-two operational guns. In order to use the guns built into the bunkers for defence, gaps in some of the bunkers were widened to provide a field of fire over the terrain beyond the fortifications. Two 15cm guns on wheeled chassis at the Portzic battery were pushed out of their bunkers and set up in an open field position. On 8 September the German defenders received anti-tank weapons and hospital supplies flown by He111 long-range transport aircraft from Zellhausen airfield near Aschaffenburg.

Even so, the collapse of the German resistance was merely a question of time. At the end of August the German authorities began to demolish and mine the harbour. The planned mining of the Bay of Brest was abandoned after the auxiliary minelayer *Pelikan* was sunk by US aircraft. On 27 August the new enclave commander, Generalleutnant Hermann-Bernhard Ramcke, reported 37,058 men present.[76] On 12 August command had been transferred to Ramcke, commanding officer of 2nd Parachute Division, after his repeated complaints to Führer HQ about the alleged lack of determination on the part of the former enclave commander Oberst von der Mosel.[77] At his side stood the Commandant, Naval Defences Bretagne, Vizeadmiral Otto Köhler, whose command post was located in the bunkers near the naval academy. In Ramcke's eyes the Kriegsmarine men were 'totally softened by the years they had spent in Brittany', and he accused them of having no fighting spirit.

When Ramcke reported that entire U-boat crews had gone over to the enemy en masse, Dönitz became personally involved and in defence of the U-boat arm demanded proof of these reports.[78] After making enquiries at Skl, Ramcke was informed that the men complained of were not from the U-boat flotillas but from the coastal security units. Nevertheless, the Kriegsmarine commander-in-chief challenged the general either to prove his assertions regarding the navy or retract them in a statement to the person who received the original report. In a radio signal to the Commandant, Naval Defence Bretagne on 4 September, Dönitz thanked Vizeadmiral Köhler and his men for their achievements to date, but bound them to hold out:

> I know that you personally and your men will do everything to defend fortified Brest in the battle sectors of the Kriegsmarine to the last breath, and force the enemy to fight for every square metre of soil. Every day you deny the enemy access to this important port, you help the hard-fought army in the west in its struggle. Fight hard and with dogged determination, and turn the struggle for fortified Brest into a glorious page in the history of the Kriegsmarine.[79]

Like his commander-in-chief, Admiral Theodor Krancke, Commander Group West, strove to rouse his troops by sending this signal to Brest on 10 September: 'Your actions and your steadfastness will contribute their share to bringing the palms of victory to our Führer and his German people.'[80] At the time Group West was already pulling back eastwards.

In the end urgings to hold fast could have little effect in the face of the inferiority in materials possessed by the German defenders. In the galleries and bunkers the situation became ever more intolerable. Margarethe Wiese, former employee at the Kriegsmarine yard, worked in one of these galleries during the siege as an auxiliary nurse:

> In the naval arsenal galleries, where I found myself during the siege there were no WCs, only buckets. When the firing eased off a bit for a while at night, the soldiers would carry these buckets out and throw the contents into the harbour basin, together with the corpses. In the arsenal galleries there were about three hundred wounded. Some died each night. The bodies were stacked in a corner and lay there for days until they could be tossed into the water at a favourable moment. In the final two weeks these nocturnal expeditions were no longer possible.[81]

After taking the Armorique peninsula to the east of the city on 31 August, from there US forces could see into, and fire into, the rear of the fortifications, the harbour and U-boat bunker. The enclave area was continually shrinking and lay under constant artillery fire. Desertions increased as apocalyptic scenes were played out in the galleries. Margarethe Wiese wrote:

> The wounded, amongst them many amputees, the blinded, men with spinal injuries, etc, lay in the galleries in the rock in wooden three-tiered

bunks. These beds came from a barracks and were infested with vermin. It was worse for those with a plaster cast, for the vermin crawled in under it. There was just enough water to boil for the food, but not enough for the wounded to wash each day. Clothes could not be washed at all ... There were people whose hair turned snow white overnight. There was never an empty bed in the arsenal galleries. Wounded were brought in daily, daily some died. ... The final weeks were so horrendous that they defy description. The rotors of the ventilation plant, insofar as they worked at all, just swept the stinking air back and forth for weeks. The draught did not quite reach the overflowing buckets and the heap of corpses. The almost incessant bombardment kept the rock in perpetual vibration, sometimes chunks of rock would break off the dripping walls.[82]

In one of his last situation reports on 12 September, the naval commandant spoke of Brest as a territory ploughed by bombs and shells, but added: 'The mass of the naval men are fighting heroically despite lack of training and armaments.'[83] At this point the first US troops were already in the suburbs. The naval flak had only three serviceable guns, and of the formerly hundred-man complement of 3rd Battery/Marine Flak Division

US artillery firing on the German defences at Brest, August 1944.
(US National Archives)

Generalleutnant Bernhard Ramcke (second from right), commander of
the Brest fortifications, in conference in the field, August 1944.
(Bernhard Ramcke, *Fallschirmjäger*, Oldendorf 1973)

805 there were only seven still alive by 12 September.[84] Of the 37,000 men
reported present in the fortifications when the defence began, by now only
a fifth of them were fit enough to fight, and of the original 800 heavy guns
only thirteen were still firing.[85] The number of wounded grew daily. In
order to keep the most important roads within the ruined city open, the
fortress commandant had whole trams set on fire and the wreckage blown
up to prevent the roads becoming blocked by houses collapsing after air
attacks.[86]

The Americans worked their way forwards under the protection of their
artillery, mortars and fighter bombers. To prevent unnecessary losses, they
avoided venturing out at night. In the German galleries the suicide rate
and drunkenness increased and military discipline broke down. Erich
Kuby experienced the final days of the siege in the extensive galleries
below the naval academy:

On the way I had to pass through the great dining hall of the U-flotilla,
an arched concrete room, the walls and floors of which glistened with
damp. They held a Catholic mass there which I attended. A soldier in
the front row was howling audibly. About eighty other soldiers did not
participate but nearly everybody took Holy Communion. A surprising
religiosity is suddenly breaking out amidst this Nazi-volk.[87]

In one of the galleries in the city centre, the Sadi Carnot shelter, there was an unexplained explosion on the night of 9 September which killed the last of the French inhabitants still in the city, including the mayor, and a large number of German soldiers.[88]

While Ramcke was handing down death sentences for desertion at impromptu court martials amidst the ruins, the last German soldiers on the island of Ushant opposite Brest decided on another end to their war. They surrendered to the islanders, and when the German S-boat *S112* approached the island looking for them, it came under fire from its own countrymen and was forced to turn away. In the fortifications more and more men refused to keep fighting. Paratrooper NCO Adolf Klein at St Pierre-Quilbignon, west of Brest, was in a command of a mixed platoon of paratroopers and naval ratings:

> We moved our position to bunker 42 near the water tower. The trench system consisted of Tobruk bunkers interconnected by communications trenches and an accommodation bunker.At dawn on 14 September 1944 the Americans attacked. We engaged them at very short range with mortars, there was no rifle or MG fire. I ran the length of the trench – deserted – the naval ratings had fled to the accommodation bunker

US infantry on the outskirts of Brest, September 1944.
(US National Archives)

without weapons, ready to surrender. I forced them back into the trench at gunpoint. This was no use, when I went up to them they returned to the accommodation bunker. In these circumstances the position could not be held.[89]

On 15 September the American lines were only 1,500m (1,600yds) from the naval commandant's bunker at the naval academy.[90] During the night the Germans finished mining the warship harbour and blocking the pens in the U-boat bunker using sunken lorries and small vessels. On 17 September the naval commandant reported once more having repelled American attacks on the bases 'Portzic' and 'Ölberg' in the immediate vicinity of his command post. In the galleries below the naval academy preparations were already in hand to capitulate. At midday on 18 September 1944 the deputy Fortifications Commandant and Commandant, Sector West, Oberst Hans von der Mosel, surrendered. General Ramcke had fled previously to Pointe des Espagnols opposite the U-boat bunker from where he was expecting a flying boat to take him to Germany to make his report. Unfortunately for him this was not possible and, after an attack by US armour against this last outpost still held by German forces, even Ramcke gave up and became a prisoner of war on the evening

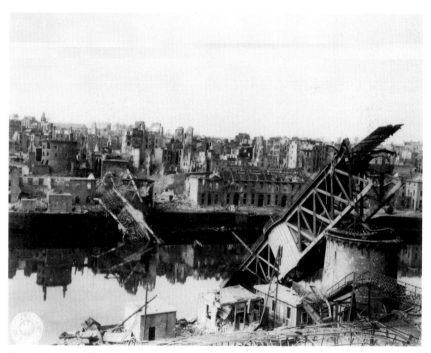

Brest city centre after the fighting ended, September 1944.
(Archives Municipales, Brest)

of 19 September. In his last radio message he assured Berlin that he had kept firing until all his ammunition was exhausted and, loyal to his oath, had fulfilled his duty as enclave commandant to the last round.[91]

Thus the battle for fortified Brest was finally ended and the survivors left the bunkers:

> The scene, as we came out after weeks in the dark, stinking galleries: the city, totally destroyed, the smoking ruins, the pitiably haggard people; the harbour basin full of rubbish, corpses, furniture, wrecked ships and lorries, typewriters, radio sets, machine-parts – on the ebb tide almost none of it covered by the water.[92]

US soldiers gazing in wonder at bomb damage to the ceiling of the Brest U-boat bunker, September 1944. (Imperial War Museum)

The American troops were astounded at the unexpectedly high number of prisoners:

> Instead of the two or three hundred we expected to have to worry about, there were men from all branches of the German forces: their numbers ran into the thousands. ... It was a strange situation. Three or four US soldiers surrounded by maybe fifty to a hundred Germans all apparently more interested in holding on to their private belongings than what would now happen to them as prisoners.[93]

According to the concluding report by his commanding general, the US VIII Corps took about 38,000 German prisoners and buried 1,059 dead German soldiers.[94] Up to 9 September 1944, in the evacuation of Brittany and the defence of Brest, the Naval Commandant Bretagne recorded Kriegsmarine losses of sixty-two officers and 3,315 NCOs and men.[95] The exact number of Germans who fell during the fighting for Brest remains unknown.

German PoWs on the Place Wilson, Brest, September 1944.
(Archives Municipales, Brest)

The US forces succeeded in conquering the German enclave but at great material cost. Whether in retrospect it was the right course is disputed amongst American military historians, who see it as a tactical victory but a strategic blunder.[96] During the siege, the German garrison had enough time to damage the harbour installation so seriously that its immediate use as a supply base was not possible. The Americans had stuck too doggedly to Brittany in their planning for a supply base. When it became clear in August 1944 how costly it was going to be to capture Brest, and other ports were already being taken into consideration, General Middleton was ordered by Allied HQ to continue the siege of Brest but avoid serious losses amongst US troops.[97]

After the fortified ports of Cherbourg and St Malo, Brest was the only German Atlantic base which the US forces overwhelmed in battle. It was not only the destruction to its harbour installations but also the great distance between Brest and the American front line in the summer of 1944 which made it impractical, for the Allied formations had already advanced far to the east.

Not until British troops had secured the undamaged port of Antwerp on 4 September did the Allied High Command finally turn its back on

The ruins of the mercantile harbour Brest; in the background the demolished outer mole, September 1944. (Archives Municipales, Brest)

Removal of German troops to captivity by train, Northern France, 1944.
(Mémorial Fort Montbarey, Brest)

Brest. Although fighting in the Scheldt estuary continued to the end of November 1944, the French Atlantic ports were no longer of interest to Allied HQ. At this time Allied forces could unload vessels at the Channel ports, and also on the French Mediterranean coast after the Allied landings there. A third of the supplies for US troops went over the relatively intact railway system along the Rhône. The US military historian A Harding Ganz concluded of the American activities in Brittany: 'It was simply a false strategy to send two armoured divisions in the opposite direction, hundreds of miles westwards, when the decisive operation was taking place in the east.'[98]

The German soldiers taken prisoner at Brest were first collected together in camps outside the city before being taken to England and shipped from there to the United States. On the way to the collecting point, years of stored hate within the French population was unloaded on them:

> When we drove up the mountain behind Renan it was already dark. Nevertheless the villagers recognised us, insulted us, threw stones at us, poured their chamber pots over us, a full pot hit the co-driver of a lorry on which people of my squad were seated. Everywhere the same cry: 'Hitler kaputt! Boche!' K, sitting on the rear flap of the lorry behind me, was hit by a stone behind the ear, and was unconscious and bleeding for some time. We drew in our heads, raised up the collars of our greatcoats and experienced a spiritual exercise in European history.[99]

Captured German generals at Trent Park: in Luftwaffe uniform, rear
centre, General Bernhard Ramcke; with walking stick, General Dietrich
von Choltitz, November 1944. (Bundesarchiv, 146-2005-0136)

Bernhard Ramcke and other high-ranking officers were taken to the
generals' camp at Trent Park outside London, where Ramcke later sang
his own praises about the destruction of Brest to General Dietrich von
Choltitz, former German city commandant of Paris, in a conversation
eavesdropped by the British secret service. Choltitz, who saved Paris from
destruction, saw the conduct of the paratrooper general as a plain war
crime and distanced himself from it, while Ramcke now limited his deeds
to the military facts.

   The destruction of Brest was to have its consequences for Ramcke after
the war. Accused by the French authorities of having committed various
war crimes at Brest, besides the shooting of French civilians and the
looting of private property, also the intentional destruction and burning
down of civilian houses, Ramcke was detained in France between 1946
and 1950. In 1951 in Paris he was sentenced to five years, six months'
imprisonment, for which he was allowed out after only three months, on
account of time served and his age. He soon came to notice again in the
West German Federal Republic when at a Waffen SS reunion at Verden an
der Aller in 1952 he referred to SS men as 'the blossom of the German
Volk'. His speech caused irritation and outrage in neighbouring countries
and endangered the work of European co-operation then just beginning,
so that even Federal Chancellor Konrad Adenauer was obliged to become
involved in the dispute.[100]

7

The Last Bastions

Whilst US forces and the French Resistance (FFI) gradually tightened the screws around the German Biscay naval bases, the yard workers in the U-boat bunkers worked to get the last U-boats there serviceable. Dönitz ordered that work on the *Schnorchel*-equipped U-boats should have priority, a task which, in his words, the yards were to expedite with 'rigour, determination and calm as long as possible and using all means'.[1] However, because of the difficult transport situation after the Allied air raids on the French road and rail system, not all boats could be got ready. Many parts remained at the wrecked railway yards, calling for much improvisation on the part of the yard workers. At Brest, for example, the Kriegsmarine yard made up a missing *Schnorchel* out of an old ship's propeller shaft.

At the same time, the yard personnel no longer required were evacuated by sea to the south. On 5 and 6 August 1944 boats of 2nd Minesweeping Flotilla brought out more than a hundred workers heading for the south from Lorient.[2] U-boats evacuated yard workers and specialists from Brest for La Pallice and Bordeaux. At St-Nazaire, before the fortification was sealed, the Kriegsmarine brought out about a thousand men from 6th VP-boat Flotilla, 8th Minesweeping Flotilla and the yard for their return to Germany.[3]

The evacuations were dangerous. Off the Biscay coast Allied warships and aircraft hunted for the remnants of the German naval forces, sinking numerous VP-boats and minesweepers. Of fifteen U-boats which were making for La Pallice and Bordeaux, by 16 August seven had been lost in the Bay of Biscay. Once British fighter bombers had sunk the destroyer *Z24* and the torpedo boat *T24*, the last two larger Kriegsmarine units on the Biscay coast, off Royan, all that remained were coastal protection units and *Sperrbrecher*, none of them offensive warships but converted merchant ships or fishing trawlers, which retired to the protection of the harbours.[4]

On 21 August the destruction of the Biscay harbours which were no longer required was ordered. At Bordeaux work was begun mining and blocking the harbour on the morning of 24 August. Twenty-one merchant

ships, the destroyer *Z37*, four minesweepers and two *Sperrbrecher* were
sunk in the harbour basin and the Gironde river. The inner harbour at
Nantes was made unnavigable by the scuttling of German supply ships
there. At this time, there were two U-boats each in the bases at Brest,
Lorient and St-Nazaire, three at Bordeaux and six at La Pallice.[5] On 26
August Dönitz ordered that all these submarines were to sail as soon as
possible for Norway, 'from where the U-boat war will be continued with
the old spirit and the new weapons.'[6]

  This order signalled the end for the German U-boat bases in France.
The boats – some with makeshift crews, many U-boat men having been
surprised by the invasion while on home leave – left the French ports on
the long and dangerous voyage to Norway. Most got there, only *U445*
being lost to air attack in the Bay of Biscay. The last boat to leave, from
St-Nazaire on 23 September, was *U267*. Five boats remained behind,
repairs not having been completed in time. Dönitz urged the U-boatmen
who had not sailed, 'to defend the bases to the last man and the last round
with total dedication and the steadfast heart of the U-boat veteran.'[7]

  It was planned initially that Bordeaux and La Pallice should serve as the
alternative bases for repairs to those U-boats still operating in the North

Allied fighter bombers attacking German naval units in the roadstead at
Royan, August 1944. (Imperial War Museum)

Atlantic, and as supply bases for the closed ports farther up the coast, but the army could not provide enough weapons and materials for the planned supply. From 16 August, all persons and goods arriving in Paris for the Atlantic coast were sent back to Germany. Because of Resistance activity and the lack of escorts, no transports were possible from the coast to Paris, and thus it was decided not to evacuate the yard workers at La Rochelle or Bordeaux. Fighting with the French Resistance was reported at both cities on 24 August.

The last two serviceable U-boats, *U534* and *U587*, left Bordeaux on 25 August. Some of the yard workers were evacuated to La Pallice, the remainder setting off for Germany with the personnel of 12th U-boat Flotilla and other German troops. On 26 August harbour commandant Ernst Kühnemann reported that the harbour had been mined and blocked as scheduled. An attempt to blow up the U-boat bunker with torpedo heads was unsuccessful. The demolition of the quay installation ordered by OKW was abandoned after the explosives required for the job blew up, together with their bunker, shortly beforehand. After the war it was discovered that a German NCO who had been holding discussions with the Resistance was responsible for the premature explosion, thus saving the historic quays and the old stone bridge over the Garonne. The FdU West, Kapitän zur See Hans-Rudolf Rösing, bearing in mind the anticipated resumption of the U-boat war, had urged that Bordeaux should only be evacuated under heavy enemy pressure, but the commanding officer of 64th Army Corps had already set off for Poitiers.

The German commanders in southwestern France were surprised by the order to retreat given on 19 August 1944.[8] The coastal fortifications with their built-in weapons, and all important ammunition, fuel and provisions compounds, were to be blown up, and the units ready to march out next day. The order found the commanding officers completely unprepared. Most of the units were not motorised, so that large numbers of men had to retreat on foot. They were divided into three groups. In each of these infantry, fortifications permanent staff, administration staff, military intelligence, aircraft observers, harbourmasters, ships' crews, U-boatmen, naval artillery detachments and yard workers were thrown together for the six-hundred-mile march to southern Germany through territory controlled by the Resistance. It made no sense because of the size of the groups and the fact that US forces were advancing at so fast a rate. In the various Kriegsmarine shore services at this time alone there were 115,000 naval artillery personnel stationed on the Atlantic coast, with another 33,000 men on the VP-boats and minesweepers of the Commander, Security West.

There were serious disagreements between the various Wehrmacht branches in the preparations for the retreat, and cohesion disintegrated.

The harbour at La Rochelle, August 1944. (Author collection)

The new solution was: 'Save yourselves who can.' While the Kriegsmarine ordered its troops into the La Rochelle fortification, the army units headed northeast and, despite having been forbidden to do so by the Commander-in-Chief West, seized naval vehicles by the simple expedient of requisitioning them wherever they were found. Some naval men, despite their lack of training and weapons, were even used to protect army and Luftwaffe units against attacks by the French Resistance. The request by the Commanding Admiral Atlantic Coast to order at least the Luftwaffe heavy flak batteries into La Rochelle, where they would reinforce the artillery already there, instead of sending them on the long and uncertain trek to Germany, was turned down by the Commander-in-Chief West, with the observation that the Luftwaffe had already obtained the permission of the Reichsmarschall to withdraw all its batteries. Skl recorded bitterly that the army simply moved out 'while the navy with the bulk of its men has to stay back in southwestern France'.[9]

Workers at the Blohm & Voss yard in Bordeaux set off for home on 24 August. Very few of them ever reached Hamburg. When in October 1944 Walter Blohm approached OKM, there was no news as to the whereabouts of the greater part of the staff, about six hundred men. Blohm asked what he should tell their families. Finally, the families received wages or other financial support to the end of November 1944.[10]

After the last German soldiers left the city of Bordeaux on 27 August 1944, the whole southern Biscay coast, except for the two fortified areas on the Gironde estuary, had been evacuated. When the mass of the

Bordeaux abandoned, in the Gironde a partially sunken blockship, August 1944. (Ullstein-Bilderdienst, Berlin)

returners reached the Loire on 10 September, having endured countless air attacks and skirmishes with the Resistance while getting there, the northern bank was already occupied by US forces and the bridges were down. Without adequate supplies of ammunition, provisions or radio contact to Germany, the commanding officer, Major Botho Elster, decided against a senseless sacrifice of the men in his charge by attempting to force a breakthrough to the northeast, and on 16 September surrendered with almost twenty thousand men at Beaugency, southwest of Orleans.[11] It was a courageous decision, for which the Reich War Court at Torgau condemned him to death in his absence, the sentence not being lifted until 1998.

At Lorient they had been totally surprised by the events in northern Brittany. The head of the engineering department at the Kriegsmarine-werft Lorient, Peter Charton, noted in his diary:

From the beginning of August events tumbled over themselves. Nobody knows any longer where the enemy actually is. ... On 3 August the Hennebont camp was abandoned and the men accommodated in the rock compound (Ploemeur) or in the bunker. One day later Westmark was also evacuated. Their people had to creep down to Keroman. On 3 August the admiral's birthday was celebrated in the arsenal with

General Wilhelm Fahrmbacher and Vizeadmiral Walter Matthiae, Lorient,
1944. (Wilhelm Fahrmbacher & Walter Matthiae, *Lorient*, Weissenburg
1956)

lobster as the last meal before his departure. On 5 and 6 August the
minesweepers of 2nd Minesweeping Flotilla left Lorient, heading south
in order to be decommissioned there. The crews would then have to
make for Germany on foot. This gives us the opportunity to make
available to the Homeland a section of our people – mainly skilled
foremen. ... The spare-parts compound at Hennebont has not yet been
evacuated. I was promised they would let me know how much time they
wanted. On 7 August they started work again. Towards midday US
tanks came past.[12]

The later enclave commandant, General Wilhelm Fahrmbacher, stated
after the war in his recounting of events there that it would have been easy
for the Americans at this point in time to have taken Lorient if they had
decided on a surprise armoured attack.[13] The German defence was still
totally disorganised, and many sectors of the main front line were
unoccupied. The American advance came to a halt, however, on 7 August
after receiving German artillery fire from Lorient. That day the US 4th
Armored Division lost thirty-five vehicles and 105 men. In consequence
of these losses, the commanding officer, General John Wood, over-
estimated the fighting strength of the German fortification. His estimate
of 500 guns was well above the actual number of 197. At the Kriegsmarine
yard, work was suspended when the Americans arrived and the workers

summoned into their shipyard alarm companies (WAK). When the suspension of repairs was reported to Paris, the surprised response was: 'Why? Is Lorient under attack?'[14] The subordinate staffs had become totally confused about the situation in France.

On his own admission, Fahrmbacher gave fortified Lorient only a few days to survive at the beginning of the siege. He thought the chances of a successful defence were very slim because of the number of troops he had. Thus there was only one army battalion, all of the men having ear or hearing problems, a squadron of Cossacks, the reserve company of the fortification permanent regiment 25, and a Ukrainian mounted detachment.[15] The artillery was mainly captured French, Russian and Yugoslav guns with almost no armour-piercing shells. Contrary to Fahrmbacher's expectations, the fortification was not attacked and instead for Lorient there began a siege which lasted almost nine months. There would be little exchange of fire, and then mainly artillery duels.

St-Nazaire was also spared an American attack. Here, as at La Rochelle, the German defenders had a huge surrounding area within the perimeter which at St-Nazaire also included Escoublac airfield. This would become an important communications point with Germany.

Within the fortifications, at first they took stock. At the beginning of Sepember 1944 Lorient had provisions for forty-eight days, St-Nazaire for forty-three, La Rochelle for eighty and the enclaves on the Gironde for

Inspection of the fortified front at St-Nazaire by the fortifications commander, Generalmajor Hans Junck (centre), 1944/1945.
(Luc Braeuer collection, Batz sur Mer)

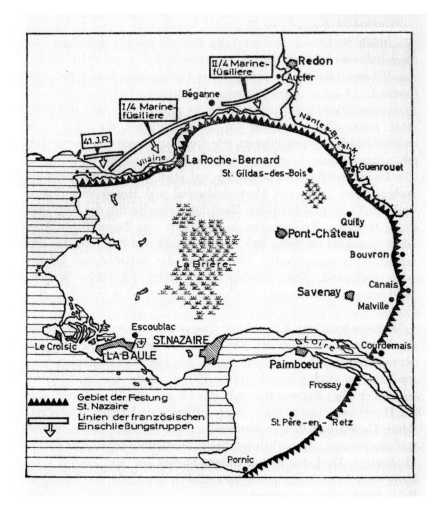

Fortified enclave of St-Nazaire (within serrated line): French lines to the
north (marked with arrows). (Jacques Mordal, *Die letzten Bastionen*,
Oldenburg/Hamburg, 1966)

about seventy days.[16] The supply situation differed widely from place to
place. At La Rochelle and St-Nazaire they could obtain food from the
large surrounding area; Lorient and the two fortresses on the Gironde had
little space. At Lorient the use of what area they had was complicated by
American forces occupying tall structures in the city overlooking the
fortified territory which they could keep under constant artillery fire. The
reports of the strengths at the fortifications for the end of August give an
overview of the exact composition of the troops holding them. Thus there

were 24,700 men at Lorient, mainly naval men and 2,200 volunteers from the east, besides 6,300 army and 1,200 Luftwaffe troops. At St-Nazaire the complement of 29,900 men included 11,200 from the army, 2,000 Luftwaffe and 11,400 navy. La Rochelle had a presence of 11,483 men, mainly navy and 440 yard workers.[17] There were far fewer occupants of the two fortified areas on the Gironde estuary: 4,987 men at Gironde-North (2,000 navy) and 3,641 men (728 navy) at Gironde-South.

General Fahrmbacher described his measures after sealing the enclave: 'The aim, a long-term resistance, was clearly indicated. In this sense training and conversion instruction, grouping of the artillery, raising the fighting power in the sectors, the creation of supply installations and the psychological factor were in the foreground.'[18] The conversion training of mariners to infantry included marksmanship and courses for company leaders, platoon leaders and officer-aspirants of all branches of service. At Keroman a military hospital was set up with space for six hundred wounded. It was never close to being filled, for there was never any heavy fighting. In a former OT barracks compound on the Île de Croix there was another emergency hospital. In order to unburden these military hospitals, in September 1944 about three hundred seriously wounded men from the August fighting were put aboard the hospital ship *Rostock*, the converted *Sperrbrecher 19*. The ship left Lorient for Germany, but shortly after sailing was stopped by a Free French MTB and escorted into Plymouth by a British destroyer, where crew and wounded went into captivity.

The main front line of the Lorient enclave was only 60 per cent ready in the summer of 1944. Fahrmbacher had the gaps closed with temporary trenches. Entanglements of tree branches replaced barbed wire, and bombs and artillery shells were dug in to serve as land mines. Because of the lack of mines, dummy minefields were laid to confuse enemy attackers. Important road junctions were made impassable by digging deep craters or burying bombs primed to explode. The most important access roads were protected by 8.8cm U-boat guns. In order to improve the military versatility of the troops, particularly the naval men, Fahrmbacher introduced infantry training, and for the naval flak, training in engaging ground targets. The Keroman bunker complex was developed into the last bulwark. Because the roof afforded a good view over the surrounding territory, the enclave staff had its command post there from time to time.

The main provisions compound was also at Keroman. Feeding the complement proved very difficult, because the Kriegsmarine had removed important facilities such as the bakery and abattoir outside the harbour after the bombing in the spring of 1943. These had to be brought back, the abattoir to a former torpedo bunker, a former French bakery in the wreckage of the city centre and an old mill in the town being recommissioned. For the orderly issue of clothing a central store was instituted.

A steam power plant, fuelled with a mixture of coal dust, pitch, tar and railway sleepers in place of the scarce coal, provided power for the most important workshops. Recourse was also had to other forms of generating power such as windmills and water wheels, U-boat batteries or steam engines. As autumn approached, the rubber outer casing of the redundant barrage balloons was tailored into trenchcoats for men in the field. The Kriegsmarine yard built emplacements and sockets for the naval guns, converted two French lorries into armoured scout vehicles each armed with an 8.8cm flak gun, and recommissioned an old Renault tank which had been used previously at Lorient airfield to roll the airstrip flat. The sheet-metal workshops turned out cooking implements and entrenching tools.

At St-Nazaire the outer terrain had been expanded well to the east and north before the arrival of US troops, providing the enclave with a surface area of 1,500 sq km (580 sq miles), in its expanse the largest of the Atlantic fortresses. The main front line of provisional field positions and infantry trenches ran from the coastal town of Pornic, south of the Loire estuary far inland to Frossay and Bouvron and the Nantes–Brest Canal. Beyond that, the Vilaine river formed a natural border of the enclave down to the sea. Command of the fortification passed into the hands of Generalmajor Hans Junck, the former commander of 265 Infantry Division, latterly in the Rennes region, but which in the summer of 1944 had withdrawn across Brittany to St-Nazaire. Junck set up his command post in a villa at the seaside resort of La Baule, about 30km (20 miles) from the front line perimeter. The officers of the enclave staff occupied the former rest homes for the U-boat flotillas; the casino became a military hospital.

As at Lorient, the guns were removed from decommissioned naval vessels and chassis for them constructed at the St-Nazaire yard. To compensate for the shortage of mobile heavy guns in the fortification, the yard built a makeshift railway battery from goods wagons fitted with 10.5cm flak guns. The central defensive piece was the 240mm railway gun of 280 Marine Artillery Division, transferred from its location on the coast near Batz sur Mer to a tunnel near Pontchâteau in the centre of the fortification. From here the gun could be shunted to prepared positions providing a field of fire over nearly all areas within the perimeter.

At the beginning of the siege, St-Nazaire had only 250 tonnes of coal, severely limiting the production of power. Four submarine hunters, whose engines could be powered by heavy oil available in a larger quantity (2,500 tonnes), provided steam for the French electricity plants, so that at least in the quarters closer to the port the men could have heating on two weekdays, but from January 1945 only on one weekday plus Sundays. The

Vizeadmiral Ernst Schirlitz (left) and French
naval Captain Hubert Meyer, May 1945.

positions on the perimeter had to do without electricity. What petrol was available was reserved for staff vehicles; the remaining lorries were converted to gas engines.

The fortification at La Rochelle enclosed 400 sq km (150 sq miles) and was well protected against attack on the land side by its many marshes and minefields. From the Île de Ré the heavy naval coastal battery Karola with its two 20.3cm twin turrets from the heavy cruiser *Seydlitz* controlled access from the sea. The Kriegsmarine yard turned bulldozers and self-propelled anti-tank guns into makeshift panzers, gave lorries armour, and built two armoured flak-trains armed with 3.7cm and 8.8cm flak guns. The former Commanding Admiral Atlantic Coast, Admiral Ernst Schirlitz, took command of the enclave. Important German services withdrew in October 1944 into an area of La Pallice protected by an anti-tank ditch and set up in the U-boat bunker. French citizens living in the harbour district were required to move out. In August the bunker had been the target of several air attacks but had emerged unscathed. The enclave hospital was set up in the former casino along the promenade at La Rochelle.

Besides the battalion of permanent troops, the Kriegsmarine supplied most of the defenders at La Rochelle. The standing force reported on 18 September 1944 was around 14,000 men. Of these 8,118 were naval personnel, amongst them 1,078 members of the security force, 691 from 3rd U-boat Flotilla, 1,684 yard workers and various other units. It was advantageous for the inexperienced naval force to have as its opponent the Free French FFI, since they were well-matched in their lack of fighting experience and weapons. Thus there were no major engagements and the two sides adopted a modus vivendi which at La Rochelle bore the hallmarks of the relationship between Vizeadmiral Schirlitz and the French negotiator, Captain Hubert Meyer, a man of Alsace in the service of the French navy and who, in the course of the siege, won the trust of the German commander and thus prevented the destruction of the town.

The French Resistance made up the greater part of the Allied besiegers. At Lorient alone there were 12,000 of them, including many men from the department of Morbihan and the Breton northern coast, poorly armed, and often lacking any military equipment or uniforms. These men besieging the enclaves were converted into regular troops and assembled

Members of the French Army of Resistance (FFI) at St-Nazaire, 1944.
(Luc Braeuer collection, Batz sur Mer)

under proper military command in October 1944. Thus at Lorient for example 19th Infantry Division came into being, made up of the newly formed Infantry Regiments 71 and 178, an armoured reconnaissance unit and some artillery and pioneer units. The division was armed with a motley collection of German captured weapons, including armour and guns, as well as French rifles, guns and armour from every epoch, and the soldiers issued with uniforms from British and American stocks.

Off Lorient and St-Nazaire only elements of the US 94th Infantry Division were stationed there, and none farther south than the estuary of the Loire. La Rochelle and the two bases on the Gironde were besieged exclusively by the FFI. The opposing trench occupants spied on each other. Between some of them, no-man's-land would be no wider than a few hundred yards, so that each could observe the other's change of sentries.[19] By the end of December 1944 there had been few direct confontations around the various enclaves aside from a few exchanges of artillery fire.

At Lorient on 28 October, however, the Germans attacked the right bank of the Etel river held by French Resistance fighters and succeeded in gaining control of the river. The attack near the village of Sainte-Hélène was even mentioned in the Wehrmacht bulletin. German soldiers holding out in the fortifications were stylised into heroes by official propaganda. Under the title 'You are our example', the *Mitteilung für die Truppe* reporting in October 1944 wrote about the defenders at Lorient and concluded that the Fatherland would be saved, 'If every German everywhere does his duty, faithful to death, as the men at Lorient.'[20] The men inside the enclaves saw their fate differently. Ernst P wrote to his wife from St-Nazaire: 'One feels nothing in the bones and wonders every day when this damned existence will ever end.'[21] At La Rochelle, former signals petty officer of 44th Minesweeper Flotilla, Karl Diederich, headed a company of naval men protecting the front line between Esnandes and Nantilly:

> We did not believe in the great Final Victory. Except for one crazy coxswain. At the beginning of the Ardennes Offensive he cried out in euphoria, they are coming to free us. Incredible but true. ... Our main worry was: how will it all end here? The rumour was circulating that if we blew up the big Overseas-Mole they would shoot every tenth man.[22]

To maintain morale for the troops in the enclaves, Naval High Command West set up a radio link with Germany. Over the so-called *Kamaradschaftsfunk* men could send their families a brief message. The message was sent from the appropriate naval station to the families on a prepared postcard, some even being engraved on a gramophone record. By the end of 1944 over 300,000 such messages had been transmitted from the enclaves to Germany. Post went from the Escoublac airfield, occasionally with officers and shipyard specialists as passengers, such as, for example,

German ratings taken prisoner by a US patrol near Lorient, August 1944. (US National Archives)

the chief of staff at the Lorient fortification, Baader, who later went missing in the defensive fighting in Czechoslovakia. The enclave commanders used to issue newsletters containing general local information and extracts from German newspapers transmitted by the naval signals network for the Atlantic coast. In the bunker barracks at Keroman, cinema films were shown and theatrical performances put on. Films, books and food could be exchanged with St-Nazaire. Whether political newspapers dropped by air such as *Front und Heimat*, *Völkischer Beobachter* or magazines such as *Der politische Soldat*, *Offiziere des Führers* and other Nazi publications ever found their readers is unknown. In January 1945, La Rochelle was given an unwished-for honour by the Propaganda Ministry when the film *Kolberg*, about holding out through thick and thin, was air-dropped and had its first release for propaganda purposes in the enclave.

Even so, the number of deserters increased. According to a tally made at Lorient on 31 October 1944 by the commandant, up to that date 112 men from all branches of service had defected to the enemy.[23] Many were eastern troops and soldiers of Volksgruppe III, men who under Nazi nationality policy in occupied Poland had obtained German citizenship by renunciation of Polish citizenship and then been immediately conscripted into the Wehrmacht: 400 of these had already deserted at Lorient. Similar figures applied for St-Nazaire where in the same period 610 men defected of which the majority, 596 men, were eastern troops or from Volksgruppe III. As soon as possible the eastern troops were disarmed, removed from the front line and given duty to the rear, for example, on building work. Despite the misgivings of the Commander-in-Chief West, soldiers of Volksgruppe III were left within the defensive system because Naval High Command West considered that it would cause an unacceptable weakening of the front line to withdraw them.

Desertion was a capital offence, and two men caught while attempting to escape at Lorient, and three at Gironde-South, were executed. On 4 November, the Commander-in-Chief Kriegsmarine, Dönitz, ordered that the name of every deserter was to be transmitted to Germany in order that he should stand court martial at the end of the war while his family would be taken into custody (*Sippenhaft*).[24] The more difficult the war situation became, the more inflexibly did Dönitz crack down on any sign of weakness within the Kriegsmarine. Already in April 1943 he had stated that every naval man who deserted and was caught would receive the death penalty, and he would turn down all appeals for clemency. In this he was more radical than Hitler, who had declared that desertion as an act of youthful light-headedness would not attract the death penalty.[25]

OKW was of the opinion that, in view of their reported strengths, the enclaves were not being proactive enough, and so in apparent ignorance of the situation, at the beginning of September 1944 the enclave commanders were ordered to act.[26] Operations by assault troops and raids against specific targets would tie down the enemy at the perimeter and encourage fighting spirit amongst the troops. This had happened at the outset of the sieges in the form of raids to straighten the front lines or occupy important observation points. On 9 August 1944 St-Nazaire reported to Skl that a company of 7th U-boat Flotilla had been engaged in a ground action, and on 8 September ten companies of naval infantry, composed of men from 10th Minesweeper Flotilla and other units, advanced along both banks of the Loire against French and American formations. As far as possible the boat crews were kept together and operated in common. Initially, those besieged at St-Nazaire appear to have been very active. On 29 August, commando raids resulted in the demolition of two bridges over the river Vilaine and the church tower at Rieux to prevent its use for artillery spotting. In a raid on 15 September 1944 it was reported that the enemy suffered seventy-two dead and a large quantity of weapons and ammunition fell into German hands.[27] From the Gironde, German motorised commando parties raided as far as Saintes, Cognac and Archiac. On the other hand the Kriegsmarine yards concentrated on defence. At Lorient Peter Carton wrote of the defensive preparations in the naval base:

> For myself I am taking command of 10.WAK (explosives company, Keroman) and thus I have a view of the planned defences at Keroman which in my opinion are pretty measly. The three permanent companies (two fortification detachments and one from 14.UJ-Flotille) occupy the developed positions. Attacks are to be made by the poorly trained WAKs instead of the other way round. The WAKs get a half day's training every 14 days. They have no heavy weapons. God help us if it comes to a fight.[28]

In November 1944 the commander of Naval Command West, Admiral Krancke, suggested that, as a precaution in case that the food supply ran out in the future, a large complement from each enclave should break out and attempt to conquer more ground, enabling those men who remained behind in the enclaves to hold out longer.[29] This was a ludicrous idea considering their morale, physical state and lack of military equipment. A breakout through the lines of the FFI would probably have been possible, but not through rested, veteran American and French regular troops with air supremacy. When the Wehrmacht embarked upon its last major offensive in the Ardennes in December 1944, Krancke, still living in a world far from the real one, urged the enclaves to take up an active struggle aimed at tying down enemy forces.[30] While the Christmas edition of the St-Nazaire fortress newspaper was duty bound, in view of the Ardennes offensive, to speak of a 'breakthrough in the west', and pledged to hold out, trusting in the Führer, at Lorient Peter Charton confided in his diary:

> From the start it is clear to me that the Ardennes offensive can only be a brief flickering of serious German resistance. We are convinced that the war can no longer be won, and count on Adolf Hitler giving up when the enemy reaches the Rhine. ... For us here there is naturally no point in calling a halt to it ourselves for that would release many more enemy troops for the advance into Germany. Perhaps the German

government could obtain concessions at the armistice negotiations for handing over the occupied enclaves undamaged.[31]

Grossadmiral Dönitz in his 1944 Christmas address to the men of the Kriegsmarine stated:

> The year 1944 has brought us bitter setbacks and demanded of us harsh sacrifice. Our enemies willed that it should break us, but it has only made us more dogged. The war at its zenith will continue to demand sacrifices. Next year will find us ready, however: we look towards it with determination. That every man will give his best, of that I am certain. Unshakeable in our belief and fanatic in our will, we will achieve final victory.[32]

In a very much more personal special call to the enclaves, Dönitz appealed once more to the will of the defenders, 'hard as steel'. Naval officers such as the former senior director at the Kriegsmarine Yard Lorient and later naval commandant there, Konteradmiral Walter Matthiae, in September 1944 had already questioned the sense in holding out at the enclaves. Although he left it in no doubt that no commandant would 'be starved into surrendering', the admiral had several other questions for his superiors to answer:

(1) Will it be possible to keep us supplied from the Reich if our food potential becomes exhausted?
(2) As regards the overall war situation, is any real purpose served by the enclaves holding out despite starvation if they are not tying down enemy forces?
(3) In the framework of extending the food potential, is there a possibility that the enclaves will be relieved when new weapons are introduced?
(4) Is it intended even to a limited extent to return U-boats to the bases once the new types enter service, and are the enclaves, holding out as long as humanly possible, significant by placing special political pledges into the hands of the leadership?[33]

Group West apparently did not reply. Higher authority gave no thought to whether holding out had any purpose, while Dönitz continued to speak of fighting to the last man in precisely the manner to which the Nazi leaders were accustomed. In March 1945, for example, Hitler stated that the enclaves in the west should preferably have a naval commandant, 'since many an enclave, but never a ship, was lost without a fight to the last.'[34] On the other hand, the French secret service took a different view of the German resolve to hold out: 'Behind a handful of convinced Nazis with an iron will to resist stands the disciplined bulk, whose morale is reflected

German and French sentries at the demarcation line of fortified La Rochelle, 1945. (Hubert Meyer, *Entre Marins*, Paris 1966)

by international developments.'[35] German soldiers had begun gradually to turn away from National Socialism. Karl Diederich recalls from the time besieged at La Rochelle: 'In a sergeants' drinking spree in company quarters at Esnandes someone shot at a portrait of Hitler. Next day it had disappeared.'[36] Admiral Krancke, as Commander-in-Chief, Naval High Command West, spoke of holding out at the end of 1944, 'so that what has been achieved by the garrisons in the enclaves shall not have been in vain.'[37]

The commandants of the enclaves had in fact sought early contacts with their FFI counter-parts. At La Rochelle, Admiral Schirlitz had been negotiating with the French naval captain, Hubert Meyer, since September 1944; at Gironde-North on 16 September talks were held at Médis near the front line between the enclave commandant and the FFI. OKW had approved these conversations two days before, provided that they helped the enclaves hold out longer. When at the Gironde, however, Oberst Pohlmann agreed to receive the French pier station of Le Verdon as a pledge in the negotiations, although the Commander-in-Chief West and the Kriegsmarine had already agreed previously to blow it up, OKW stepped in. The previous enclave commander, Generalmajor Fritz Meyer, had wanted to agree a compromise with the French commander in the Médoc not to demolish the pier station, so long as the French did not attack the enclave.[38] The French had rejected the proposal. Therefore the station was already doomed. Pohlmann and Meyer were then ordered back to Germany for court martial. The Commander-in-Chief West, Generalfeldmarschall Gerd Rundstedt, observed with regard to the events: 'There must be no consideration regarding the population nor for retrospective psychological effects.'[39] Therefore the mole and the pier railway station of Le Verdon were demolished as ordered on 17 November 1944.

An odd agreement was reached at La Rochelle. The commander of the French troops, Colonel Henri Adeline, signed the La Rochelle Convention on 18 October 1944, ratified two days later by the German enclave

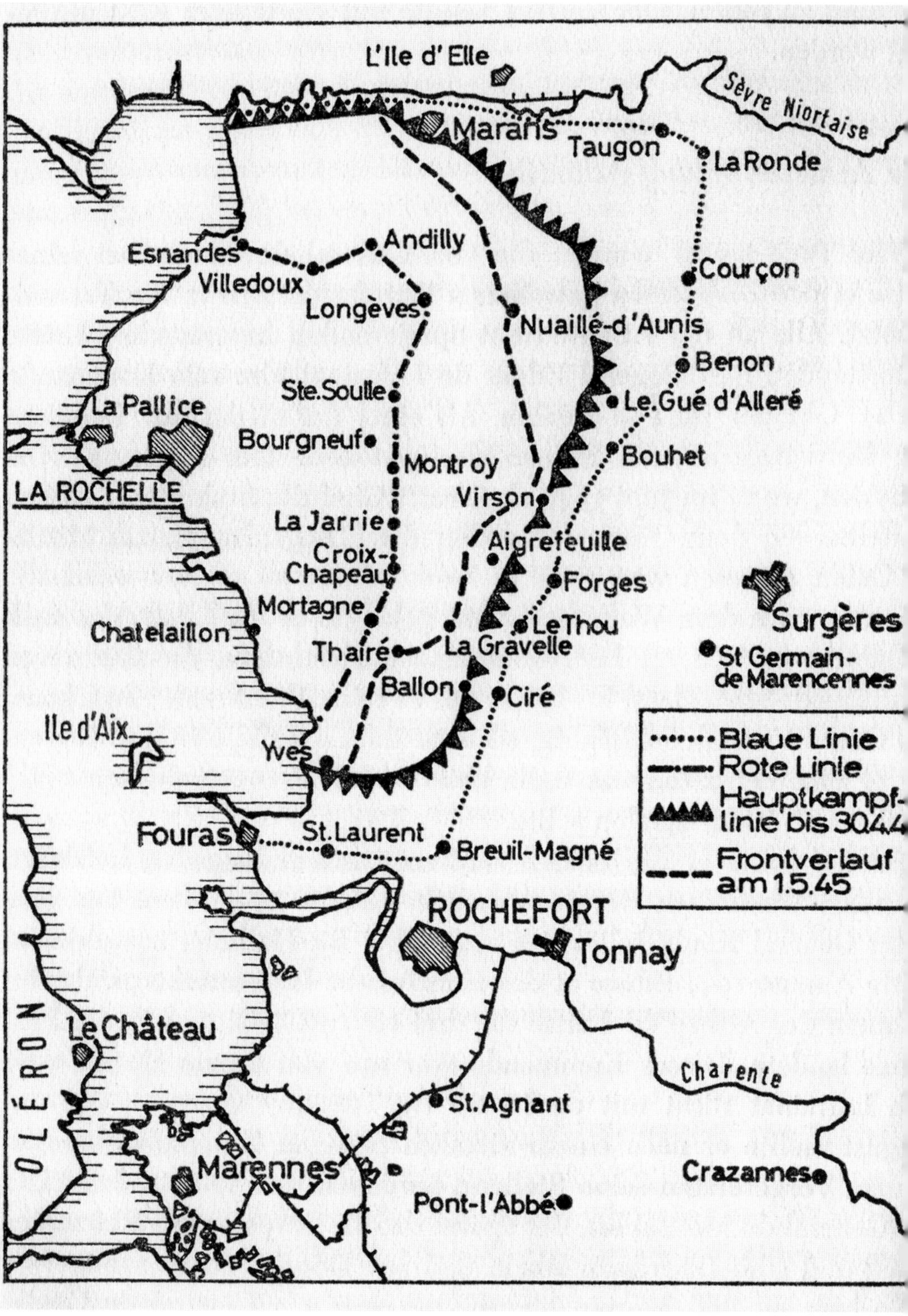

L'Ile d'Elle

Sèvre Niortaise

Marans
Taugon
La Ronde

Courçon

Andilly

Esnandes
Villedoux
Longèves
Nuaillé-d'Aunis
Benon

La Pallice
Ste.Soule
Le.Gué d'Alleré

Bourgneuf
Bouhet

LA ROCHELLE
Montroy
Virson

La Jarrie
Aigrefeuille

Croix-
Chapeau
Forges

Mortagne
Le Thou
Surgères

Chatelaillon
Thairé
La Gravelle
St Germain-
de Marencennes

Ballon
Ciré

Ile d'Aix
Yves

Fouras
St.Laurent
Breuil-Magné

ROCHEFORT
Tonnay

Le Château

OLÉRON
St.Agnant
Charente

Marennes
Crazannes

Pont-l'Abbé

.... Blaue Linie
—·—·— Rote Linie
▲▲▲▲ Hauptkampf-
linie bis 30.4.4
— — — Frontverlauf
am 1.5.45

Negotiator Hauptmann Reinhold Mueller (right) in front of the train bringing food for the French inhabitants of the St-Nazaire enclave, December 1944. (Reinhold Mueller, *Unter weisser Flagge*, Bad Nauheim 1966)

commandant, Vizeadmiral Schirlitz. The Germans bound themselves not to advance beyond the existing perimeter of the enclave, in exchange for which the French agreed neither to attack La Rochelle nor the offshore island of Île de Ré.[40] Fighting between the respective sides was permitted, but only between a red line and a blue line straddling the existing perimeter (see map opposite). Schirlitz also agreed by his signature to relinquish all further acts of destruction in the harbour and the French likewise agreed that the civilian population would abstain from Resistance activities and acts of sabotage.

At St-Nazaire Hauptmann Reinhold Mueller held talks, approved by the enclave commandant, with the FFI regarding supplies to the population. Mueller would also lead the surrender discussions with the Americans on 8 May 1945 at Cordemais for the handover of the St-Nazaire enclave. Often the fate of whole cities depended on a handful of such men. When on 10 April 1945 the sub-prefect of St-Nazaire learned that the French High Command was planning an attack on St-Nazaire in order to regain the Loire estuary, he went at once to Paris and convinced General de Gaulle to cancel it. Thus St-Nazaire was spared the dreadful fate of Royan, victim of a British air raid on 5 January 1945 in which 1,500 townspeople were killed and the town razed to the ground only months before the end of the war. The historical port of La Rochelle owes its survival relatively intact to the talks between Vizeadmiral Schirlitz and Captain Hubert Meyer.

Opposite: Map showing the enclave of La Rochelle, 1944/1945. The serrated line is the main front line until 30 April 1945, the line of dashes immediately inside it shows the front line as at 1 May 1945. The 'blue line' outside the perimeter (dotted line), and the 'red line' (dot and dash) from Esnandes to Yves inside it, were negotiated in October 1944 by Vizeadmiral Schirlitz and French naval Captain Hubert Meyer as the boundaries within which the respective sides agreed to confine hostilities. (Jacques Mordal, *Die letzten Bastionen*, Oldenburg/Hamburg, 1966)

French troops after the attack on Royan, April 1945. (Hubert Meyer, *Entre Marins*, Paris 1966)

The latter found little sympathy for his action from the FFI and he received many death threats for his alleged treason.

The negotiations between Germans and French had as their priority the feeding of the civilians still living within the enclave perimeters. While OKW had ordered on 18 September 1944 that the population, apart from the men of military age, were to be expelled for fear that the available food supplies for German troops and French civilians might not be enough despite rationing, the US forces would not permit it, quoting the Hague Convention which provides that the garrison of a fortress is responsible for supplying the civilian population with provisions.[41] Only at Dunkirk did a German enclave commandant succeed in ousting the civilian population at the beginning of a siege. Thus in November 1944 there were 8,500 French civilians in the enclave at Lorient, 40,000 at La Rochelle and 110,000 at St-Nazaire. Most of them had been found somewhere to live in the region surrounding Lorient and St-Nazaire after the Allied bombings and were then surprised by events in the summer of 1944. Few of them were still living near the ruined harbour areas.

At Lorient the Red Cross set up a food supply line using a trawler for the voyages back and forth between Vannes and Lorient.[42] At the beginning of 1945 when the Red Cross negotiated an agreement with US forces for the evacuation of about 1,400 enclave inhabitants, many preferred to remain where they were.[43] At St-Nazaire, the German liaison officer to the French civilian administration, Hauptmann (R) Reinhold Mueller, a pre-war secondary schoolmaster in English and French, organised the provisioning of the French population in the enclave at the request of the French sub-prefect of St-Nazaire.[44] Because most of the people from the towns bombed to rubble in 1943 could not afford to feed themselves, the German officer contacted the French units beyond the perimeter. In the talks at Cordemais on the stretch of railway line between St-Nazaire and Nantes, the French side agreed to make available a train to evacuate two thousand people, mainly the old and infirm, out of the enclave. The first such run was made in December 1944 and repeated four times before the enclave capitulated, so that almost ten thousand people were able to leave in the period beforehand. On the inward journey this *train de pitié* brought in medicine and food for the civilian population. Distribution was handled by the Red Cross. At La Rochelle the Red Cross supplied the civilians from March 1945 from the Swedish-flag trawler *Messidor*. This vessel was under French navy command and made four runs each month from Rochefort to La Rochelle bringing in about 90 tonnes of food each time. Later, as a result of the negotiations, an exchange of prisoners of war was arranged with all enclaves, although it appears that the French and Americans found it increasingly difficult as the war neared its end to find German volunteers to be repatriated into the enclaves.

Because the deliveries of food were reserved exclusively for the civilian population, the German complements had to make do with what they had, and as time went on food stocks began to dwindle. From Germany, Group West, which had relocated to Bad Schwalbach, organised the supply to the enclaves. Together with an airlift by long-range aircraft, in December 1944 a supply U-boat came round from Germany bringing fats, cigarettes, shoes, shirts, medicaments, Panzerfäuste and spare parts to St-Nazaire. Others were to follow. By 25 March 1945 the Luftwaffe had made eleven drops over Lorient, thirty-two over La Rochelle and twenty-three over the Gironde enclaves, while at St-Nazaire, which had the Escoublac airfield still operational, aircraft landed on fifty-two occasions. Nevertheless, the air bridge fell short of expectations. This was due to weather conditions and technical problems, but also to the fact that the machines had to fly over a liberated area and suffer its anti-aircraft fire. Thus in November and December 1944, nineteen machines of 143 involved in supply flights were lost to enemy action.

At Lorient foodstuffs were strictly rationed and the remaining cattle herded into a depot on the former airfield, where cabbage was being cultivated on the runway. Despite the proximity of the sea, fishing was not possible on a large scale as a result of fuel shortages. The good apple harvest in the autumn of 1944 came in useful for syrup and preserves, but from the beginning of January 1945 there was not enough food to go round and hunger set in. Coastal artilleryman Hubertus Michling recalled:

> The rations began to diminish. Even the flour for bread was eked out by the addition of sawdust, as we found out from the bakers. Fields of potatoes towards the perimeter were harvested and then re-dug over and over and replanted, and that under enemy fire. After the winter passed we searched under the apple trees for fallen fruit and ate whatever we found, frozen or not.

The German supply problems were known to their opponents. French army intelligence reported at the beginning of 1945 about the situation in Lorient: 'Lorient is the fortification in which they have the worst problem. The Germans scour the area they control or in no-man's-land for whatever they can find. German patrols often said they were out of potatoes or more or less ripe wheat.'[45]

At St-Nazaire there was little shortage of food on account of the large arable area within the defences. Strict rationing guaranteed the occupation force there a basic diet. French farmers who had remained on their farms within the defended area were obliged to surrender their cereals to the enclave commissariat. Meat was available in sufficient quantity and stored in a refrigerated plant near the U-boat bunker. To some extent, the enclaves exchanged foodstuffs amongst themselves, transport being possible by the use of small craft. Every three weeks a large boat left Lorient under cover of darkness for St-Nazaire. After a six-hour voyage there would be an exchange of mail, cattle meat, cereals and fuel. On 8 September 1944 the small tanker *Mary* left Lorient with an escort of three armed patrol boats (KFKs) for St-Nazaire, and also made two trips to collect heating oil from La Pallice, before being intercepted by Allied warships and sunk. Later *U255* made the runs between the various ports, operating out of St-Nazaire.

Occasionally, German troops would foray beyond the enclave perimeter in search of food. Thus in January 1945 a party of marauders from La Rochelle arrived at Marans, outside the perimeter but within the agreed red-blue hostilities corridor and captured 590 head of cattle, 576 sheep, 270 lambs, 61 pigs, 17 horses, 148 tonnes of wheat and 17 tonnes of beans.[46] The date had been chosen because the French community just outside the perimeter had re-established peacetime customs such as the annual cattle market, which explains the mixed nature of the bounty. Although the Germans were driven out by French forces two days later, the success of the commando action was radioed with pride to Germany.

These sorties were the exception, however, and thus it remained quiet around the enclaves apart from the daily exchanges of artillery fire but nevertheless several hundred Germans lost their lives in them once they were sealed. The actual number is not known, but a survey of the losses in the enclaves up to 25 November 1944 gives an impression of the intensity of the fighting. According to the survey, including the losses during August, 1,930 soldiers fell near Lorient and 2,400 near St-Nazaire.[47] The losses south of the Loire Estuary were relatively small in comparison, 191 near La Rochelle and 310 near the two enclaves on the Gironde. There was no heavy fighting subsequently, except for the already-mentioned storming of the right bank of the Etel near Lorient in October 1944, and the naval engagement with French forces near the occupied small islands of Houat and Hoëdic off Lorient on 15 December 1944.[48] The daily artillery exchanges also took their toll.

At the beginning of May 1945 the stock of bread at Lorient was only sufficient for five days. There was enough fat for two weeks and meat for two months but nothing else. At the perimeter, troops gathered stinging nettles which the field kitchens mixed with flour to make soup.[49] Their military training enabled the troops from all branches of service to combine into a uniform garrison which amounted finally to five Wehrmacht infantry regiments, two infantry battalions, a reserve battalion, a Wehrmacht pioneer battalion and a Wehrmacht signals detachment. The fighting value of these units was not great as a result of their poor physical

Changing the guard in front of Keroman III U-boat bunker at Lorient, March 1945. (Luc Braeuer collection, Batz sur Mer)

condition after months cooped up in the enclave on a poor diet. Fortunately for them, they were never called upon to fight rested Allied troops.

The men in the Gironde enclaves were less fortunate. After the provisional French government decided in January 1945 to liberate these fortified areas by force, the initial intention having been stalled by the Ardennes campaign, in April 1945 battle-hardened French troops were brought out from occupied Germany and sent to the Atlantic coast, amongst them General Leclerc's 2nd Armoured Division. On 15 April they attacked the enclaves of Gironde-North and Gironde-South. Because of the small, poorly equipped German force holding them, it is not surprising that the two enclaves, attacked by two divisions supported from air and sea, fell within a few days. What was the purpose is a question that remains unresolved. Just a few days before the end of the war the French lost 364 dead and 1,567 were wounded, and another eighteen French soldiers fell during the landings on the island of Oléron at the end of April 1944. The German losses are not known.

General Charles de Gaulle (left) and General Edgard de Larminat at the Biscay Front, April 1945. (Hubert Meyer, *Entre Marins*, Paris 1966)

Probably it was a matter of honour for the French government of General de Gaulle to liberate some bit of mainland French territory themselves. The commander of the French Army Division Atlantique, General Edgard de Larminat, had been one of the first officers to join the Free French forces in 1940. In a letter dated 10 April 1945, Larminat notified Admiral Schirlitz that he was revoking the La Rochelle Convention agreed in October 1944. At the same time he expected the German admiral to continue to protect the harbour installations with a warning that to destroy them would be seen by the French government, considering the war situation, as deliberate sabotage and a breach of international law, bringing punishment in its train for those responsible. On the other hand, should the installations not be destroyed, the French High Command would take all measures it could to handle the German garrison at La Rochelle honourably and – in the case of a return to Germany – preferentially.

After Skl had intercepted a radio signal on 19 April 1945 in which the French requested the enclave commander to spare the town, the OKW stepped in. The commandant at La Rochelle was ordered on 21 April 1945 to break off all contact with General de Larminat at once. According to an instruction from the head of the Wehrmacht planning staff, General-oberst Jodl, Schirlitz was to defend the port 'to the uttermost'. Jodl's position was that offers to exchange prisoners were to be refused, and enemy threats to be answered with the warning that for every such German combatant killed, five French prisoners in German hands would be executed.[50] On 28 April 1945 the Wehrmacht planning staff established that 'the development of the situation is leading to numerous rumours and much speculation in the remotest outposts.'[51] In order to counteract this, in the view of the OKW it was necessary 'more now than ever to ensure the feeling of constant and close contact to the most senior command levels by running orientation and clear instructions.' Jodl

pointed out that 'all that matters now is to obey, and carry out the orders of the Führer to the last'. At this point in time Germany already lay in ruins and the Nazi leadership had withdrawn into the bunkers beneath the Reich Chancellery. Fortunately, the will of the responsible officers in the enclaves 'to keep firm in their allegiance' was not holding up in the face of the military situation. Whereas Schirlitz had officially informed his

Surrender of the St-Nazaire enclave by Generalmajor Hans Junck, 11 May 1945. (Luc Braeuer collection, Batz sur Mer)

French opposite number of his will to resist, whether he would have gone so far as to destroy La Rochelle if ordered seems more than doubtful.

At the same time the enclave commandant at Lorient, having regard to the low energy reserves and little ammunition, was considering firing off all his ammunition at the Allies should they attack, and then surrendering. It did not come to that. On the evening of 7 May 1945 the enclave commandants received radio signals informing them of the imminent capitulation of the German Wehrmacht. On the morning of 9 May French units occupied La Rochelle. On 10 May General Fahrmbacher capitulated at Lorient. General Jungk surrendered on 11 May 1945 to US General Kramer, and St-Nazaire thus became the last town in France to be liberated.

Capitulation and captivity

For German servicemen in the enclaves, capitulation meant mixed relief and concern at the same time. Relief at having survived the war despite deprivation and struggle, concern at what being a prisoner of war would mean: 'How, during all this time we had been hungry, had had hope and had overcome all hardships, all for nothing. We were starving, our

French troops entering La Rochelle, 9 May 1945. (Hubert Meyer, *Entre Marins*, Paris 1966)

Landing of French naval infantry in the port of Saint-Martin-de-Ré, May
1945. (Hubert Meyer, *Entre Marins*, Paris 1966)

uniforms were in rags and we looked
like scarecrows,' wrote Hubertus
Michling, former naval artilleryman
in the Lorient enclave.[52]

At Lorient a flotilla of French
MTBs took possession of the
harbour for the French navy. The
officers inspected the bunker
installations of Keroman with
curiosity: 'The U-boat bunker was
intact, and it was a strange feeling
to wander the bunker halls, see the
workshops still functioning and the
Germans still manning the power
plant.' At St-Nazaire a German
pilot awaited the French MTBs and
led them through the sunken
blockships into the harbour:

The German ships in the harbour all had their German crews
on board, just the flags had
disappeared. A German officer,
who handed me a water tap and

German naval ratings at La Pallice, May
1945. (Hubert Meyer, *Entre Marins*, Paris
1966)

an electric cable, asked me if we used 110 or 220 volts. ... These men
looked neither haggard nor unkempt, they were not nomads but just
troops, definitely correct troops, even very correct, who apparently
could speak a bit of French but at the same time had the downcast mien
of the defeated.[53]

The German prisoners of war now faced an uncertain future. At La
Rochelle, French naval infantry occupied the U-boat bunker on 9 May
and set up a prison camp on the terrain behind it. Amongst the prisoners
was former signals petty officer Karl Diederich:

On 9 May 1945 capitulation. Marched through La Rochelle into the
Prien Camp depressed. End of May into the Chatelaillon Camp near
La Rochelle. Unfortunately an army camp. 'Mariners wear your blues,'
we were advised, 'They treat naval men better.' An error! The French
navy yes, but not their army. At the camp we were thoroughly fleeced.
That was the last we saw of our sea-bags.[54]

In their memoirs German prisoners of war complained about the bad
treatment by the French guards, appalling hygiene conditions and poor
rations for the heavy labour in the ruins or harbour. According to Karl

Diederich, at La Rochelle whips were used on the prisoners and in the prison camp at the former Lorient airfield he observed how German military police were given brutal treatment by the French guards who confused them with SS men.

A different picture is seen in the report of a French officer on the organisation of the French navy prison camp in the harbour at La Pallice. According to his statement, a German navy officer and his adjutant took charge of the general administration of the camp. In this he was supported by a German camp company consisting of six officers, 637 men and thirty medical orderlies who were responsible for the general administration, the kitchens, cleaning and general housekeeping.[55] The German inmates were divided off into four work companies each headed by a German officer. In general, the French lieutenant commander acknowledged that his German prisoners worked with a will. Besides clearance work and minesweeping they took on special tasks. A formal naval diver at the La Pallice yard worked on the harbour locks in June 1945.[56] At the end of May 1945 at a prison camp near Poitiers the former chief engineer of *Sperrbrecher 16* offered to lead the work to raise the ship, sunk in La Pallice harbour on 10 August 1944. He estimated six to ten weeks for the task and asked for twenty-five prisoners to assist, amongst them former crew members. It was love for his profession which motivated his offer, he

German troops removing a bomb with French guards looking on, La Rochelle, May 1945. (Hubert Meyer, *Entre Marins*, Paris 1966)

wrote, and offered as proof of his goodwill his co-operation with the head of the French power station whom he had helped supply electricity to the Île de Ré in September 1944 by salving an engine from the sunken *Sperrbrecher*.[57] There were also examples to the contrary. At La Rochelle in June 1945 a German staff surgeon in the Lafond prison camp was transferred away for his hostile attitude towards the French authorities in the former German naval hospital, in particular, having done what he could to prevent the French navy setting up their own naval hospital.[58]

Besides the hard labour, German prisoners recalled the very short rations and bad treatment by the French. Because of poor hygiene and lack of nourishment, dysentery was common. For this reason a number of prisoners stepped forward when the call went out for men to crew the former German minesweepers. In Karl Diederich's eyes, volunteering for minesweeper duty meant salvation from camp life:

> On board we were given fair treatment by the French seniors and guards in charge of us. Above all, the commander was a correct officer. We received good food, the same meals as the French members of the crew, a little less by way of tobacco. At the outset we even got 250cc of wine daily. It was soon stopped because the 'comrades' got drunk and sang Nazi songs.

The former signals petty officer had his station on the bridge beside a coxswain's mate and was responsible for flag semaphore and Morse traffic between the ships.

His was not an isolated case, but rather the rule, for most German prisoners of war along the coast were either put to work in rebuilding the ruined port towns or particularly in minesweeping. The latter was dangerous work and the French authorities sought volunteers from the prison camps, promising better food and an early return home. For minesweeping at sea, those boats found in the French harbours at the conclusion of hostilities were pressed into service. Thus the former German auxiliary minesweeper *M4626*, a steam trawler built in 1937 at Seebeckwerft, Wesermünde, operated with a mixed Franco-German crew out of Lorient and La Pallice. The chief mechanic and the stokers were former German crewmen. The boat was worked by thirty-eight Germans who inhabited the fore part of the ship, and only twelve French, housed in the poop. On large units such as the minesweepers of the *M35* and *M40* classes the imbalance was even greater: on *M434* the ratio was eighty Germans to twelve French. The accommodation was clearly separated, the French crew having received instructions from their officers to limit contact with the German prisoners to what was necessary.

Otherwise, no great difference existed between German and French aboard the minesweepers, the respective nationalities sharing the same food and the same dangers. Thus the French former commander of *M4626* wrote in his memoirs:

> As regards the circumstances on board, naturally the French were the guards and the German ratings their prisoners. Above and beyond that, however, they were first of all sailors on the same ship sharing the same risks. For that reason I saw them more as crew than prisoners, provided they behaved. The conditions were underpinned with trust and the work shared out harmoniously. As for the food, it was rationed throughout France, and that went for us too. There was only one galley, and so French and Germans ate the same meal as the commander.[59]

Those German sailors not able to knuckle under the French giving orders were sent back to the prison camp.

German prisoners made attempts to escape the dangerous employment. The French commander of *M434* reported for the year 1945 a total of nine successful escapes and for the period from January to September 1946, twelve frustrated attempts. According to the French files, some of the men committed suicide.

On 3 December 1946 the first 105 minesweeping volunteers were released from duty and brought by French corvette to Germany. Karl Diederich was given his freedom a week later, on 10 December. The French commander had taken his personal leave of each man beforehand. The men were transferred to a French destroyer which brought them into Hamburg to be discharged: they were told that this special treatment was by way of gratitude to the garrison at La Rochelle who had kept their word and not blown up the port. Hauptmann Mueller at St-Nazaire was released in December 1945. Other German prisoners were detained until 1947 in France. The former German enclave commandants were court-martialled by the French and imprisoned. Ernst Schirlitz was released in October 1947, while the commandants of Lorient and Gironde-North, Wilhelm Fahrmbacher and Hans Michahelles, remained in French custody until August 1950; Fahrmbacher later became a military adviser to the Egyptians.

The French who had worked for the Germans in the ports were also required to justify their actions. At Brest there were brawls between Free French naval personnel stationed in Britain and naval gendarmes who had remained in service in France.[60] A number of officers were relieved of their posts, although many were reinstated later. Sentences such as the ejection from office of the head of French naval ordnance at Brest with loss of pension rights, for collaborating with the occupying power by making flak shells for the Wehrmacht and openly saluting German officers, remained the exception. The Admiralty also came under scrutiny, although nobody was called to account. Officially, the activity of French naval personnel in

Konteradmiral Hans Michahelles, commander of the Gironde-Nord
fortifications, as a prisoner of the French, April 1945. (Hubert Meyer,
Entre Marins, Paris 1966)

the occupied zone was seen as service to France, which meant that the
French navy could continue to receive manpower and important materials
for the reconstruction.[61] The fact that French engineers, officials, officers,
men and workers spent more than four years working for the occupiers
and were an important factor in the use of the French Atlantic bases by
the Kriegsmarine was shrouded in silence and forgetfulness in the France
of the post-war era.

8

The Bunkers Today

The former U-boat bunkers in the ports on the French Atlantic coast are witnesses in stone to Nazi claims to supremacy over Europe, and a monumental expression of Hitler's delusions of grandeur. For the French towns involved, their construction signified military defeat. Leaving aside Bordeaux and La Rochelle, for years after the war, as at St-Nazaire, for

The U-boat bunker Keroman III, Lorient, 2011. (Martin Kaule)

example, they were not part of city planning. After being ignored for many years, today they are once more under the eye of French town planners, and these wartime structures have been turned into peaceful places of cultural history.

Each bunker influenced the post-war development of its appropriate town or city in a different way, according to its situation. At Brest and Lorient, where the bunkers were built outside the town, they were taken over in 1945 by the French navy and were less of a presence than at St-Nazaire, where even today the bunker dominates the inner city and harbour basin. At La Rochelle and Bordeaux, on the other hand, the U-boat bunkers are to be found in the harbour installations in the suburbs, far from the city centres and public perception.

The ruins of Brest, September 1944. (Archives Municipales, Brest)

Brest

When the German enclave at Brest capitulated on 18 September 1944, the city and port were a field of rubble. The first returners amongst the population found a scene of devastation:

> More impressive than the sight of it is the silence, a deathly silence hanging above the ruins, and the depressing atmosphere. At the same time one smells the smoke. It affects all the senses: sight, hearing, smell. ... The total absence of animal or plant life, dead and twisted trees, not the least flap of a bird's wing nor the twitter of a sparrow. Nothing but ruins and desolation. What can one do about so much rubble, about a totally obliterated city?[1]

Five thousand houses in the inner city were destroyed, another five thousand damaged. The U-boat bunker alone stood undamaged at the western edge of the warship harbour. Although a couple of British Tallboy bombs had penetrated the bunker ceiling on 5 August 1944, the Germans left the installation standing because the wounded were sheltered in the galleries behind the bunker.[2] Inside the harbour the Kriegsmarine had rendered the dry docks and wet pens unusable by sinking lorries, smaller harbour craft and diverse equipment, but by the evening of 18 September the French navy had regained possession of its formerly most important Atlantic base. In a symbolic act, a flotilla of the former Free French navy, the Forces Navales Françaises Libres (FNFL) equipped with British MTBs, was the first French navy unit to enter the harbour after its liberation. It berthed at the U-boat bunker, since all other quay areas were destroyed or mined. It would be some considerable time before the harbour could be used again by large vessels.

A total of 900 wrecks lay in and around Brest at the end of the fighting. The two great dry docks at Laninon were blocked by scuttled *Sperrbrecher* and their gates blown off. Near the Flotilla Quay in the warship harbour was the hospital ship *Oakland*, sunk by US aircraft before the enclave capitulated. The entrances into the U-boat bunker were blocked by several scuttled tugs and a VP-boat. In the great building dock in the rearward reaches of the naval arsenal was the scuttled wreck of *U415*. Most workshops had been destroyed by the bombing and artillery bombardments during the fighting. Nevertheless, the arsenal resumed work within a short space of time.

In October 1944 more than a thousand workers were occupied in clearance work in the arsenal. In order to avoid incidents with German prisoners of war clearing mines and rubble under US supervision there, the new French naval commandant had been ordered simply to ignore them.[3] The first repairs were carried out in the U-boat bunker, since this was the only installation in the arsenal with an electricity supply and protection against the elements. In the workshops, the still usable machine tools were retrieved from the rubble and repaired, or replacements obtained from Germany as reparations, or supplied by the Allies. On 15 March 1945 the cruiser *Dusquesne* made fast at the Flotilla Quay and in October 1945, after the arsenal river had been cleared, entered the great building dock. After the dry docks and wet pens in the U-boat bunker had been repaired, the new French navy submarine station at Brest was set up there. The holes in the bunker roof caused by RAF bombing in the previous summer were given a temporary cover.

Up to the end of December 1944 only the roadstead was open to warships. In January 1945, after the quays were repaired, the first Liberty ships entered the mercantile harbour to unload urgently needed goods such as coal, fertiliser and cement, but even in June 1945 entry into the harbour was very difficult due to the wrecks. In one of the access channels a French navy tanker had several metres of hull ripped open, damage which would have sunk a normal freighter. By September 1945 the mercantile harbour still had only a single berth open to process Liberty ships, then came another, as well as two places for smaller merchant ships to come alongside.

The complete clearance of the ruins in the naval arsenal deprived Brest of the last remaining masonry dating from the sixteenth-century royal arsenal. The reconstruction of the city followed a completely new arrangement. The walls which had enclosed it since the time of Vauban, near the thick fortifications of the castle, the only historical structure standing less than half damaged, were pulled down. The city architects wanted the city open to the sea and so they designed a completely new ground plan.

While temporary accommodation for the population was set up in a broad ring around the city, in the city centre whole trams lay buried below the rubble and ruins. After this had all been cleared, and German prisoners of war had rummaged through it for usable materials and forgotten ammunition, the city had the appearance of a flattened featureless surface with a few undamaged structures jutting upwards. Later, the prisoners helped in the reconstruction work.

Ruler-straight streets on the American pattern set the tone in modern Brest, which is typical of model city reconstructions of the 1950s with its almost monotonous facades. Only the castle and the old promenade above the mercantile harbour have retained the impression of old Brest. In order to give its inhabitants some sense of the historical dimension of their city, in the year 2000, based on an idea from the artist Gwenaëlle Magadur, a blue line was painted along the streets and pavements, following the course of the former fortress walls from the time of Vauban: a timid attempt at approaching the way that old Brest used to

The former U-boat bunker in modern Brest. (Hans Krohn)

look before it disappeared in the confusion of war, and providing its citizens of today with a fragment of history in the search for historical identity. Efforts have also been made to maintain a few historical artefacts, such as the foundation walls of the former city gate in the centre or the impressive remains of the fortress walls to the north of the city. Below the city centre lies the Sadi Carnot bunker, the great air-raid tunnel, now reopened, a place where so many people lost their lives in September 1944, and which will remain as a reminder of that terrible phase in the city's history into the future.

The U-boat bunker is an important venue for remembering the period of German occupation, and opens to visitors in the summer. It is within a prohibited military area, but can be seen from the coastal road between the Recouvrance district and the St Anne de Portzic lighthouse. The French navy continues to use the bunker for its minesweepers, and the pens serve as berths for minor vessels for the naval base, as do the galleries below the naval academy. The rear walls of the bunker are pockmarked by numerous shell hits, the scars of battle around the German enclave of Brest: the head of a Tallboy bomb which penetrated the bunker ceiling in August 1944 decorates the wall of a pen.

Reminders that Brest was the site of battle appear from time to time with the discovery of forgotten munitions. Thus when the new tram system was planned, the intended routes were sounded out down to a depth of 4m (13ft) to detect unexploded bombs. In July 2009, around the new tram depot to the west of the city, 6 tonnes of ammunition of all calibres was found and de-primed. The last still-visible evidence of the German occupation, the bunkers along the former defended perimeter, are disappearing beneath the undergrowth, or making way for city development projects.

More accessible due to their location and more visible for the modern generation are the installations of the former Atlantic Wall and the artillery bunkers for the German coastal batteries which set the tone along the embankments at the entrance to Brest Bay. Stretched out in a line along this area, they form part of the long history of the coastal defences and have become part of the French memorial landscape.

Lorient

As at Brest, on 8 May 1945 the German enclave at Lorient presented a landscape of devastation, a consequence of the many bomber raids and artillery duels during the siege between the summer of 1944 and the capitulation. The U-boat base at Keroman withstood it all undamaged. The three great bunkers on the perimeter of the ruins remained enthroned above the almost totally destroyed city. The base was given over to the French navy in full working order and was used by them for the re-creation of the French submarine arm.

At Keroman the French navy stationed its own submarines surviving from the war and U-boats received from the Kriegsmarine: *Blaison* (*U123*), *Millé* (*U471*), *Laubie* (*U766*), *Bouan* (*U510*) and *Roland Morillot*

Entrance to the transfer cradle of Keroman II. (Martin Kaule)

(the Type XXI boat *U2518*). They also brought here four German two-man U-boats of the *Seehund* type found at the Dunkirk enclave and a number of submarines given to them by the Royal Navy.[4] The workshops in the U-boat pens, the slip and mobile cradle and the Keroman III dry docks were all fully functional and at the war's end the only industrial enterprise in the city still running. However, the naval arsenal was a heap of rubble and had to be rebuilt.

First submarine to enter the submarine centre, reinstated on 19 May 1945, was the *Curie* (ex-HMS *Vox*) in July that year. On 6 July 1946 the base was named officially 'Base Stosskopf' after the engineer officer at the Lorient naval arsenal arrested in February 1944 for passing information about U-boat movements and later executed at Natzweiler concentration camp. The French used the Keroman II barracks with a capacity for a thousand men as quarters for their submarine personnel; at the end of the 1950s it was modernised to accommodate five hundred men. Between 1957 and 1973 new barrack structures including an officers' mess, a canteen, sports facilities and a sailor's home were built.

Lorient became the home base of the Atlantic Squadron of the French submarine arm with a complement of about two thousand men. German U-boats, particularly the Type XXI *U2518*, influenced French naval architects in their plans for the first French post-war submarines. Thus the diesel-electric *Narval*-class submarines of the 1950s were clearly inspired by the Type XXI U-boat. The final example of this type is the *Espadon* which can be seen today in the lock bunker at St-Nazaire.

The Kriegsmarine *Tauchtopf* on the west side of Keroman III was used to train French submariners in escaping from sunken submarines at great depths. The Keroman base was also used to build up the French nuclear submarine arm in the 1960s. Besides trials of the new propulsion technology aboard the experimental boat *Gymnote*, the crews for the new atomic submarines were trained aboard. The control room of a modern submarine was built in Keroman I. New bases for atomic submarines were set up at Cherbourg, Brest and Toulon, so Keroman was shut down after the decommissioning of the last diesel-electric submarines between 2002 and 2005. When, in the wake of the restructuring of the French navy, these boats were taken out of service ten years earlier than planned, the submarine base at Lorient was closed down fifty years after the end of the war.

As a result of the long usage of the installation and its continuing maintenance, most areas of the former German inner fittings remained intact, though weather conditions on the coast had caused some of the outer concrete to start crumbling, which the French navy protected with netting. The Keroman base was turned over to the city of Lorient, which now had the great task of restoring the area while keeping it as a war

The post-war French submarine *Flore* on the railed transfer cradle
between Keroman I and II. (Martin Kaule)

memorial. Thus there arose a unique location for organisations dedicated
in the most varied manner to the theme of the sea.

In the process of the conversion, chandlery companies moved into the
great halls of Keroman I and II, where yachts could also lay up for the
winter. On the quay to the west of the installation the Cité de la Voile, a
modern museum and archive dedicated to ocean racing, was set up, and a
marina installed in front of the former U-boat quay. Although the overall
site has been changed by the addition of a number of halls between the
bunkers, the mobile cradle was retained in its original dimensions. Today
it is the resting place of the French submarine *Flore* of the *Daphné* class.
This boat was commissioned at Lorient into 2nd Submarine Squadron in
1964 and operated until 1989 in the
Atlantic and Mediterranean. After
being decommissioned in 1995, it
was brought to Lorient to become
the foundation exhibit for a submarine museum. Unfortunately, the
former transporter carriage of
the slipway, exposed to the elements
unprotected for years, had deterior-
ated so much that it was scrapped a
short while ago.

The storage halls, Keroman I. (Martin Kaule)

Yacht in front of Keroman III. (Martin Kaule)

Today the visitor to Keroman will find a cultural complex with a mixture of technical history, water sports and tourism with bars and restaurants. A visit to the archive can be followed by a boat trip across the Lorient roadstead to the unchanged bunker Keroman III. The first museum within the Keroman complex, the submarine museum, dedicated to the submarine world around Lorient, was opened in 1999 in the former *Tauchtopf* tower.

Amongst the exhibits are many wrecks from the war period such as *U171*, mined when entering the harbour. In another section a U-boat museum was opened in 2010. This is a museum with a wide appeal, occupying the first chamber of Keroman I near the post-war French submarine *Flore* and the former barracks. Passing through a 10m (33ft) high, 30-tonne armoured door to the former U-boat base the visitor enters the world of the U-boatman and can experience for himself how life aboard must have been, from the engine room to the control room and making dive manoeuvres. On a platform built into the box below an

One of the cathedral bunkers, now bricked up, in the modern Lorient fish dock. (Martin Kaule)

original ceiling crane from the German era, one can watch a film dedicated to the Keroman bunker complex and its significance in the twentieth century.

Only a few yards from the Keroman bunker complex in the fish dock are the two cathedral dome bunkers from the initial period of the German base. The historic turntable has been removed and the bunker entrances walled up, but the dome bunkers have been preserved as original and are used today as warehouses.

At the end of the Second World War Lorient was one of the most ruined cities in France. Long after the end of the war, the German air-raid bunkers were prominent, being the only structures to have survived the bombing. To dismantle them would have been expensive, and as the work of reconstruction was begun, many of them were built over or surrounded by new housing developments but, nevertheless, their presence was a continual reminder of the German occupation. Then at the beginning of the 1980s thoughts turned towards the old history of Lorient as the home port of the French East India Company, and the end of the bunkers hove into sight. In 1982 the first to go was the 60m (200ft)-long German air-raid bunker on the north side of the old harbour, in order to clear the quayside area and reopen the city's historical centre to the public. Later, during the building of a new harbour link, the great bunkers of the torpedo arsenal behind Keroman were broken up. In 1999 French builders needed three months to break down a torpedo bunker only 40m (130ft) long by 24m (80ft) wide, using several small explosions. From 1995 onwards, the other five bunkers of the torpedo arsenal disappeared when a new building area was prepared.

In recent years more and more German bunkers have gone from the city scene as the city centre has been modernised. In the summer of 2006 the air-raid bunker of the former 10th U-boat Flotilla behind the former French sailors' home on the Cours Chazelles was broken up. The same fate is intended for the naval territory at the top of the Old Harbour, where Saltzwedel Barracks of 2nd U-boat Flotilla, now reduced to the air-raid bunker in the courtyard, was located in the old French harbour barracks destroyed in the war. It was planned to pull it down in 2012 during the conversion work, prompting many citizens of Lorient to ask when on earth the last remnants of these bunkers will finally go. The destruction of the city and the suffering of the civilian population is remembered in an air-raid bunker, uncovered during building work in 1993, and converted into a memorial below the Place Alsace-Lorraine in the city centre. A remembrance stone in the village of Caudan marks the spot where the German enclave of Lorient surrendered on 10 May 1945.

Rear side of the Saint-Nazaire U-boat bunker with stairway to the deck terrace. (Martin Kaule)

St-Nazaire

At the end of hostilities the St-Nazaire U-boat bunker passed to the French navy, which used it for repairs and conversions to both warships and merchant vessels and as a depot until 1948. Apart from a period between 1953 and 1959 when it functioned as a shipyard to build eight minesweepers for the French navy, from 1948 the bunker was used as a civilian warehouse. St-Nazaire was 85 per cent destroyed by the many bombing raids during the war. Only the massive body of the U-boat bunker remained intact above the rubble of the city centre. The rebuilding of the city followed a new north-south axis, while an artificial green belt separated the new centre from the harbour and the original city arterial roads. This division disappeared in the 1980s when St-Nazaire underwent a facelift and reopened itself to the sea. Blocking this corridor to the water, like an enormous concrete barrage, was the U-boat bunker, almost 300m (980ft) long and 19m (60ft) high, and so from 1995, as part of the planning scheme for the Ville-Port project, St-Nazaire began to reshape the harbour terrain with its industrial wastelands and giant bunker.

The bunker was not broken up but used as a binding element. In 1997 the Spanish architect and city planner Manuel de Sola Morales had the rear walls of four bunker boxes demolished so as to allow a view of the waters of the harbour basin. From the newly created square behind the U-boat bunker, a ramp leads up to a terrace on the bunker roof. Finally, since 1998 two of the former bunker boxes have housed the Museum Escal'Atlantic which deals with the history of the trans-oceanic liner trade and tells the visitor of a time in the nineteenth century when St-Nazaire was, after Le Havre, the second most important French trans-oceanic port and home to a significant shipbuilding industry.

In a subsequent part of the project in 2007, another box, the Alvéole 14, was converted into a centre for contemporary art and music, transforming the wartime structure into a peaceful place of culture, a textbook example of the successful conversion of such installations, especially since the raw and impressive form of the concrete bunker suffered only minimal change. The centre for new art forms, 'LiFE', is above the former wet-box harbour, and the exhibition room can be opened on to the harbour by way of a large folding door. The venue for contemporary music, 'VIP', inside the

Lighting installation in the interior of the St-Nazaire U-boat bunker, 2011.
(Martin Kaule)

bunker, encloses a hall for about six hundred with a bar and theatre boxes and also houses the exhibition centre archive. The former communications track in the interior of the bunker between the workshops to the rear and the wet boxes or dry docks was carpeted and connects the various cultural facilities in the bunker. A stairway leads from this gallery through the ceiling to the bunker roof where the former radar cupola from Berlin's Tempelhof airport serves as a potential exhibition space for artistic and music projects.

The former German sluice bunker at St-Nazaire now houses a museum dedicated to the historical development of the city and port. The bunker and its roof are accessible and the French post-war submarine *Espadon*, based on the German Type XXI U-boat, can be seen in the lock chamber. Not far from St-Nazaire at Batz sur Mer, in a former German coastal battery artillery-control bunker, is a museum well worth a visit, dealing with the era of German occupation at the French Atlantic coast.

La Rochelle–La Pallice

A peculiarity of La Rochelle is that the German U-boat base in the harbour area was at La Pallice, west of the historical old town with its picturesque harbour. By virtue of an agreement between the commandant of La Rochelle enclave, Vizeadmiral Ernst Schirlitz, and the French spokesman, naval Captain Hubert Meyer, La Rochelle and La Pallice were left intact. In the historic old town there is a built-over air-raid bunker housing a private museum, but no other visible testimony to the German presence during the occupation. Only at the old casino and in a former barracks to the northeast of the town, the seat of 3rd U-boat Flotilla at La Rochelle, are there still air-raid bunkers to be seen. There is a different picture in the harbour at La Pallice, dominated on the eastern side of the harbour basin by the U-boat bunker.

The undamaged installation surrendered to the French navy at the capitulation was used in 1945 as a naval training centre for U-boats taken over from the Kriegsmarine. La Pallice was thought of as a substitute for the former French naval base Rochefort further inland.[5] When the La Rochelle enclave surrendered, the U-boat *U766* was in one of the bunker wet boxes, where it had served as an emergency power plant during the siege and was handed over undamaged. A few weeks later, under the command of Lt Cdr Pierre Brunet the boat made a trial dive off La Pallice. Two-thirds of his crew were former U-boatmen plus one interpreter. In the dive trial in the autumn of 1945 the boat reached a depth of 187m (613ft), only leaks in the cooling cycle of the diesels being reported. The French navy then had the engines removed for overhaul in the bunker from November 1945 to March 1946. The trials were then resumed. During an emergency dive on 17 July 1946, *U766* proved its full

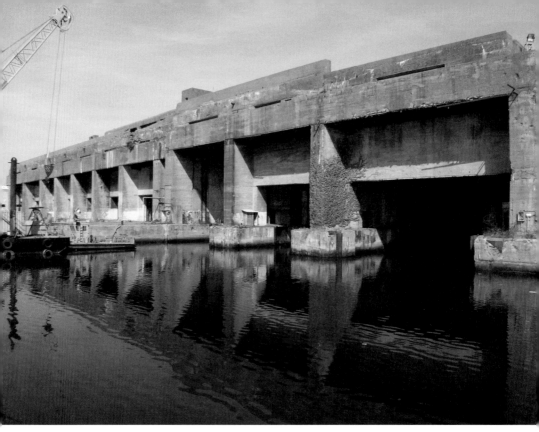

Harbour side of La Pallice U-boat bunker. (Thomas Balk)

efficiency, the French officers being particularly impressed by its fast rate of dive. The boat was commissioned into the French navy as *Laubie* in June 1947. Another former German U-boat restored to usefulness was *U510* found at St-Nazaire. It was towed to La Pallice and, with the aid of various parts discovered in the U-boat bunkers and also cannibalised from the wreck of *U415* at Brest, was repaired and in June 1947 commissioned into the French navy as *Bouan*.

In October 1947 the French navy decided against any future military use of the harbour and U-boat bunker. In the 1950s, however, La Pallice played an important role against the background of the Cold War, the Berlin blockade and the beginning of the Korean conflict. The US military command considered whether their only supply base in Europe, the port of Bremerhaven, would remain usable in the event of a military conflict. Fearing the loss of this important base, they eyed the French coast as they had done in the two world wars and for a short time re-bestowed upon it strategic and geographic significance. At the beginning of 1952 the US Army practised unloading supplies off La Pallice and bringing them ashore from landing craft and amphibious vehicles over the beaches and through the harbour.

Finally, La Pallice became an important NATO port and until 1966 was the garrison town of the US 106th Transport Battalion and the seat of several US barracks, one of them immediately in the harbour area, on the spot which had formerly been the torpedo arsenal of the Kriegsmarine. The US army used the old German bunkers to store ammunition. There were other American logistics bases at the ports of St-Nazaire and at Bassins in the Gironde. In case of emergency, lorries would bring up supplies from here along the route Poitiers–Tours–Orléans–Nancy to Germany. In the summer of 1962 US troops stationed at La Rochelle acted as extras for the Hollywood spectacular *The Longest Day* about the Allied landings in Normandy, which was filmed on the Île de Ré. This renewed military use of La Pallice finally ended when Charles de Gaulle ordered the Americans to leave France and took the country out of the NATO alliance in 1966.

Until the end of the 1970s there used to be a small French navy base in the southern part of the U-boat bunker, used by three patrol boats which kept watch on the stretch of sea fronting the French rocket-testing site at Biscarosse. Pioneer troops of the French army stationed at La Rochelle kept landing craft in the wet boxes. In 1981 the U-boat bunker and harbour area with the bunker sluice was used as the backdrop for the film

Rear side of the La Pallice U-boat bunker with power plant alongside.
(Thomas Balk)

The U-boat bunker at Bordeaux seen from the harbour basin: the
rounded-top *Fangrost* beams can be seen covering the roof, 2010.
(Thomas Balk)

Das Boot. Parts of the bunker have been used from time to time for
warehousing by the La Rochelle Chamber of Trade and Industry. Today
the U-boat bunker is empty and since it lies in the prohibited military area
of the port is inaccessible. The same goes for the sluice bunker at the
harbour exit.

Bordeaux
The Bordeaux U-boat bunker is in the Bacalan district to the north of the
town. It can be found on the northern side of the backwater basin of the
former mercantile port, now a yacht marina, amidst an industrial area.

Entrance to wet pens 6 and 7 at Bordeaux: the original numbers have survived. (Thomas Balk)

At the end of May 1945 the French navy decided not to use it for military purposes. They already had enough submarine bunkers at Lorient, Brest, St-Nazaire and La Pallice, of which they had taken possession in outstanding condition, so that from a military point of view they had no need of it provided they had the right of seizure in the event of war.[6]

For a while some civilian trades were housed there, but in general the structure was abandoned for long periods and, in comparison to the bunkers at Lorient and St-Nazaire, eventually had rather a sorry look about it. In its interior, besides many German inscriptions, much of the equipment has been preserved, such as the armoured doors at the entrances, ceiling cranes, armoured shutters at some of the U-boat access points, dock gates and other internal artefacts. Between 1997 and 2001, within the framework of an EU project to improve the quality of life on both banks of the Garonne, the city of Bordeaux renovated part of the U-boat bunker and upgraded it by the installation of lighting along the walls in the wet boxes and along the front facing the harbour. As at St-Nazaire, the Bordeaux bunker is used as a cultural centre, if on a very modest scale and for some years has been an exhibition site for large photographic installations on the concrete walls inside the bunker, as a stage for various cultural events which require a lot of space, and also for classical concerts in an unusual setting.

View of the interior of the Bordeaux U-boat bunker, 2010. (Thomas Balk)

Nowadays about a third of the whole is accessible to the public: the other wet boxes contain half-sunken rotting harbour barges and old sailing boats, while the workshop area to the rear serves as a storage area for lumber of all kinds. The bunker cannot be visited beyond the cultural sites. Of the former accommodation for 12th U-boat Flotilla, a barracks compound at Claveau, only the air-raid bunkers remain; the rest was pulled down in the 1990s.

One of the wet pens, Bordeaux U-boat bunker. (Thomas Balk)

9
Conclusion

The occupation of the French Atlantic coast in the summer of 1940 was the fulfilment of a long-cherished strategic dream for the German navy. For the first time in German naval history it had direct access to the world's oceans. The much promised 'Gateway to the Atlantic', which had been part of discussions about improving the outlet situation, seemed to have been achieved, and had fallen into the hands of the Kriegsmarine completely unexpectedly. From the strategic point of view, the seizure of the French Atlantic coast was a success, but it was necessary to make it capable of being utilised, for pure possession was not a military advance.

The Kriegsmarine began immediately to set up French harbour installations for the shipping war against Great Britain. Besides supplying German U-boats with fuel and torpedoes, the French Atlantic ports were to serve as the backbone for the operations of German surface forces in the North Atlantic. It was soon apparent that the possibilities of use were seriously limited by the damage the French navy inflicted before the occupation, and the geographical position of the ports within range of English airfields. In addition, progress was dogged by the slow recruitment of the necessary technical personnel to set up the Kriegsmarine yards, the sluggish fitting out of the bases with the necessary materials, and the lack of auxiliary warships of all kinds.

If the French navy had not been able to defend its ports successfully, it had at least ensured that not a single seaworthy French warship nor a drop of oil fell into German hands. Dock gates and cranes were blown up. The smallest vessels such as tugs and harbour craft fled to southern England, so that even in that respect it was necessary to replace them from German ports. A further crippling factor was the unknown mine situation off the French coast, made worse by the Luftwaffe mining the waters outside the French ports in the summer of 1940, an action much criticised by the Kriegsmarine, and the long drawn-out discussions at Skl on the most suitable harbour for the heavy German units, Brest or St-Nazaire. All this makes it clear how unprepared the Germans were for reaping the benefits from their acquisition of the French ports.

The French coast had fallen easily into the laps of the German admirals, but they delayed in taking advantage of it. Although the naval commandants, with their better knowledge of the regional circumstances, advised against using Brest for heavy warships, in October 1940 *Seekriegsleitung* decided to develop the great French naval port with its broad natural roadstead into the new main base for the German fleet. When some of the latter, in the shape of the battleships *Scharnhorst* and *Gneisenau*, finally entered the port of Brest in March 1941 it was still far from being a functioning base. The worst fears of the doubters within the naval planning circle were realised. Not only was Brest only capable to a limited extent of carrying out major repairs on the battleships, the base also lacked the necessary defensive measures. It was no coincidence that a bold Canadian pilot should succeed in April 1941 in torpedoing *Gneisenau* at her berth in the warship harbour. Despite the successful attack by British torpedo bombers on the Italian fleet at Taranto in November 1940, this important ship was in the roadstead without anti-torpedo protection.

In view of this amateur-looking organisation, the bombs which hit the same ship in dry dock a little later seem like a prelude for the end of the operations by large German warships. Only a couple of months afterwards the *Bismarck* was sunk in the North Atlantic, and once her escort the heavy cruiser *Prinz Eugen* had also fled into Brest, the Royal Navy rolled up the German supply system in the Atlantic after breaking the naval codes. This deprived the Kriegsmarine of the pre-conditions for further successful forays into the Atlantic by heavy ships, especially since more extensive British air reconnaissance had closed down the possibilities of the Denmark Strait for undetected breakouts. *Prinz Eugen* was bombed and damaged at Brest and in July 1941 *Scharnhorst* received bomb damage at La Pallice, but a major commitment by the workforce and a huge camouflage operation enabled repairs to be made, to the extent that the three heavy ships were able to retire to Germany through the English Channel in February 1942.

The Channel Dash marked the end of large surface raiders on the oceanic supply routes and the demarcation point between the Raeder and Dönitz eras at Naval Command. From now on, the Atlantic coast became the U-boat theatre alone, with the occasional arrival and departure of blockade-runners from Bordeaux under escort by the destroyers and torpedo-boats stationed in the Gironde for their protection, these Kriegsmarine naval units being the last of any size in the west.

From July 1940 the U-boat arm had begun the phased transfer of its front U-boats to the Atlantic/Biscay coast, and in the course of the war

Lorient would be developed into the principal German U-boat base and the seat of the BdU and his staff for some while. Nazi propaganda had hailed the taking of the Atlantic coast as a great victory, and the increase in sinkings by U-boats in the summer of 1940 seemed to confirm this, but in reality the situation in the bases at the beginning had a provisional look about it. In particular, the lack of skilled workers limited the capabilities of the newly founded Kriegsmarine yards on the Atlantic, to the extent that recourse was had to recruiting staff from the French naval arsenals and private French shipyards. It must be remembered that many of the German naval commandants or shipyard managers preferred to keep this staff shortage secret, otherwise the reason will not be obvious why the Naval Commandant Bretagne responded to enquiries from Paris in October 1940 that French naval ratings working at Brest should wear the uniform of yard workers.

The dependence on French collaboration grew over the years. This co-operation initially made possible the control and protection of French personnel, whether ratings or yard workers, by the French authorities. Thus the French harbour commandant at Brest and the head of the French shipyard in the Lorient naval arsenal acted at first as their consciences dictated, since no official directives were forthcoming from Vichy. Whilst collaboration with the German naval centres was later legitimised by the French Admiralty in Vichy, and extended within the framework of a policy of collaboration with the Third Reich, this did not mean that all French naval officers, engineers and workers went along with it. Besides outstanding examples such as the refusal of the head of the Brest shipbuilding yard to repair a damaged French destroyer for service in the Kriegsmarine, or the espionage activities of the two French naval officers, Jean Philippon at Brest and Jacques Stosskopf at Lorient, there are many indications that the workforce rejected the German occupation.

Nevertheless, it is a fact that French workers collaborated with the German Kriegsmarine for more than four years of the occupation period. Whether they did this voluntarily or because they had no choice owing to lack of alternative employment is difficult to judge almost seventy years on. Nevertheless, one must be conscious that there were open protests in the arsenals against transfers to work service in Germany, the workers at the French munitions factory in Brest declined to make flak shells for the occupying force, and some acts of sabotage were committed within the arsenals, although not of a meaningful size given the dimensions of the installation. Of course, it must not be overlooked that sabotage attracted the death penalty, and many acts of resistance in the yards were camouflaged as technical defects or glossed over by the French authorities.

On the other hand, it must also not be forgotten that some French yard workers in the U-boat bunkers got there by applying to a German labour bureau, and many Frenchmen had very well-paid positions in the numerous bunker construction sites in the harbours and along the coast. Neither in the U-boat yards nor on the bunker construction sites was there any forced labour, except that performed by interned Spanish Republican fighters under the supervision of the French police.

The involvement of French building concerns and various suppliers in the construction of the German U-boat bunkers, and the activity of the private and national French shipbuilding industry – whether in the arsenals at Brest and Lorient or the mercantile harbours at Nantes, St-Nazaire and Bordeaux – were part of the economic collaboration of French industry with the Third Reich. Even though a detailed academic examination of the role of the private French shipbuilding industry during the German occupation remains to be undertaken, from the present state of our knowledge it is certain that both the private and state yards were paid for their work. Above all, against a background of a dwindling force of skilled German workers due to conscription into the Wehrmacht, the Kriegsmarine was forced into this co-operation. Besides resorting to the labour force in France, from October 1942 onwards some French shipyard workers were forced to work for the Reich shipbuilding industry in Germany (*Reichseinsatz*). The so-called worker question remained the biggest problem for the German armaments industry during the Second World War, right up until the end.

The importance of the French Atlantic coast for the German naval planners received its first telling blow with the withdrawal of the heavy ships from Brest. Although the Channel Dash was a tactical victory, from the overall strategic point of view it was a defeat, for heavy ships would not be used again in an offensive role in the Atlantic. Based in Norway as a 'Fleet in being' they tied down some of the Home Fleet: *Scharnhorst* was lost on 26 December 1943 with most of her crew while attacking a convoy bound for the Soviet Union. It was a far easier matter, on the other hand, to protect U-boats in harbours on the Atlantic coast, and from November 1940 Organisation Todt began building the first bunkers at Brest, Lorient and St-Nazaire. Setting up these shipyards under concrete enabled the Kriegsmarine to use French bases for the Battle of the Atlantic until the summer of 1944, despite increasing losses due to Allied advances in radio reconnaissance and anti-submarine methods. That the U-boat bunkers were not attacked in the early stages of construction was one of the great errors of British aerial warfare. In the autumn of 1942, when the Allies resumed attacking the U-boat bunkers in response to their increasing losses in merchant shipping, it was too late. While they destroyed the surrounding cities, the U-boat bunkers remained almost intact. Not until August 1944 did they have a bomb big enough to inflict some damage, but by then the U-boats had begun to evacuate French ports.

The question whether there was any military sense in holding on to the so-called Atlantic enclaves was answered in August 1944 by Group West. When Skl asked if Allied supply lines could be disrupted significantly by destroying the French Atlantic ports, they were told that neither the natural harbours at Brest and Lorient, nor St-Nazaire, La Pallice and Bordeaux, could be totally wiped out to the extent that the Allies would be unable to use them to unload ships, for they also had nearby beaches.[1] Thus the only option available to interrupt the Allied supply line if it came that way was to defend the harbours which – as shown – was successful until the Allies' fast advance eastwards and the use of the southern French ports in Provence rendered these insignificant. In his reflection on the last battles in the west in 1945, the German military historian John Zimmermann concluded that the Wehrmacht Command Staff demanded until the very end only 'fanaticism instead of professionalism' and 'senseless defeat instead of responsible dealings with the lives of its subordinates'.[2]

Thus discipline to the last was required, even in the Atlantic enclaves. This meant that those within the enclaves were neither available to take an active part in military events such as the Ardennes offensive in December 1944, as Naval High Command had requested, nor could they bind down enemy troops heading away to the east from their position in the west. Their survival depended on the decisions of the enclave commandants, who all recognised the hopeless situation and, despite the officially announced policy of holding out no matter what, attempted to establish contacts with the enemy to lighten the burden of everyone involved. The extraordinary La Rochelle Convention is the best example of this. At the latest, by the time that Antwerp became available as the Allied port for supplies, the Atlantic coast enclaves had lost all military significance and were no more than well guarded, self-administering prison camps awaiting capitulation.

The setting up of German U-boat bases at Brest, Lorient, St-Nazaire, La Pallice and Bordeaux brought fundamental change to these French coastal towns. Former mercantile ports became warship harbours and paid for the privilege with their almost total destruction in the course of the war. Today the memory of the German occupation in these towns is preserved not only by the permanently visible, all-dominating presence of the U-boat bunkers in the harbour districts, and by the remains of the Atlantic Wall along the coasts, but it is also to be found in the facades of the *villes nouvelles* of Brest, Lorient and St-Nazaire. While the collective French desire post-war was to rid itself of the painful memory of the occupation period – including the half-hearted cleansing of the French navy at the end of the war, the culpable officers being transferred or given temporary suspensions – the inhabitants of the coastal towns and cities were left with a permanent reminder in the form of the U-boat bunkers.

These unlovable foreign bodies drew attention to a dark period of French history at the time of a new beginning. Long ignored by the local authorities, but still evoking a past epoch which in the literal sense simply would not go away, these former military installations were only recently opened for new, peaceful purposes. Beyond the museum in the Keroman bunker at Lorient there are hardly any museums on the Atlantic coast which involve themselves more closely with the story of the U-boat bunkers and their role in the Second World War, and do not limit themselves just to technical fascination. Quite a number of private museums were set up in the affected ports after the war, but these were historical collections rather than venues for a critical explanation of history – collaboration and the question of how people lived their everyday lives during the occupation, in all its aspects. People did not want to hear the word 'collaboration' with all its implication of moral blemish; a man had worked to feed his family, had spent many a night in a shelter while the Allies bombed his town to rubble, and with a bit of luck he had come through it – that should be enough said. Only a few after the war questioned the moral legitimacy of their own activities during the occupation.

After 1945, with regard to its role in the use of the ports in occupied France, the French navy derived benefit from the official myth that everybody was somehow connected to the Resistance. That this was not the case has been demonstrated herein. However, it is not an indictment of the conduct of French workers, whose behaviour, when all is said and done, was determined by politics. In this review of the events in the French Atlantic ports during the Second World War we have seen that, despite the conditions of the occupation, time and again there were examples of that mutual respect upon which later modern Franco-German friendship could be built. In that sense, the story of the German naval bases in France serves both as a memory and an admonition.

Notes

Introduction

1. Figures according to Werner Rahn, 'Deutsche U-boote im Ersten und Zweiten Weltkrieg', in Stephan Huck (ed), *100 Jahre in deutschen Marinen*, Bochum 2011, p.57.
2. Michael Salewski, *Von der Wirklichkeit des Krieges. Analysen und Kontroversen zu Buchheims Boot*, Munich 1976.
3. Wilhelm Fahrmbacher and Walter Matthiae, *Lorient. Entstehung und Verteidigung des Marine-Stützpunktes 1940/1945*, Weissenburg 1956; Reinhold Mueller, *Unter weisser Flagge vor Saint-Nazaire 1944–1945*, Bad Nauheim 1966.
4. Sönke Neitzel, *Die deutschen U-bootbunker und Bunkerwerften*, Koblenz 1991; Lars Hellwinkel, *Der deutsche Kriegsmarinestützpunkt Brest 1940–1944*, Bochum 2010.
5. Hellwinkel, *Der Kriegsmarinestützpunkt*.

Chapter 1

1. From Werner Rahn, 'Strategische Optionen und Erfahrungen der deutschen Marineführung 1914 bis 1944', in Rahn, *Deutsche Marinen im Wandel*, Munich 2005, p.202.
2. Werner Rahn, *Reichsmarine und Landesverteidigung 1919–1928*, Munich 1976, p.130.
3. Wolfgang Wegener, *Seestrategie*, Berlin 1929, p.63.
4. Ibid, p.20.
5. Rahn, *Reichsmarine und Landesverteidigung*, pp.131f.
6. Ibid, p.131; see also Jost Dülffer, *Weimar, Hitler und die Marine*, Düsseldorf 1973, p.187.
7. Alfred Thayer Mahan, *The Influence of Sea Power upon History*, vol I, 5th edn, London 1894, pp.30f.
8. Stefan Kiekel, *Die Reichsmarine zwischen Küstenverteidigung und Weltmachtstreben*, Bonn 2007.
9. Gerhard Schreiber, 'Die Rolle Frankreichs im strategischen und operativen Denken der deutschen Marine', in Hildebrand, Werner et al, *Deutschland und Frankreich 1936–1939*, Munich 1981, pp.188ff.
10. Michael Salewski, *Die deutsche Seekriegsleitung, 1935–1945*, vol I, Frankfurt 1970, p.41.
11. See the memorandum made available in October 1938 by Fregattenkapitän Hellmuth Heye from Skl (Ops Abt) 'Seekriegführung gegen England', in Salewski, *Die deutsche Seekriegsleitung*, vol III, Munich 1973, pp.27–63.
12. See the letter from A V to the Staff of OKM(M), dated 8 March 1939, in 'Sammlung Raeder', Kriegsfragen (8.3.1939–1.3.1943), BA/MA RM/6-81.
13. Regarding the idea of using Polarnoje see Michael Salewski, 'Basis Nord – eine fast vergessenen Episode aus dem 2.Weltkrieg', in *Schiff und Zeit* 3 (1976), pp.11–17.
14. Dülffer, *Weimar, Hitler und die Marine*, p.523.
15. 'Gedanken des ObdM zum Kriegsausbruch am 3.9.1939', quoted from Gerhard Wagner (publ), *Lagevorträge des ObdM vor Hitler 1939–1945*, Munich 1972, p.21.
16. The situation regarding other surface craft was even less favourable. Here there were six German light cruisers against sixty-one on the Allied side. The Kriegsmarine had thirty-four destroyers and torpedo boats against 255 British and French vessels of this class.
17. Wagner, *Lagevorträge*, p.21.
18. See Hitler's Instruction Nr 1 of 31 August 1939 in *Hitlers Weisungen für die Kriegführung 1939–1945. Dokumente des OKW*, Walther Hubatsch, Frankfurt 1962, p.21.
19. KTB (War Diary) Skl, 5.10.1939, pp.52ff; also Hans-Adolf Jacobsen and Jürgen Rohwer, 'Planungen und Operationen der deutschen Kriegsmarine im Zusammenhang mit den Fall

Gelb', in *Marine Rundschau* 2 (1960), p.67; Salewski, *Seekriegsleitung*, vol I, pp.212ff.

20. Extracts appear in Jacobsen and Rohwer, ibid, pp.74f.
21. Hans-Martin Ottmer, *Weserübung*, Munich 1994.
22. Friedrich Ruge, *In vier Marinen*, Munich 1979, p.204.
23. Jürgen Rohwer and Gerhard Hümmelchen, *Chronik des Seekrieges 1939–1945*, Hamburg 1968, p.43.
24. Ibid, p.45.
25. KTB Skl, 14.5.1940, p.139; Salewski, *Seekriegsleitung*, vol I, p.220.
26. Rohwer and Hümmelchen, *Chronik*, pp.47 and 48.
27. Ibid, p.45.
28. Wagner, *Lagevorträge*, p.103 (21 May 1940).
29. Karl-Heinz Frieser, *Blitzkrieg-Legende*, Munich 1995, pp.395ff.
30. Hubatsch, *Hitlers Weisungen*, pp.59ff.
31. Message no. 4872 of 15 June 1940 quoted in *L'armistice de juin 1940 et la crise franco-britannique*, Marine Nationale, Etat-major Général, Service historique, Vincennes 1959, p.57.
32. Stephen W Roskill, *The War at Sea*, vol I, London 1954, p.232.
33. KTB Skl, 17.6.1940.
34. Per Caroff, *Les Forces Maritimes à l'Ouest 1939–40*, Service historique de la Défense-Marine (SHM), Vincennes 1954, pp.303ff.
35. Roskill, vol I, p.234.
36. List of ships evacuated to Britain in *L'armistice de juin 1940*, Vincennes 1959, pp.92ff. For the list of target destinations for the naval forces running from Brest see Caroff, pp.311f.
37. Survey of the aerial mining operation, see Sönke Neitzel, *Der Einsatz der deutschen Luftwaffe über dem Atlantik und der Nordsee 1939–1945*, pp.258ff.
38. KTB Skl, 12.6.1940, p.135.
39. KTB Skl 19.6.1940, p.200.
40. Roskill, vol I, p.234.
41. Jean Philippon, *Le blocus du Scharnhorst et du Gneisenau*, Paris 1967, p.20.
42. Reminiscence of Henri le Rochais, former crew member of the submarine *Ouessant*, in *Plongée* 442 (1983), p.55.
43. 'Rapport du C V Le Chuiton fait à Toulon le 14.11.1940', SHM Vincennes TTD 113.
44. Message no. 5025–26 of 18 June 1940 at 2240hrs, quoted from Hervé Cras, *L'Armistice de juin 1940*, Vincennes, 1959, p.57.
45. Detlev von Plato, *Die Geschichte der 5. Panzerdivision 1938–1945*, Regensburg 1978, pp.100–103.
46. 'Protocole de rendition de Brest le 19 juin 1940', SHM Vincennes TTD 113.
47. 'Rapport du Capt de Frégate Lahalle', SHM Vincennes TTD 113.
48. Philippon, *Le blocus*, p.54.
49. Ordre 2e Région Maritime – Etat-major du 19 juin 1940, SHM Brest 5 E 56.
50. Report of the Special Plenipotentiary of the ObdM B No 115/40 of 3.7.1940 respecting the inspection of the ports of Anwerp, Bruges, Ostend, Dunkirk, Calais, Boulogne, Le Trait, Le Havre, Cherbourg, Brest, Lorient, St-Nazaire and Nantes, BA/MA RM 45 IV 768.
51. Note on the enquiries made by Vice Admiral Traub on the relationship with the German authorities after the German entry into Brest (of 4 July 1940), S.5, SHM Vincennes TTD 113.
52. As note 50 above.
53. KTB Naval Commander, Brittany, 21.6.1940, BA/MA RM 45 IV 463.
54. Ibid, 23.6.1940.
55. KTB Skl, 22.6.1940, pp.238f.
56. Friedrich Ruge, *Im Küstenvorfeld*, Munich 1974, pp.52ff.
57. See the list of the fishing steamers impounded by the Kriegsmarine as captured or prize material, as an appendix to a letter from the 'Syndicat des Armateurs de Chalutiers de Lorient' of 6 August 1940 to the Head of the French 'Intendance Maritime' at Lorient, SHM Brest 11 E; see also Ruge, op cit, pp.54ff.
58. The otter system was employed in the sweeping of moored mines by a single ship. A long hawser with serrated edges was streamed off the ship's quarter at depth and angled across the direction of travel by use of an underwater kite. When it contacted the cable of a moored mine the teeth of the hawser sawed through the cable, thus releasing the mine to

the surface to be destroyed by rifle fire. The kite was attached at a predetermined depth to a cigar-shaped float at the surface, the 'otter'.

59. Activity report, Gruppe II, Sonderstab, Cmmdg Adm Brest, 28.6.1940, BA/MA RM 45 IV 765.
60. Activity report, Sperrwaffenkommando Brest, 1.8.1940 (no number), BA/MA RM 45 IV 765.
61. Extract from a report by Reg Baurat Dreher on the activity of the Dockyard Work Group Wilhelmshaven, 22.7.1940 at OKM A Wa A 1B Nr 17903/40, dated 28 October 1940, to the Naval Commander Brittany.
62. Hafenschutz-Flotille Brest B Nr, G 174, 28.9.1940, BA/MA RM 45 IV 765.
63. Günther Naims and Lothar Frädrich, *Seekrieg im Ärmelkanal*, Hamburg, Berlin & Bonn 2003, p.66.
64. Ruge, *Im Küstenvorfeld*, p.59.
65. Extract from Hermann Böhme, *Entstehung und Grundlagen des Waffenstillstandes von 1940*, Stuttgart, 1966, p.365.
66. Roskill, *The War at Sea*, vol I, p.335.
67. KTB Marinebefehlshaber Bretagne, 24.8.1940, BA/MA RM 45 IV 765.
68. KTB Skl, 23.9.1940, p.311.
69. Wagner, *Lagevorträge*, p.106 (20.6.1940).
70. KTB Skl, 22.6.1940, pp.238f.
71. OKM B Nr A Ich 1323g.GKdos, 9.7.1940, NA/MA RM 45 IV 747.
72. OKM K III Nr 1027/40 GKdos 17.7.1940, observation on statement at Chef KII about use of shipyard capacity in France, p.5, BA/MA RM 7 1227.
73. Commdg Admiral France B Nr GKdos 284/40 A 1, 23.7.1940, BA/MA RM 45 IV 747.
74. Ibid.
75. KTB Skl, 1.8.1940, p.10.
76. KTB Skl, 4.10.1940, p.42.
77. Ibid.
78. KTB Skl, 4.10.1940, p.42.
79. KTB Skl, 9.10.1940, p.99.
80. KTB Skl, 9.10.1940, p.100.
81. Report by the Amtsgruppe Werften KV Ta Nr 1420/40 GKdos, 17.10.1940, regarding a service journey to Paris, Brest, Lorient, St-Nazaire and Nantes, BA/MA W 04/7758.
82. Ibid.
83. OKM Skl U IId Br Nr 7529/40, 16.9.1940, BA/MA RM 35 II 157.
84. 'Werftorganisation im Raume Frankreich', OKM K III A 1811/40 geh 28.10.1940, BA/MA RM 35 II 157.
85. Commdg Adm France-I/c Shipyard B Nr G 1621 TS, 3.12.1940, BA/MA RM 35 II 157.
86. 'Werftdienstordnung', Marinewerft Wilhelmshaven and Marinearsenal Kiel, 13.4.1938, Marine-Dienstvorschrift Nr 145.1.
87. OKM K III A 1874/40 of 12.11.1940, BA/MA RM 35 II 157.
88. OKM K V Tc 12202/40 g II Ang 27.11.1940, 'Niederschrift über die Besprechung bei KV am 12.11.1940 über die Beschäftigung und den Ausbau der Werften and über Personalfragen für Schiff- und Maschinenbau', p.6, BA/MA W-04/192664.
89. 'Aufteilung der deutschen Arbeiter bei der Kriegsmarinewerft Lorient nach Ihren Stammbetrieben (Stand 1 August 1942)', as an appendix to the war diary of the Oberwerftdirecktor der Kriegsmarinewerft Lorient, BA/MA RM 45 IV 410.
90. 'Entsendung von Gefolgschaftsmitgliedern von Privatfirmen in die besetzte Gebiete', OKM K V Nr 21455/40 of 13.11.1940, BA/MA RM 35 157.
91. Cmmdg Adm France-I/c Shipyard B Nr G 1680 T, 30.11.1940, RM II 157.
92. Telex Naval Cmmdr Bretagne B Nr G 1351, 10.8.1940 to Cmmdg Adm France, BA/MA RM 45 IV 770.
93. Cmmdr Naval Defences Brest B Nr G 97/40-Naval Cmmdr Bretagne, 20.7.1940, BA/MA RM 45 IV 774.
94. Harbour Cmmdr Lorient B Nr 102/40 g, 3.7.1940, BA/MA RM 45 IV 768.
95. OKM K IV Nr 610 Gkdos, 3.10.1940 (Repair prospects for surface ships in the French-Belgian area), report of the journey of Kapt z See (Ing) Heimberg – OKM K IV A to Nantes, St-Nazaire, Brest, Cherbourg, Le Havre, Boulogne, Calais, Dunkirk, Ostend and Antwerp, BA/MA RM 45 IV 751.

96. Ingénieur Mécanicien Général L Le Puth, 'Quelques souvenirs de la vie lorientaise de 1940 à 1945', in *Académie de Marine, Communications et mémoires* (q955), p.83.
97. Telex Group West Gkdos 02671 Aop, 21.10.1940, BA/MA RM 45 IV 751.

Chapter 2
 1. Wagner, *Lagevorträge*, p.147 (14.10.1940); Salewski, *Seekriegsleitung*, vol I, pp.269f and 375ff; Gerhard Bidlingmaier, *Einsatz der schweren Kriegsmarineeinheiten im ozeanischen Zufuhrkrieg*, Neckargemünd 1963; Gerhard Wagner, 'Überlegungen der deutschen Marineführung zum Einsatz und Verlust der Schlachtschiffe während des Zweiten Weltkrieges', in MGM (1/1974), pp.99–108.
 2. Wagner, *Lagevorträge*, p.147 (14.10.1940).
 3. KTB Skl, 26.11.1940, p.344.
 4. Salewski, vol I, pp.378f, n.13.
 5. For the operations of the *Admiral Scheer* see Theodor Krancke and Jochen Brennecke, *Das glückhafte Schiff: Kreuzerfahrten der 'Admiral Scheer'*, Biberach 1955.
 6. See Jochen Brennecke, *Eismeer, Alantik, Ostsee. Die Einsätze des Schweren Kreuzers 'Admiral Hipper'*, 5th edn, Munich 1975.
 7. KTB Skl, 25.12.1940, p.279.
 8. Roskill, *The War at Sea*, vol I, p.292.
 9. The attack on the convoy was facilitated by British 'Force H' having left Gibraltar on 6 February 1941 to bombard Genoa.
10. KTB Skl, 15.2.1941, p.195.
11. See telexes from Commandant, Naval Defence Brittany, Gkdos 144/41 of 2.2.1941 to the Commanding Admiral France and the Naval Commander Western France in respect of the Brest experience of the *Admiral Hipper*, BA/MA RM 45 IV 803.
12. Brennecke, *Eismeer*, p.154.
13. See note from torpedo boat *Kondor* to the OKM, signal Group West, 30.12.1940, BA/MA RM II 179.
14. Kriegsmarine Werft Brest B Nr G 151, 13.1.1941, BA/MA RM 35 II 179.
15. Telex *Richard Beitzen* B Nf G 35/40 of 13.11.1941 quoted from FdZ, B Nr G 581 M of 13.2.1941, p.4, BA/MA RM 35 II 179. Regarding the problem of distillate supply to German bases in France see [Konteradmiral Ing] Paul Zieb, *Logistische Probleme der Kriegsmarine*, Neckargemünd 1961, pp.110f.
16. Observation to K IIIA 2284/40 geh, 30.12.1940, BA/MA W-04/192664; Commander of the cruiser B Nr Gkdos, 160 M, 28.2.1941, BA/MA RM 35 II 157.
17. 2 Adm Flotte B Nr Gkdos 482 A I, 1.3.1941, BA/MA RM 45 IV 805.
18. Ibid.
19. KTB battleship *Scharnhorst*, 23.3.1941, result of the shipyard meeting on board, BA/MA RM 92 5196.
20. Disposition OKM K V ta 3307 of March 1941 to the request for machine tools for the Kriegsmarine Yard Brest, to the Commdg Admiral France and the Kriegsmarine Yard Wilhelmshaven, BA/MA W-04/19264.
21. KTB Skl, 7.4.1941, p.91
22. KTB Skl,12.4.1941, pp.155ff.
23. KTB Skl, 12.4.1941, p.156.
24. KTB battleship *Gneisenau*, 16.4.1941, BA/MA 92 5247.
25. KTB battleship *Gneisenau* extract engine, 20.5.1941, BA/MA 92 5248.
26. KTB battleship *Scharnhorst*, KTB engine-room, 23.3–31.3 1941, BA/MA RM 92 5196.
27. Report made to Brest 13.5.1941 (without provenance), SHM Vincennes TTD 114.
28. Post-war statement by Kpt zur See Hoffmann to the French naval historian Jacques Mordal at a meeting in Paris, in Jacques Mordal, *La Marine à l'épreuve*, Paris 1956, p.84.
29. Copy Skl U IIa Nr 1243/41 Gkdos (undated), BA/MA W-04/192664.
30. KTB Skl, 12.4.1941, p.159.
31. Commdg Adm France Nr 52/41 Gkdos, 19.5.1941, BNA/MA RM 35 II 179.
32. KTB Skl, 24.5.1941, p.361.
33. KTB Skl, 26.5.1941, p.390.
34. Fritz Otto Busch, *Schwerer Kreuzer 'Prinz Eugen'*, Hanover 1958, p.59.
35. Denis Richards and George Saunders, *Royal Air Force 1939–1945*, vol I, London 1953, p.237.

36. KTB Skl, 5.7.1941, p.62.
37. Draft of the conversation of 17.4.1941, BA/MA RM 45 IV 820.
38. Description of structure of decoy, Brest OKM K 1 Ge Nr 2058/41 Gkdos, BA/MA RM 45 IV 821.
39. Letter from Cmmdt Sea Defence Brittany B Nr Gkdos 508/41 to Cmmdg Adm France, 21.4.1941, BA/MA RM 45 IV 820.
40. Ibid.
41. Cmmdt Sea Defence Brittany B Vr G 5249 to Naval Cmmdr Western France, 5.7.1941, BA/MA RM 45 IV 820. The suggestion that the church tower could be used as a navigational aid was disproved by Luftwaffe experimental flights on 9 October and it was left intact.
42. Ibid.
43. Draft of conferences with Cmmdg Adm France, 19.4.1941, with Cmmdt Sea Defence Brittany on 20.4.1941 and on 21.4.1941 about air raid measures in Brest, BA/MA RM 45 IV 820.
44. KTB Skl, 21.12.1941, p.330.
45. Draft of the conference on decoy installations in the western France area by the Cmmdg Adm France, 24.6.1941, BA/MA RM 45 IV 820.
46. Bohn, Roland, *Raids aériens sur la Bretagne durant la Seconde Guerre Mondials*, vol I, Bannalec, 1997, pp.108ff.
47. Wagner, *Lagevorträge*, p.272 (25.7.1941).
48. KTB Skl, 21.7.1941, p.214.
49. KTB Skl, 2.10.1941, p.23.
50. Karl Dönitz, *Zehn Jahre und Zwanzig Tage, Erinnerungen 1935–1945*, 10th edn, Bonn 1991, pp.159f.
51. Wagner, *Lagevorträge*, p.305 (13.11.1941).
52. Ibid, p.336 (29.12.1941).
53. Winston S Churchill, *Reden 1938–1940*, vol I, Zürich 1946, pp.104ff.
54. Ibid.
55. Bohn, *Raids aériens*, vol I, p.154.
56. Richards and Saunders, *Royal Air Force*, vol I, p.349.
57. Erich Raeder, *Mein Leben*, vol II, Tübingen 1957, p.263.

Chapter 3

1. Memorandum 'Gedanken über den Aufbau einer U-bootswaffe', 1.9.1939, taken from Salewski, *Seekriegsleitung*, vol III, pp.64–9.
2. Wagner, *Vorträge*, p.106 (20.6.1940).
3. KTB Marinebefehlshaber Bretagne, 27.6.1940, BA/MA RM 45 IV 463.
4. Dönitz, *Zwanzig Jahre*, p.109.
5. KTB Marinebefehlshaber Bretagne, 28.6.1940, BA/MA RM 45 IV 463.
6. KTB Skl, 25.6.1940, p.265.
7. KTB Skl, 26.6.1940, p.276.
8. KTB Skl, 28.6.1940, p.296.
9. KTB Marinebefehlshaber Bretagne, 28.6.1940, BA/MA RM 45 IV 463.
10. BdU Opns/Abtg B Nr Gkdos 1049, 2.7.1940, fol 169, BA/MA RM 45 IV 747.
11. KTB Marinebefehlshaber Bretagne, 2.7.1940, BA/MA RM 45 IV 463.
12. 'Bericht über die zur Zeit in Lorient vorhandenen Mittel zur Versorgung von U-booten' as appendix to Skl/U Ic Nr 2033/40 Gkdos of 30.7.1940, BA/MA RM IV 748.
13. Dönitz, p.110.
14. See order for U-boat repair yard Lorient, OKM K IIIA Nr 1175/40, 31.8.1940, BA/MA RM 35 II 157.
15. OKM Skl/U 1c N Nr 2033/40 Gkdos of 30.7.1940, BA/MA RM IV 748.
16. OKM K IIIA Nr 1811/40, 28.10.1940, BA/MA RM 35 II 157.
17. Jak Mallmann-Showell, *Deutsche U-boot-Stützpunkte und Bunkeranlagen*, Stuttgart 2003, p.50.
18. Werft Lorient G 213 III, 22.1.1941 to OKM K V, BA/MA W 04 19264.
19. Copy Skl U IIa Nr 143/41 Gkdos (oD), BA/MA W 04 19264.
20. Neitzel, *Die deutschen Ubootbunker*, p.165.
21. Dönitz, p.400.

22. KTB Marinebefehlshaber Bretagne, 16.11.1940, BA/MA RM 45 IV 463.

23. Planning of the former leader of the OT Head Office, Xaver Dorsch, for the Historical Division of the US Army, from Hedwig Singer, *Quellen zur Geschichte der OT*, Osnabrück 1987–1998, vol I, p.466.

24. For the French building industry during the occupation, see Danièle Voldman, 'Le bâtiment, une branche sollicitée', in Alain Beltran, Robert Frank and Henry Rousso, *La vie des entreprises sous l'Occupation*, Paris 1994, pp.91–116.

25. From Neitzel, *Die deutschen Ubootbunker*, p.23.

26. Franz Seidler, *Die OT. Bauen für Staat und Wehrmacht, 1938–1945*, Koblenz 1987, p.128.

27. Report of the Finistère Prefect on criminal offences committed by foreign workers, 1941–1942, ADF 200 W 46.

28. Quoted from Neitzel, op cit, p.23.

29. Seidler, *Die OT*, pp.160ff.

30. Neitzel, p.16.

31. Ibid, p.49.

32. KTB, Oberwerftdirektor Kriegsmarinewerft Lorient, 21.10.1942, BA/MA RM 45 IV 410.

33. Martin Middlebrook and Chris Everitt, *The Bomber Command War Diaries*, 1985, p.337.

34. Neitzel, p.29.

35. Middlebrook and Everitt, p.338.

36. Richards and Saunders, *Royal Air Force*, vol I, p.349.

37. From Roland Bohn, *Chronique d'hier, La Vie du Finistère, 1939–1945,* vol III, p.291.

38. Memories of Marinebaurat Otto Feuerhahn, Head of Ship Construction, U-boat Repairs, Kriegsmarine shipyard, Brest, quoted from Neitzel, op cit, p.154.

39. Ibid, p.155.

40. Ibid, p.160.

Chapter 4

1. Newspaper *La Dépêche*, 25.6.1940, p.1, Brest Municipal Archives.

2. Harbour commandant, Lorient B Nr 102/40, 3.7.1940, BA/MA RM 45 IV 768.

3. 'Travaux des Arsenaux de la Marine et des Chantiers travaillant pour le Marine de Guerre', prepared at Vichy for the Ingénieur Général du Génie Maritime Norguet (no date). The document was given to Norguet unsigned and was returned on 3 August 1940 to the C-in-C French navy, SHM Vincennes, TTA 25.

4. Note No. 39 FMF 4, 10.8.1940, SHM Vincennes TTB 60.

5. Commdg Adm France to Building Director, B Nr Gkdos 3279, 10.12.1940, BA/MA RM 45 IV 805.

6. Harbour construction department Brest, 31.12.1940, BA/MA W 04 19264.

7. Telex *Richard Beitzen* B Nr G35/40, 13.1.1941, quoted from: FdZ B Nr G 581 M of 13.2.1941, p.4, BA/MA RM 35 II 179.

8. OKM K III Nr 1027/40, 17.7.1940, observation on statement at Chef KII about use of shipyard capacity in France, p.5, BA/MA RM 7 1227.

9. Report of 2 Fleet Admiral, Konteradmiral Siemens, about the shipyard situation at Brest Fleet Command, 2 Adm Flotte B Nr Gkdos 482 A I) of 1.3.1941, BA/MA RM 45 IV 805; Effectifs du personnel ouvrier par Direction pour le port de Brest, 1.1.1941, SHM Vincennes, TTB 147.

10. KTB, Oberwerftdirecktor, Kriegsmarine Werft Lorient, BA/MA RM 45 IV 410.

11. Note No. 19517 FMF 3/SECA, 30.9.1940, SHM Vincennes TTA 107. Also Jean-Claude Catherine, 'Face à la Kriegsmarine', in *Revue Historique des Armées* 195 (1994), p.93.

12. For Admiral Darlan see Hervé Couteau-Bégarie and Claude Huan, 'Darlan', in *Vingtième Siècle – Revue d'histoire* 36 (1992), pp.3–9.

13. 'Brest en guerre', *Souvenirs du Médecin Général Mirguet*, Paris 1956, p.27, AMB 8 S 3 Fonds Thomas.

14. *La Délégation française auprès de la Commission allemande d'armistice. Recueil de documents publié par le gouvernement français*, vol II (30.9.1940–23.11.1940), Paris 1950, p.450.

15. Wagner, *Lagevorträge*, p.189 (4.2.1941).

16. Ob d M K III M Nr 11530/41, 23.9.1941, BA/MA RM 35 II 157.

17. Information given to the author by Herr Adolf Nidrich, former shipyard worker at Kriegsmarine Yard Lorient, 25 April 2005.

18. Rapport fait à Brest le 13 mai 1941 (lacks provenance), SHM Vincennes TTD 114.
19. Port de Brest-Direction des Constructions Navales No 2630 A, 26.12.1940, SHM Vincennes, TTB 145.
20. Secrétariat d'Etat à la Marine-Direction Centrale des Industries Navales No 17001 IN.O, 13.9.1942, SHM Vincennes 1 BB2 224.
21. 'Compte-rendu d'un entretien avec l'amiral Schultze, Admiral Frankreich, et l'amiral Kinzel, chargé des arsenaux, en présence du Chef d'état major allemande', DSMMZO No 378 Cab, 1.8.1942, SHM Vincennes TTB 28.
22. DSMMZO No 451 Cab, 2.9.1942, SHM Vincennes TTB 28.
23. DSMMZO No 427 Cab, 28.8.1942 SHM Vincennes TTB 28.
24. Regarding the use of French forced labour in Germany see Helga Bories-Sawala, *Französen im Reichseinsatz*, vol III, Frankfurt, Berlin, Vienna 1996; also Robert Frankenstein, 'Die deutschen Arbeitskräfteaushebungen in Frankreich', in Waclaw Dlugoborski, *Zweiter Weltkrieg und sozialer Wandel*, Göttingen 1981, pp.211–23.
25. Anne-Laure Le Boulanger, *La question de la Main-d'oeuvre dans le Finistère 1940–1944*, Magister, Université d Bretagne Occidentale, Brest 1977, p.110.
26. Robert Frank, 'Deutsche Okkupation, Kollaboration und französische Gesellschaft 1940–1944', in *Europa unterm Hakenkreuz*, Berlin, Heidelberg 1994, p.93.
27. Marine Nationale/Légion de Gendarmerie Maritime Cie de Brest No 85/2, 19.2.1942, copy of report by Commandant of the Company to the Under-prefect of Brest, ADF 200 W 76.
28. Copy of the note from the Secretary of State to the Navy and Colonies/Marine Direction centrale des Industries Navales/Bureau du Personnel No 2613 IN2, 29.5.1943 to the Chef de l'Arrondissement Maritime Brest, SHM Brest 5 E 81.
29. KTB Oberwerftdirecktor Kriegsmarine Werft Lorient, Oct 1942, BA/MA RM 45 IV 410.
30. Report to the Director des Industries Navales de Lorient on the activity at the Keroman shipyard during the month of March 1943, Keroman 27 March 1943 from l'Ingénieur des Industries Navales GIRAUD, chargé du chantier Keroman, SHM Vincennes TTD 142.
31. The historian Philippe Burrin coined the term 'accommodation', Burrin, *La France à l'heure allemande 1940–1944*, Paris 1995.
32. Report RZ 57/21.000, sent 15.4.1943, Archives Nationales 3 AG 2 362.
33. Cmmdg Adm France B Nr A III 14928, 28.10.1940 to OKH Gen Qu/Abt K Verw: OKW, OKM, Skl, BdU, Mainebefehlshaber Bretagne, BA/MA RM 45 IV 770.
34. KTB Skl, 17.2.1941, p.215; also Ruge, *Im Küstenvorfeld*, p.77.
35. Arrondissement Maritime de Lorient No 350 E M, 7.4.1943, Organisation des Services du 3ème Arrondissement Maritime, 1.4.1943, SHM Vincennes TTD 142.
36. List of all German navy craft in the command region of Naval Commander Western France (undated, but the list must have been prepared after the disbanding of the service office Naval Commander Bretagne in December 1940 since otherwise the craft would have belonged to this command authority), BA/MA RM 45 IV 245.
37. Copy document, Sperrwaffen (harbour protection) Kommando Brest, B Nr 8741, 14.1.1941, to Naval Commander Western France, BA/MA RM 45 IV 811.
38. Report of KKptn von Tirpitz as an appendix to the letter from Senior Yard Staff France, B Nr G 15420 W, dated 19.11.1942, p.1, AN AJ40 1284.
39. Ibid.
40. 'Vortrag KKpt von Tirpitz (Mar Grp Kdo West OW Stab) über Folgen eines Bruchs mit der französischen Marine', appendix to GKdos B Nr 2186/43 W 1 (undated), AN AJ40 1287.
41. Ludger Trewes, *Frankreich in der Besatzungszeit* 1940–1943, Bonn 1968, p.261.
42. Hans Umbreit, *Der Militärbefehlshaber in Frankreich 1940–1944*, Boppard 1968, p.299.
43. List of the naval units stationed at Brest, appendix to KTB Marinebefehlshaber Bretagne, 22.11.1940, BA/MA RM 45IV 463.
44. See list (undated) of seventy-six impounded hotels and guesthouses at Brest, AMB 4H 4.38.
45. OKM K IIIA Nr 1811/40, 28.10.1940, BA/MA RM 35 II 157.
46. Situation plan of the accommodation barracks at Lorient on the eastern side of the yard harbour, 15.8.1940, BA/MA RM 45 IV 757.
47. See the memoirs of former head of 6th U-boat Flotilla at St-Nazaire: Wilhelm Schulz, *Über dem nassen Abgrund*, Berlin, Bonn and Herford 1994, p.169; also the commander of *U552*, Erich Topp, *Fackeln über dem Atlantik*, 4th edn, Hamburg 2001, pp.87f.

48. Herbert A Werner, *Die eisernen Särge*, Hamburg 1970, p.153.
49. Marine-Kriegs-Abtg West 2 Zug Nr 4/469, 15.3.1941, AMB 4 H 4.37.
50. Kmmdt der Seeverteidigung Bretagne, B Nr 27y8/41, 29.1.1941, AMB 4 H 4.37.
51. Letter, Kreiskommandantur 623 (No B number), 14.10.1940, AMB St Pierre 4 H 4.10.
52. U-boat Archive Cuxhaven: Kmmdt der Seeverteidigung Bretagne-Wehrbetreuung-Bretagne Programm Nr 3 (7.12.1941) and Nr 6 (1.2.1942). Programm Nr 3 'From Shanghai to St Pauli' was a presentation by the crew of *Scharnhorst*. See Heinrich Bredemeier, *Schlachtschiff Scharnhorst*, Jugenheim 1962, pp.166ff.
53. At times there were up to eight brothels in Brest for the German occupying force, amongst them one especially for officers and another for OT members; Insa Meinen, *Wehrmacht und Prostitution im besetzten Franckreich*, Bremen 2002, pp.16ff.
54. Statement to the author by Gerhard Gramm, former *Gneisenau* crewman, 26.12.2004.
55. Statement to the author by Hans-Joachim Spallek, administration rating at Kmmdnt der Seeverteidigung Bretagne.
56. Statement to the author, 25.5.2007, by Helmut Obst, armourer, Marine-Artillerie-Zeugamt Lorient, February–June 1942.
57. Statement to the author by Hans-Joachim Spallek, administration rating at Kmmdnt der Seeverteidigung Bretagne.
58. Memory of Kpt zur See Bethmann, ship's administration officer *Gneisenau*, Kieler Stadt und Schiffahrtsmuseum, 144/98.
59. Max Laferre, *Le siège de Brest*, Quimper 1945, pp.111ff.
60. Jean Leizour, *Locmaria-Plouzané, La Libération 26 août–3 septembre 1944, La Guerre 1939–1945*, Soissons 1989, p.40 (Archives du Mémorial du Finistère).
61. Memories of Erwin Jankowski, crewman *Scharnhorst*, and Robert Bangel, crewman VP-boat 716, recounted to the author on 3.2.2004 and 11.6.2002 respectively.

Chapter 5
1. Léontine Drapier-Cadec, *Recouvrance des souvenirs*, Brest 1963, p.37.
2. Rapports du préfet du Morbihan, AN F1 CIII 1172 quoted from Catherine, *Face à la Kriegsmarine*, p.90.
3. For memories of his activity on the staff of the German military commander in France, see Walter Bargatzky, *Hotel Majestic*, Freiburg 1987.
4. Announcement in newspaper *La Dépêche*, 9.7.1940, p.3, AMB.
5. *La Dépêche*, 11.11.1940, p.3, AMB.
6. Report of the 'Inscription Maritime-Quartier de Brest', 22.10.1942, SHM Vincennes TTB 28.
7. Police report, 25/26.7.1940, Archives Municipales Brest 1I 3.36.
8. Gustave Mansion, head of the public air raid protection service at Lorient, in *Lorient 1943, chronologie d'une destruction annoncée*, Archives Municipales Lorient.
9. 'Memories of Laurent Georget', Lorient, in *Lorient 1943*.
10. Catherine, *Face à la Kriegsmarine*, p.91.
11. Jean-Yves Besselièvre, 'Les bombardements de Brest (1940–1944)' in *Revue historique des Armées* No. 2 (1998), p.104.
12. Drapier-Cadec, *Recouvrance*, p.65.
13. Gustave Mansion, *Lorient 1943*.
14. Laurent Georget, *Lorient 1943*.
15. Paul Fontaine, *Lorient 1943*.
16. Xavier Allainguillaume, *Lorient 1943*.
17. Inscription Maritime – Quartier de Brest compte-rendu du mois de mars 1942, SHM Brest 2p2 12.
18. Télégramme Quimper à Brest No. 2561 63/62, 29.9.1942, AMB 4 H 4.38.
19. Letter, 'Entreprise Renvoisé', 1.10.1942, AMB 4 H 4.38; letter from Entreprise Générale de transports et Déménagements to Etablissement PLOUÉ père et fils LE CALVEZ, dated 1.10.1942, AMB 4 H 4.38.
20. Note from l'Entreprise BARBÉ et Cie, dated 9.10.1942, AMB 4 H 4.38.
21. Note from Ateliers & Chantiers GOURIO, dated 10.10.1942, AMB 4 H 4.38.
22. Note from l'Entreprise Jean GRIGNOU (undated), AMB 4 H 4.38.
23. Note from l'Entreprise F Rivière & Fils, 8.2.1941, AMB 4 H 4.45.
24. Fahrmbacher and Matthiae, *Lorient*, p.18.

25. Letter from Otto Feuerhahn, 26.1.1988, U-boot Archiv Cuxhaven; information from Georg Goerke, former foreman at the Kriegsmarine Yard, Brest, 25.7.1987, U-boot Archiv Cuxhaven.

26. Port de Brest – Intendance Maritime/Service de l'Habillement, Couchage, Casernement No. 156-D, 7.10.1941, SHM Brest 5 E 065.

27. See payrolls of the Service des Subsistances et des Services HCC of the Intendance Maritime Brest for the period 1941–1944, with confirmation of employments at the 'Naval Abattoir Brest' and the 'Local Naval Admin Office Brest', SHM Brest 146y.

28. Marine Nationale/2ème Région Maritime DIM No 273-D, 14.8.1940, AMB 4 H 4.45; Marinestandortverwaltung Brest B Nr 155b, 4.2.1941, AMB 4 H.4.45; Marinestandortverwaltung Brest B Nr 461, 28.3.1941, AMB 4 H.4.45.

29. Kommandant, Seeverteidigung Bretagne, B No. 35, 2.1.1941, to Ortskommandantur Brest, forwarded to Marine-Baudienststelle Brest, AMB 4 H 4.45.

30. Deutsche Waffenstillstandsdelegation für Wirtschaft VO Nr 1204/42, 31.12.1942, AN AJ40 1267.

31. Quoted from Catherine, *Face à la Kriegsmarine*, p.90.

32. KTB Marinebefehlshaber West Frankreich, 13.8.1940, BA/MA RM 45 IV 457.

33. Ortskommandantur Brest to Commissaire Central, 8.10.1940, AMB 4 H 4.41.

34. Drapier-Cadec, *Recouvrance*, p.38.

35. Reports by the Préfet of Morbihan (AN F1 CIII 1172) per Catherine, op cit, p.91.

36. Report of the Police Municipale, Brest, 19.8.1940, AMB 1 I 3.36.

37. Police report, 13/14.1.1941, AMB 1 I 3.36.

38. Ortskommandantur Brest, 19.7.1940, AMB 4 H 4.41.

39. Police report, 4/5.8.1940, AMB 1 I 3.36

40. Police report, 2/3.12.1940, AMB 1 3.36.

41. Kreiskommandantur Brest to Mayor of Brest, 18.11.1940, AMB 4 H 4.43.

42. KTB Marinebefehlshaber Westfrankreich, 24.7.1941, BA/MA RM 45 IV 459.

43. Note from the sous-préfecture, Brest, 6.3.1942, ADF 200 W 70.

44. Note from the sous-préfecture, Brest, 6.11.1942, ADF 200 W 70.

45. Catherine, *Face à la Kriegsmarine*, p.91.

46. Letter No. 691 D, 22.2.1941 from Direction des Armes Navales Brest to the Direction Centrale des Industries Navales, SHM Vincennes TTD 114.

47. KTB Skl, 25.10.1944, p.430.

48. KTB Skl, 22.7.1942, p.434

49. Police report, 6/7.4.1941 and 27/28.4.1941, AMB 1 I 3.36.

50. Police report, 10/11.8.1941, AMB 1 I 3.36.

51. KTB Marinebefehlshaber Westfrankreich, 29.9.1941, BA/MA RM 45 IV 459.

52. Ibid, 20.8.1941.

53. Ibid, 5.4.1941, 29.9.1941, 458/9.

54. Ibid, 12.9.1941.

55. From Regina M Delacor, *Weltanschauungskrieg im Westen*, in MGZ 62/2003, pp.71–99.

56. KTB Marinebefehlshaber Westfrankreich, 15.2.1942, BA/MA RM 45 IV 460.

57. Ibid, 1.5.1941, IV 458.

58. Police reports, 11/12.6.1942, 9/10.9.1942, AMB 1 I 3.36.

59. KTB Skl 2.1.1943, pp.20ff.

60. Umbreit, *Der Militärbefehlshaber*, p.51.

61. For the collaboration by the French police, Bernd Kasten, *Gute Franzosen*, Sigmaringen 1993.

62. Neitzel, *Die deutschen U-bootbunker*, p.163.

63. KTB Skl, 6.9.1942, p.119.

64. Eugène Kerbaul, *Chronique d'une section communiste de province (Brest, January 1935–January 1943)*, Bagnolet 1992, p.259.

65. KTB Skl, 5.1.1943, p.65.

66. Monthly reports of the Préfet du Finistère à la Feldkommandantur de Quimper, 3.5.1943 (for April 1943) and 1.9.1943 (for August 1943), ADF 200 W 29.

67. Note from the Préfet du Finistère, 3.7.1942, ADF 200 W 70.

68. Kerbaul, *Chronique*, p.218.

69. Ibid, p.235.

70. Neitzel, p.163.

71. Ibid.
72. Ibid.
73. See 'Die Beurteilung französischer Marineoffiziere', October 1944, prepared for the Kriegswissenschaftliche Abtg des OKM by Commander Ruault-Frappart, former naval liaison officer Vichy, and KKpt Lange, former Group West, BA/MA RM 8 1646.
74. Telex Kriegsmarinewerft St-Nazaire-Oberwerftdirektor B. Nr. Gkdos 1578, 2.9.1941, BA/MA RM 45 IV 845.
75. Telex BdS Gkdos Chefsache, AIF 00016, 21.7.19841, to Group West, Commdg Admiral France and Naval Commander Western France, BA/MA RM 45 IV 674.
76. KTB Skl, 4.10.1941, p.71 and 11.10.1941, p.189.
77. Wagner, *Lagevorträge*, p.336 (29.12.1941).
78. BCRA 3471/RZ55, Archives Nationales, 3 AG 2 162.
79. Report sent, 20.7.1943, received by BCRA on 20.7.1943, Archives Nationales 3 AG 2 362.
80. 'Rapport sommaire sur l'activité d'un groupe de résistance branche Marine (renseignements) ayant operé dans l'Arsenal de Brest durant les années 1943–1944', (undated), p.1, AMB 8 S3 Fonds Thomas.
81. KTB Marinebefehlshaber Westfrankreich, 16.9.1941, BA/MA RM 45, IV 459.
82. Kerbaul, *Chronique*, p.235.
83. An example of this leaflet can be seen at Brest city archive, AMB 4 H 4.41.
84. Police report, 27/28.9.1941, AMB 1 I 3.36.
85. Command, Hafenschutzflotille, Gascogne, Flotillenbefehl Nr 62, 20.2.1944, SHM TTD 182.
86. Ibid.
87. KTB Skl, 13.5.1944, p.121.
88. Laferre, *Le siège de Brest*, p.111–13.
89. Per KTB, Cmmdg Adm Atlantikküste, 8.8.1944, reports that at 'Gougeoneau' near Brest, forty-nine terrorists had been 'niedergemacht', ie massacred, BA/MA RM 45 IV 418.
90. Sönke Neitzel, *Abgehört. Deutsche Generäle in britischer Kriegsgefangenschaft 1942–1945*, Berlin 2005, p.251.
91. KTB Cmmdg Adm, Atlantikküste, 7.8.1944, BA/MA RM 45 IV 418.
92. 'Versorgungslage nach Stand vom 5.8.1944', addition to KTB Cmmdg Adm, Atlantikküste, BA/MA RM 45 IV 418.
93. Quoted from Delacor, *Weltanschauungskrieg*, p.93.

Chapter 6
1. For the Atlantic Wall in France see Rudi Rolf, *Der Atlantik Wall*, Osnabrück 1998; Heinz Rudolf Zimmermann, *Der Atlantik Wall*, Munich 1982–1997; Alain Chazette, *Atlantikwall*, Bayeux 1995; Patrick Andersen Bo, *Le Mur de l'Atlantique en Bretagne*, Rennes, 1998.
2. C E Lucas Phillips, *Im Schatten der Tirpitz, der Handstreich auf Saint-Nazaire*, Preetz/Holstein 1958.
3. Jak P Mallmann-Showell, *Deutsche U-boot Stützpunkte und Bunkeranlagen*, Stuttgart 2003, p.171.
4. 'Niederschrift über die Besprechung beim Führer über den Atlantik-Wall am 13 August 1942', BA/MA RM 7/226 from Rudi Rolf, op cit, pp.114ff.
5. Letter, Kreiskommandantur 623 Br B Nr 3243/43, 16.4.1942, AMB 4 H 4.36.
6. See 'Rückverlegung von Stäben und Einheiten,' in KTB Marinebefehlshaber Westfrankreich, 30.4.1942, BA/MA RM 45 IV 460.
7. KTB Marinebefehlshaber Westfrankreich, 25.4.1942, BA/MA RM 45 IV 460.
8. Werner Rahn, *Der Seekrieg im Atlantik und Nordmeer*, Stuttgart 1990, p.400.
9. Kriegsmarinedienststelle Bordeaux, B Nr Sm 1201/42, 3.6.1942, BA/MA RM 45 IV 463.
10. KTB Skl, 5.3.1943, pp.87ff.
11. Ibid, 15.3.1943, p.287.
12. Ibid, 10.10.1942, p.188.
13. Ibid, 14.4.1943, p.268.
14. Ibid, 16.3.1944, p.322.
15. Ibid, 20.2.1944 p.448.
16. Ibid, 30.3.1944, p.615.
17. OB Group West, FüStab Gkdos No. 5100/43 A1 Chefsache, 11.9.1943, from Horst Boog, *Der globale Krieg*, vol VI, Stuttgart 1990, p.178.

18. KTB Skl, 21.7.1942, p.406.
19. Draft 'Besprechung beim Führer über den Atlantikwall, 13.8.1942', BA/MA RM 7/226, copy from Rolf, *Der Atlantikwall*, pp.114ff.
20. Of the 5,000 Canadians at Dieppe, only 2,000 returned to England. Karl-Heinz Hildebrandt, 'Die Front am Ärmelkanal, Dieppe 1942', in *Militärgeschichte* NF 4 (1992), pp.57–64.
21. Neitzel, 'Der Kampf um die deutschen Atlantik- und Kanalfestungen', in *MGM* 55 (1996), p.385.
22. Friedrich Ruge, *Rommel und die Invasion*, Stuttgart 1959, p.57.
23. Telegram OKW/WFSt/OP No. 00606/44 Gkdos, 19.1.1944, quoted from Rolf, *Der Atlantikwall*, p.208; also Skl, 19.1.1944, p.330.
24. OB West (OK Army Group D) Kampfanweisung für die Festung Brest, 8.3.1944, folio 94, BA/MA RH 19 IV 120
25. See the list of naval offices in the Brest region in: OB West (OK Army Group D), op cit note 24 above, folio 55.
26. 'Einteilung der Hilfskräfte in der Festung Brest', op cit note 24 above, folio 27.
27. DUR 2/6000, 'Rapport sur la situation du port de Brest du 30.3.1944', SHM Brest.
28. Appendix to KTB BdU, 1.3.1944, 'Die U-bootlage im January und Februar 1944', BA/MA RM 87 37 from Sönke Neitzel, 'Bedeutungswandel', in Rolf-Dieter Müller und Hans-Erich Volkmann, *Die Wehrmacht, Mythos und Realität*, Munich 1999, p.260.
29. Karin Orth, 'Warum weiterkämpfen?' in *100 Jahre U-boote in deutschen Marinen*, Stephan Huck, Bochum 2011, p.177.
30. Ibid, p.168.
31. Ibid.
32. Neitzel, *Bedeutungswandel*, p.259.
33. Heinrich Walle, *Die Tragödie des Oblts zur See Oskar Kusch*, Stuttgart, 1995.
34. Katrin Orth, *Warum weiterkämpfen?*, p.169.
35. Memoir of Kptlt Hanns-Ferdinand Massmann, ibid, p.178.
36. Jürgen Rohwer and Gerhard Hümmelchen, *Chronik des Seekrieges*, p.454, where it states that the Germans had available in the Channel five torpedo boats, thirty-four S-boats, 163 minesweepers and R-boats, fifty-seven VP-boats and forty-two artillery carriers.
37. Theodor Krancke, 'Invasionsabwehrmassnahmen', in *Marine-Rundschau* 66 (1969), pp.170–87.
38. From Andrew Williams, *U-boot-Krieg im Atlantik*, Königswinter 2007, p.283.
39. Ubooteinsatz im Invasionsraum, Appendix to KTB BdU, 10.8.1944, BA/MA RM 87/42, folio 428.
40. Rohwer and Hümmelchen, op cit, p.457.
41. KTB Skl, 7.6.1944, p.158.
42. Ibid, 5.7.1944, p.110.
43. See Alain Le Berre, 6 July 1944, 'L'opération Dredger ou un embuscade au large de Brest', in *39/45 Magazine* 43 (1990), pp.18–23.
44. KTB Skl, 7.7.1944, p.162.
45. KTB Kommandierender Admiral Atlantikküste (closing entry), 15.7.1944, BA/MA RM 45 IV 418.
46. Letter from office Fieldpost Nr 57 373 A (1944 Stab II and 5-8 Kp Gren-Regt, 898) dated 15.7.1944 to the Mayor of St Pierre-Quilbignon, AMB St Pierre Quilbignon 4 H 4.12.
47. Feldkommandantur 752-Verwaltungsgruppe Sachgebiet Arbeit, G/N 17519 H V Wi, 27.6.1944, AMB 4 H 4.38.
48. KTB Kommandierenden Admiral Atlantikküste, 12.6.1944, BA/MA RM 45 IV 418.
49. For the formal recognition of the dock personnel by the commandant of the Kriegsmarine arsenal, see Arsenal Order of the Day Nr 55, 3.8.1944, BA/MA RM 45 IV 1731.
50. 'Bericht über die Lage auf den Atlantikwerften im Juli 1944', Werftbeauftragter Frankreich/Hauptausschuss Schiffbau, B Nr WB 244 of 2.8.1944, BA/MA W 04 7132.
51. 'Compte-rendu de la situation à Brest', Note from Chef de l'Arrondissement Maritime de Brest No. 405, 19.6.1944, to the Secrétariat d'Etat à la Marine Vichy, SHM Vincennes TTD 114.
52. Order of Platzkommandantur 1 623 Br B Nr 1931/44, 4.6.1944, AMB 4 H 4.43.
53. From Neitzel, *Die deutschen Ubootbunker*, p.173.

54. KTB Skl, 17.4.1944, p.384; KTB Kommandierenden Admiral Atlantikküste, 3.7.1944, BA/MA RM 45 IV 418.
55. Ahlrich Meyer, *Die deutsche Besatzung in Frankreich, 1940–1944*, Darmstadt 2000.
56. KTB Kommandierenden Admiral Atlantikküste, 3.7.1944, BA/MA RM 45 IV 418 and 16.7.1944, BA/MA RM 45 IV 418; KTB Skl, 16.7.1944, p.353.
57. KTB Kommandierenden Admiral Atlantikküste, 3.8.1944, BA/MA RM 45 IV 418.
58. Extracts from the situation report from Lorient, printed as an appendix, letter of Direction Centrale des Industries Navales – Echelon cde Paris INO (P) No. 6098, 18.7.1944 to Vichy office.
59. 'Bericht über die Lage auf den Atlantikwerften im Juli 1944', Werftbeauftragter Frankreich/Hauptausschuss Schiffbau, B Nr WB 244 of 2.8.1944, BA/MA W 04 7132.
60. KTB Skl, 31.7.1944, pp.692ff.
61. Ibid, p.701.
62. Neitzel, *Der Kampf*, p.393.
63. Ibid, p.386.
64. KTB Kommandant, Seeverteidigung Bretagne, 4.8.1944, BA/MA RM 45 IV 464.
65. Neitzel, *Der Kampf*, pp.397ff.
66. Neitzel, *Die deutschen U-bootbunker*, p.174.
67. KTB Kommandant, Seeverteidigung Bretagne, 4.8.1944, BA/MA RM 45 IV 464.
68. Neitzel, *Der Kampf*, p.394.
69. Erich Kuby, *Nur noch rauchende Trümmer*, Hamburg 1959, p.63.
70. Kreiskommandantur 623, Br B Nr 1 342/44.III, 26.4.1944, AMB 4 H 4.37.
71. KTB Kommandant, Seeverteidigung Bretagne, 8.8.1944, BA/MA RM 45 IV 464.
72. Report Oblt zur See (MA) Jenner on 'Kampf um Brest', BA/MA RM 35 II 68
73. Ibid.
74. Neitzel, *Die deutschen U-bootbunker*, p.167.
75. Kuby, pp.79f.
76. KTB Skl, 30.8.1944, p.813.
77. Letter from the former head of the principal signals centre Paris, Sea Rescue Service West, Franz Müller, to MGFA, 24.5.1988. According to Müller, General Ramcke would never have become commandant of Brest had he not had his own radio link to Führer HQ, for the contents of his signals were not transmitted over the army or navy radio centres under fortifications commandant von der Mosel, BA/MA MSg 2 4141.
78. Neitzel, *Der Kampf*, p.400.
79. KTB Skl, 4.9.1944, p.53.
80. Telex 024470/W75, 10.9.1944, BA/MA RM 7/153.
81. Margarethe Wiese, Letter of 21.2.1959, U-boot Archiv, Cuxhaven.
82. Ibid.
83. KTB Commdg Adm Atlantikküste, 12.9.1944, BA/MA RM 45 IV 418.
84. KTB Skl, 12.9.1944, p.306.
85. KTB Skl, 11.9.1944, p.278.
86. Report, Oblt zur See (MA) Jenner, BA/MA RM 35 II 68.
87. Kuby, *Nur noch rauchende Trümmer*, p.76.
88. Laferre, *Le siège de Brest*, pp.129ff.
89. Statement by Adolf Klein, author's archive.
90. KTB Commdg Adm Atlantikküste, 15.9.1944, BA/MA RM 45 IV 418.
91. KTB Skl, 19.9.1944, p.261.
92. Margarethe Wiese, Letter of 21.2.1959, U-boot Archiv, Cuxhaven.
93. Joseph Binkoski and Arthur Plaut, *The 115th Infantry Regiment in WWII*, Washington 1948, p.162.
94. French translation of the concluding report, US VIII Corps, août/septembre 1944, *Le siège de Brest, Opérations du VIII Corps de la 3ème Armée des Etats Unis*, Brest 1969, p.25.
95. KTB Cmmdg Adm Atlantikküste, 9.9.1944, BA/MA RM 45 IV 418.
96. Binkoski and Plaut, p.166.
97. Dwight Eisenhower, *Crusade in Europe*, London 1949, p.307.
98. A Harding Ganz, 'Questionable Objective', in *Journal of Military History* 59 (1995), p.95.
99. Kuby, *Nur noch rauchende Trümmer*, p.114.
100. 'General Ramcke und der Zeitgeist', Ruth Hermann, *Die Zeit*, 27.2.1959.

Chapter 7

1. KTB Skl, 8.8.1944, p.99.
2. Peter Charton, diary notes, from Neitzel, *Die deutsche Ubootbunker*, p.174.
3. Memoirs of Hans Mirow, former Kommandant, Naval Defence Loire, in 'Der Seekommandant Loire', compiled in 1946 for the Foreign Military Studies of the US Army in Europe Historical Division, p.5, BA/MA ZA 1/339.
4. KTB Skl, 22.8.1944.
5. KTB Skl, 25.8.1944, p.338.
6. KTB Skl, 26.8.1944, p.355.
7. Ibid.
8. Welf Botho Elster, *Die Grenzen des Gehorsams*, Hildesheim 2005, p.89.
9. KTB Skl, 22.8.1944, p.283.
10. OKM Mar Rüst K IV Va 1 Az 59/44, 1.12.1944 to Blohm & Voss re closure of yard business Bordeaux, StA Hamburg 871.
11. Elster, *Die Grenzen des Gehorsams*, pp.86ff.
12. Neitzel, *Due deutschen Ubootbunker*, p.174.
13. Fahrmbacher and Matthiae, *Lorient*, p.57.
14. Ibid, p.175.
15. Ibid, p.51.
16. KTB Skl, 1.9.1944, pp.11f.
17. KTB Skl, 30.8.1944, p.413.
18. Fahrmbacher and Matthiae, Lorient, p.101.
19. Mueller, *Unter weisser Flagge vor St-Nazaire, 1944–1945*, Bad Nauheim 1966, p.119.
20. *Mitteilungen* Nr 365, Oct 1944, BA/MA RW 4/v.357, quoted from John Zimmermann, *Pflicht zum Untergang*, Paderborn 2009, p.326.
21. Quoted in Zimmermann, p.327.
22. Information from Karl Diederich to the author, 27.12.2012.
23. Fahrmbacher and Matthiae, *Lorient*, p.101.
24. KTB Skl, 4.11.1944, p.80.
25. Neitzel, *Bedeutungswandel*, p.260.
26. KTB Skl, 3.9.1944, p.42.
27. Ibid, 15.9.1944, p.207.
28. Neitzel, *Die deutschen Ubootbunker*, p.176.
29. Neitzel, *Der Kampf*, p.427.
30. Ibid.
31. Op cit, p.425.
32. KTB Skl, 24.12.1944, p.590.
33. Lage Atlantikfestungen, Appendix to KTB Marinegruppe West, 25.10.1944, BA/MA RM 35 II 69, in Neitzel, *Der Kampf*, p.418.
34. Wagner, *Lagevorträge*, 26.3.1945, p.686.
35. Yves Buffetaut, *Les ports françaises 1939–1945*, Bourg-en-Bresse 1994, p.104.
36. Information to the author from Karl Diederich, 27.2.2012.
37. Neitzel, *Der Kampf*, p.419.
38. Mordal, *Die letzten Bastionen*, p.115; see also Peter Lieb, *Konventioneller Krieg oder NS-Weltanschauungskrieg?*, 1943/44, p.491.
39. Oberbefehlshaber West 1a No 9674/44 Kdos, 26.10.1944, quoted from ibid.
40. See the extract from the Convention in Mordal, *Die letzten Bastionen*, pp.243f.
41. KTB Skl, 18.9.1944.
42. Fahrmbacher and Matthiae, *Lorient*, p.112.
43. Ibid, p.111.
44. Mueller, *Unter Weisser Flagge*.
45. Buffetaut, *Les portes françaises*, p.104.
46. KTB MOK West, 22.1.1945, p.404, BA/MA RM 35 II 69.
47. See review of the losses, KTB Marineoberkommando West, 25.11.1944, in Neitzel, *Der Kampf*, p.427.
48. Ibid, p.111.
49. Statement to the author by Hubertus Michling, 11.1.2005.
50. OKW/WFSt/OpFS, 21.4.1945, BA/MA RM 7/851 fol 53, from Zimmermann, *Pflicht zum Untergang*, p.327.

51. OKW/WFSt/Op(H), Nr 008888/45 Gkdos, ibid.
52. Hubertus Michling, *Kriegsgefangenschaft in Frankreich 1945–1948*, Schriftenreihe des Volksbundes Deutsche Kriegsgräberfürsorge, vol XL, Pössneck 2004, p.6.
53. *La 23e flottille de MTB des Forces Navales Françaises Libres*, Marine Nationale –État major – Service historique, Paris 1967, p.110.
54. Information from Karl Diederich to the author, 27.2.2012.
55. Letter from Enseigne de Vaisseau de 1ère classe RABION, head of 3 Comp of Bataillon des Fusiliers Marins to the battalion commander, 17.5.1945, respecting the organisation of the prison camp Jeumont, SHM Vincennes TTD 182.
56. Base Navale de La Pallice No. 3 SEC, 7.6.1945, SHM Vincennes, TTD 182.
57. Whether the offer was taken up by the French authorities is not known. In the French Navy files at La Rochelle, however, is a list of twenty-nine named German prisoners located in various camps in the Charente-Maritime region who were made available in August 1945 in connection with the German chief engineer's offer. The *Sperrbrecher* was raised in 1946 and re-entered service under its former name, motorship *Tulane*. She was sold to Panama in 1965.
58. Letter from Securité Navale Rochefort – Antenne de la Rochelle, 22.6.1945, regarding German Stabsarzt H at La Rochelle, SHM TTD 182.
59. Memoir of M Herrou, former French naval officer, author's archive.
60. *La 23e flottille de MTB des Forces Navales Françaises Libres*, Marine Nationale –État major – Service historique, Paris 1967, p.94.
61. Le Puth, *Quelques souvenirs*, p.83.

Chapter 8
1. Charles-Yves Peslin, *Le dernier été de Brest, août–septembre 1944. Souvenirs de siege, de l'exode, du retour*, unpublished manuscript, Archives Municipales, Brest.
2. KTB Kommandierender Admiral Atlantikküste, 12.9.1944, BA/MA RM 45 IV 418.
3. Unité Forces Navales Brest – Service d'Ordre Note No. 1, 1.10.1944, SHM Vincennes TTD 129.
4. Christophe Cerino and Yann Lukas, *Keroman, Base de sous-marins 1940–2003*, Plomelin 2003, p.60.
5. Rossignol and Le Borgn', *Reconstruction*, p.100.
6. Ibid, p.101.

Chapter 9
1. KTB Skl 3.8.1944, pp.32f.
2. Zimmermann, *Pflicht zum Untergang*, p.323.

Index